T0324493

FLEXIBILITY OF LABOUR IN GLOBALIZING INDIA

The Challenge of Skills and Technology

FLEXIBILITY OF LABOUR IN GLOBALIZING INDIA

The Challenge of Skills and Technology

JEEMOL UNNI

UMA RANI

 Tulika Books

Published by **Tulika Books**
35 A/1 (third floor), Shahpur Jat, New Delhi 110 049, India

First published in India 2008

ISBN: 978-81-89487-39-3

The study on which this publication is based and the publication
itself were made possible by the financial support of the Indo-Dutch
Programme on Alternatives in Development (IDPAD) – A Joint
Programme on Development Research of the Indian Council of
Social Science Research (ICSSR), New Delhi and Science for Global
Development (WOTRO), The Hague.

Typeset in Sabon and Univers Condensed at Tulika Print Communication Services, New Delhi, and printed at Chaman Offset,
New Delhi

Contents

Contents

Acknowledgements

The book is based on a study conducted with financial support from the Indo-Dutch Programme on Alternatives in Development (IDPAD) – A Joint Programme on Development Research of the Indian Council of Social Science Research (ICSSR), New Delhi and Science for Global Development (WOTRO), The Hague.

The focus of the study is on how workers and small enterprises fare when faced with the process of globalization and liberalization in India. While most discussions on globalization stop with the impact of the opening-up of the economy on industry, corporations, large enterprises and workers in them, we have tried to tell the story of what happens to workers and enterprises at the bottom of the pyramid. At the same time, ours is not a sob story. While workers and small enterprises do suffer, we look for the positive signs in the economy.

An effort is made to raise key questions with respect to globalization and skill formation processes (Chapter One). We may not have been successful in answering all the questions raised or testing all the hypotheses put forth. However, if we have succeeded in raising questions for further research and for development of theoretical and empirical work, we would consider our efforts worthwhile. In any event, we immensely enjoyed the process of writing this book from the bare skeleton of an IDPAD project report.

A large part of Chapter Two was written for a World Bank study on the state of India's labour, presented at a Conference on 'India: Meeting the Employment Challenge', in July 2006. Ahmad Ahsan and Ashish Narain from the World Bank, and Professor Dipak Mazumdar facilitated the work and provided detailed comments on drafts. A number of workshops were organized during the course of the study to discuss the methodology and preliminary results, and to disseminate the findings to a wider audience of academicians, policy-makers, industrialists, practitioners and NGOs. All the experts actively participated in the workshops contributing incisive comments and suggestions, which helped to develop our ideas at various stages. Professors Rakesh Basant, Sebastian Morris, Pankaj Chandra, Errol D'Souza, S.P. Kashyap, Sunanda Sen, Tirthankar Roy, K.V. Ramaswamy, R. Nagaraj, T.A. Bhavani, Arup Mitra, Ritu Dewan and Dr Jaya Prakash Pradhan constantly supported us during the course of the study. Professors Abhijit Sen and T.S. Papola supported our academic efforts and provided insightful comments on globalization and the role of skill in the process at the Policy Review Workshop held in Delhi. Professors Shiela Bhalla and Alakh N. Sharma have encouraged our work at various fora. We particularly benefited from discussions with the participants and experts at the Conference and Workshops.

Dr Shuji Uchikawa, Institute of Developing Economies, Japan helped clarify conceptual issues with regard to skill and technology, and in the framing of questions for the interviews with managers. Dr Uchikawa was particularly supportive as a host during our trips to Japan. He patiently conducted the interviews of twenty firms in Japan and five firms in the National Capital Region of India, and acted as an interpreter during the course of interviews with Japanese managers and workers. Without his support, this part of the work would have been difficult.

The owner–entrepreneurs/managers of the firms in all the regions of the study where we conducted the interviews gave us their valuable time, and provided even more valuable information. Without their support and openness about certain sensitive issues, this work would have been impossible.

The IDPAD Secretariat provided administrative support, led by Ms. Sanchita Dutta who was in touch with us throughout the course of the study. This publication would never have seen the light of day without Sanchita's constant nudging to convert it into a book. The Indian Council of Social Science Research, New Delhi extended administrative support during the course of the study. Indira Chandrasekhar of Tulika Books, placed her trust in us and brought out this wonderful volume in a short time.

The Gujarat Institute of Development Research (GIDR), Ahmedabad provided infrastructure and facilities during the study, as well as while we struggled to convert the report into a manuscript for the book. Professors Leela Visaria, Sudarshan Iyengar, R. Parthasarathy and the faculty of GIDR provided an academically lively and supportive atmosphere. Enthusiastic support from the secretarial staff and staff of the administrative, accounts and computer divisions at all times is acknowledged. We made full use of the library facilities at GIDR, and Ms Kalpana Mehta and her library staff made all efforts to help in even accessing books that were not available in the library. Ms Arti Oza provided painstaking statistical assistance and catered to our continuous demands of tabulations and re-tabulations. Ms Sarmistha Das and Archana Dwivedi provided research assistance and helped in the collection of field data.

We gratefully acknowledge the inputs and services of all these organizations and individuals, without implicating them in any possible errors in analysis and interpretation.

Finally, we would like to thank our respective families and extended/ marital families. Uma thanks her brothers Sathish and Raja, and Jeemol thanks her husband Rakesh and daughter Angika, without whose doting support nothing would have been possible. We also pay homage to Uma's parents, and thank Daddy and Mummy whose blind faith and confidence in our abilities provided us the strength to make the final home-run. We dedicate this book to our loving parents.

March 2008   JEEMOL UNNI
                                                                                          UMA RANI

Foreword

GUY STANDING

Globalization is a catchword for many related phenomena. But it is primarily about the steady growth of economic liberalization and the drift around the world to a market society, in which privatization and commercialization of social policies have followed the process in economic sectors. One of the apparent consequences has been a remarkable growth of various forms of economic inequality and economic insecurity.

This book considers a wide range of economic explanations for the growing wage gap in India, and does so in a way that will fascinate scholars for years to come. For good measure, there is also consideration of related developments in Japan.

Three points seem worthy of reflection. First, the experience of Indian development, particularly since the onset of the economic reforms in 1991, highlights the difficulty of any dualistic interpretation and the limitation of the notion of informal sector. There has been a growth in labour informalization and there does appear to be a growth in the extent of production and labour in small-scale units. But much of the informal labour that has taken place is in or around large-scale producers. The result is that India has actually created and preserved a highly flexible labour system, one which is setting patterns for other countries.

Second, the issue of *outsourcing* is inducing excited comment around the world, particularly in the USA where commentators typically cite India as the magnet for the outsourcing of jobs. That is far too facile. There is an international re-division of labour taking place, but the general equilibrium dynamics of this process defy easy description.[1]

Third, the authors of this book are surely right to warn of the limitations in conventional analysis of the links between education, skills and economic performance. The commercialization of higher and secondary edu-

---

[1] On this, see E. Paus (ed.), *Global Capitalism Unbound: Winners and Losers from Offshore Outsourcing* (New York: Palgrave Macmillan), 2007.

cation is a matter of acute social concern, or at least it should be. Education is more than schooling, and it should be about much more than developing 'employable' workers. There is a danger that the imperatives of the market society are driving out the deeper cultural aspects of education. Similarly, as the authors note in Chapter Eight, it is not necessarily correct to presume that level of formal schooling is an adequate proxy for the possession of skills. Many people with little schooling have wonderful skills, and many with schooling do not.

Overall, this is a book that is bound to provoke debate and reconsideration of some conventional perspectives. Policy-makers and economists have much to gain from it.

CHAPTER ONE

Globalization

Changing Technologies and Skills

Globalization is described as a process of growing interdependence between all peoples on the earth – an interdependence that has occurred because of the global integration of products, labour and financial markets. This phase of globalization rides on the wave of new technologies that facilitate the process of integration of markets. These technologies, in turn, require certain skills among workers so that the countries that can take advantage of the positive growth features of globalization are those with a larger share of better educated workers. Illiteracy and low levels of skill can become a bottleneck to the pace of economic growth.

These very features of globalization – high levels of technology and skills – have raised controversies regarding who benefits and who suffers in the process. They have exposed a deep fault-line between skilled–unskilled, male–female and formal–informal workers. Globalization, through trade liberalization, affects employment in three different ways. The first of these, examined most extensively in the literature, is the effect of relative demand for skilled and unskilled workers (Ghose 2000). The second impact of international trade with developing countries is the greater ease with which workers across borders can substitute low-skilled workers in the advanced countries through sub-contracting or foreign direct investment. The impact on labour markets is the volatility of earnings and hours of work, and the decline of bargaining power in the workplace (Rodrik 1997; Mazumdar 2000). These led to the third effect of international trade, that is, an increase in job insecurity in the 1990s.

The processes unleashed by globalization affect poor and unskilled workers in a variety of ways. The wage gap between skilled and unskilled labour widens partly due to technology, and partly due to trade and openness: product and labour markets become more volatile and impinge on unskilled workers, and economic power shifts in favour of more mobile factors such as capital and skilled labour (Jhabvala and Kanbur 2002). Further, in the developing countries there is a feminization of the labour force in certain manufacturing sub-sectors. In the industrialized countries of Canada, Japan and the United States, which traded with non-OECD countries during 1987–95, female employment in manufacturing reduced compared to male employment (Kucera and Milberg 2000).

Another consequence has been the informalization of labour in both the developed and developing countries, which is often discussed in terms of encouraging flexibility in the labour market. The nature of the informalization is, however, different across these countries. The sharpest contrast is evident in the fact that informal work in the developing countries is mainly generated in informal enterprises, while informalization in the developed countries occurs mainly within the formal enterprises, as much as self-employment of a particular kind. Globalization in recent decades, however, has also generated informal jobs in developed countries that are similar to those found in developing countries (Carre and Herranz 2002). Further, with cross-border investments and the creation of commodity chains, informalization of the formal sector has also begun in the developing countries. The latter implies more flexible contracts and the loss of social security benefits for workers engaged in the formal sector.

This book focuses on labour and small enterprises, and the impact of globalization upon them in a developing country like India. The positive features of this process are the growth of markets, the inflow of new technologies and a rise in productivity. It has also led to a transmission of skills to the work force and to an increase in the employability of workers. However, the jury is still out as to whether this has resulted in an increase in employment, and whether the majority of the workers have benefited in terms of an increase in wages and income.

While the book broadly addresses all these issues, its primary focus is the entry of new technology in the wake of liberalization policies in India, and to see if it has created any skill biases in the labour market. It examines at a macro level, and across various industry groups, the extent to which various segments of workers have actually benefited from this phenomenon.

The process of integration of product markets is achieved through outsourcing of manufacturing products and, more recently, of services from corporate businesses in the developed countries to the developing countries. This is also facilitated by the introduction of new technologies which allow fragmentation of the processes of production and services. The book investigates this phenomenon in a specific industry group, namely, the autocomponents industry, which has witnessed major changes in the technology and organization of production in the wake of liberalization. The focus here, again, is on its impact on the skill content of the work force and the extent to which workers have benefited.

Finally, the book presents the story of informalization or increasing flexibility in the Japanese labour market. Japan is a country with a well regulated labour market that is undergoing a rapid change. The process of outsourcing and the threat of the flexible Chinese economy next door have led to various changes in the small enterprises of Japan. The most important aspect of these changes in Japanese enterprises is the skill formation process and how Japan has been able to develop it. Even during the hollowing-out phase of Japanese industry, with firms moving to Southeast Asian countries and China due to global competition and expanding markets, there are small enterprises that have stayed on in Japan. These are firms which have specific skills that can support niche markets within the economy. The book explores these issues and proposes what India can learn from the Japanese experience.

In this introductory chapter, we seek to contextualize and locate our study in the available theoretical and empirical literature. We begin with a brief description of the strands in the literature that offer an analysis of technological change and its impact on skilled workers across countries. We then present the different hypotheses that have been tested in various studies. Finally, we present a few studies on India that have explicitly analysed these issues, and situate our study in this broad context.

Perceptions of Technology and Skill

Taking the liberty to make some broad generalizations, we may distinguish three strands in the academic literature that discuss the importance of a skilled labour force in a country that wishes to enter a phase of rapid economic growth. While all of these place great importance on the role of technology, they address the relevant issues at different levels of aggregation: the macro level, across countries or for the country as a whole; at the level of the firm or the corporate entity; and at the level of the individual worker.

The Macro Level

The macro approach considers the economic growth of countries across time, and better education and higher skills are seen as important conditions for this to occur. For an economy to enter the globalized, competitive market with new technologies, a highly skilled labour force is the minimum requirement. There are two streams of standard theory that follow this macro approach: classical and new growth literature, and the old and new trade theories.

The early growth theories of Ramsey (1928) and Harrod (1939) largely emphasize the growth effects of capital accumulation, given varying levels of initial production technology (Sen 1979). The neoclassical growth models of Solow (1957) demonstrate the crucial importance of technical change, and argue that productivity growth results from an increase in the amount of capital that each worker is put to operate upon. The new growth theory makes a significant departure from Solow's model by endogenizing technological progress as 'learning by doing' (Kaldor and Mirrlees 1962; Arrow 1962). This approach is used by proponents of the new growth theory (Romer 1986; Lucas 1988; Scott 1989) to argue that, in the long run, countries will not grow at the same rate, as was assumed by Solow who exogenized the technology factor. Capital accumulation, both physical and human, is essential for technological progress, and to a large extent this can be achieved through 'learning by doing'. This theory places a clear emphasis on skill, hitherto seen as an impediment to technological progress.

The Stopler–Samuelson trade theory describes the relationship between changes in output or goods prices, and changes in factor prices such as wages and rents, within the context of the Hecksher–Ohlin (H–O) 'factor proportion' model. It asserts that an increase in the domestic price of a commodity, brought about by a higher tariff or additional protection, will raise the real price of the factor of production used relatively intensely in producing that commodity (Stopler and Samuelson 1941, as discussed in Burtless 1995). The theorem further predicts that trade liberalization will raise the demand for and returns to the abundant factor of production, that is, unskilled labour in the less developed countries, leading to a decrease in the wage gap between skilled and unskilled labour. The factor-price equalization theory is however unlikely to apply perfectly in the real world. The H–O model assumes that technology is the same between countries in order to focus on the effects of different factor endowments. If production technologies differ across countries, then factor prices would not equalize when goods prices do.

The new trade theory argues that the comparative or competitive advantage of countries in a globalized economy depends on the level of education, knowledge and skills of their population. This assumption is based largely on the 'factor proportion' theory of the H–O model.

The Firm Level

In recent times, the role of firms in the technological revolution have come to be seen as important. Nelson and Winter (1982) present an evolutionary theory of economic change where firm behaviour and market outcomes are jointly determined. Corporate performances, it is claimed, depend on technology and the organization of enterprises, and, therefore, on the skills of their labour force. This assertion relies on the assumption that competitive power and the corporate results of enterprises increase according to their innovative capabilities, and that these in turn are functions of the levels of skill of their work force.

A side assumption of this logic is that firms will invest in training their work force. Apart from hiring and training more skilled workers, firms will also invest in and adopt new technologies. This corporate or enterprise-level view provides the micro foundations of skill-biased technological change.

The Individual Level

The third position comes from an individualistic view of income formation: better educated people can, in the long term, obtain higher personal incomes and reduce the probability of being unemployed. This view is based on the claim that labour incomes are related to labour productivity, and that labour productivity is related to education and skill levels. Human capital theory assumes that the levels of formal schooling earn returns commensurate with the training. Investment in education increases productivity and contributes to economic growth (Becker 1984; Schultz 1975). Besides returns to education and on-the-job training, the human capital analytical framework is used for studying wage differentials and wage profiles over time. Further, it is used to disaggregate the factors underlying economic growth. The human capital approach has been used to explain trade patterns across countries.

Rising Skill Premiums and Increased Wage Differentials

The growing gap in earnings between skilled and unskilled workers, first documented in the United States, is now observed in a number of other developed and developing nations. Several hypotheses have been put forward and tested to explain the rise of the premium on skill and the demand for skilled workers. Chamarbagwala (2006) documents five such different hypotheses about rising skill premium and increasing wage differentials. Broadly based on her documentation and our understanding, we present below six hypotheses within the three broad strands of theories outlined earlier. We also present the empirical evidence we could find to test each of these hypotheses.

Trade-Related Hypothesis

Trade economists argue that trade liberalization is the main source for the widening gap in the wages of skilled and unskilled workers, presenting a macro hypothesis (Thurow 1992; Leamer 1996). A simple Stopler and Samuelson (1941) analysis would suggest declining wage inequality in skill-scarce developing countries as they trade more with skill-abundant developed countries. However, empirical studies on inequality have found increasing inequality not only within the most developed countries (Leamer 1996; Wood 1994; Slaughter 1998; Beaulieu et al., 2004), but also within many developing countries (Wood 1997; Robbins 1996; Feenstra and Hanson 1996; Hanson and Harrison 1995). Not all developing countries experienced a rise in wage inequality, though: it increased in Mexico, Chile, Colombia, Costa Rica and Argentina, but decreased in the Philippines, Singapore, Taiwan and Malaysia (Das 2002; Robbins 1996).

Wood (1994) further argues that both the North and the South have access to similar kinds of capital at the same rental price, and also to technology, to the extent that technology can be embodied in traded capital and intermediate goods. By making this assumption he implies that the difference between the North and the South is actually with regard to the skills of workers. As these skills are improved through the expansion of basic education, the developing countries can begin to produce manufactured goods that require such skills. He then attributes the decline in the relative wages of less skilled workers to two trade-related phenomena: the elimination of manufacturing trade barriers, and the increase in relative abundance of workers with certain basic skills.

Skill-Biased Technological Change

A second macro hypothesis relates to the worldwide increase in skill-biased productivity experienced in the last few decades in the developed countries, with a corresponding increase in the proportion of skilled workers. Lawrence and Slaughter (1993), Berman, Bound and Griliches (1994), and Machin (1994) decisively favour the technology explanation over the trade explanation for the rising wage differentials. Emphasizing that the Heckscher–Ohlin model is about inter-sectoral shifts in employment structure, they argue that lower trade barriers cause skill-intensive sectors to expand and labour-intensive sectors to contract. The associated decline in the relative wage of unskilled workers, by contrast, gives firms in all sectors an incentive to adopt less skill-intensive techniques. The fact that the ratio of skilled to unskilled workers has however risen within most sectors suggests that (i) technical progress is biased against unskilled workers, and (ii) this bias in new technology, rather than trade, is widening wage differentials.

A skill-biased technological change is an exogenous[1] technological

---

[1] Technological change can also be endogenous if one brings in a firm-level perspective. Trade and other liberalization processes force firms to compete on price and non-price parameters. This in turn requires the adoption of new skill-biased technologies.

change in the production function that increases the factor ratio of skilled labour to unskilled labour at the same relative wage. Such technological advances would lead to persistent shifts in relative labour demand in favour of more experienced and better educated workers, resulting in a rising skill premium. The explanations for rising wage inequality have focused on relative demand shifts towards skilled labour (Bound and Johnson 1992; Berman *et al.*, 1994; Autor *et al.*, 1998; Berman *et al.*, 1998). Topel (1997) concludes that the rising wage inequality is related to rising returns to measures of skills such as education, experience and occupational status. Katz and Autor (1999) show that countries with the largest increases in wage dispersion also have the largest increases in wage differentials by skills. Acemoglu (2002) provides a simple framework to analyse skill-based technological change and skill premiums.

Though a number of models and methods now exist, the trickle-down effects of (skill-biased) technological progress on the large stratum of low-skilled workers in the developing countries are not well understood as yet (Rigolini 2004). It is argued that most theoretical models that analyse the distribution of wages and workers across skills generally assume the existence of only two skill levels, and that the worker's decisions regarding skill acquisition are driven by an exogenous, worker-specific ability parameter. Rigolini (2004) states that whenever the costs of education are positively related to the wages of skilled workers, the inter-generational elasticity of substitution plays a relevant role in determining how the long-run skill premium reacts to technological progress. He further argues that high skill premiums may no longer imply higher incentives to acquire skills for unskilled workers, and that poverty traps can persist even under high rates of (skill-biased) technological progress.

Combining the Trade and Technology Explanations

While there is no consensus yet in the literature, the discussion to date seems to employ these two hypotheses as the major explanations for the decrease in demand for unskilled labour, with larger support for the skill-biased technological change hypothesis. Acemoglu (2003) argues that trade liberalization which encouraged the import of capital goods in developing countries led to greater demand for skilled workers as a result of capital–skill complementarities and therefore increased skill premium.

Attanasio *et al.* (2004), citing the case of Colombia, show that individuals with the same characteristics and skills receive different compensation depending on the industrial sector in which they work, their occupation, and whether their job is formal or informal. The findings show that the proportion of skilled workers rose in every industry, consistent with the hypothesis of skill-biased technological change. At the same time, skill-biased technological change was greater in sectors that experienced larger tariff reductions, suggesting that skill-biased technological change was itself partly an endogenous response to increased foreign competition.

A third macro hypothesis yokes the two explanations together within a unified model of trade and technology (Zeira 2006). Additionally, skill-biased technical change is modelled in a new way, incorporating innovations that enable the replacement of unskilled workers by skilled ones. The novelty of this model is that such innovations are adopted only where the wage rates induce adoption. Hence wages, trade patterns and technology adoption are all jointly determined in this model. Interestingly, differences across countries in the adoption of technology also lead to differences in factor productivity.

The argument is that in most economies there exist primitive technologies that enable the production of all intermediate goods by unskilled workers. Some new innovations enable producers to replace unskilled workers in the production of some intermediate goods with fewer but skilled workers. Hence technical progress replaces one input with another. Such technology adoption increases the demand for skilled workers and reduces the demand for unskilled ones, so that the wage gap between the two types of workers increases. However, such innovations are not adopted by all producers, since their adoption depends on input prices, namely, the wage ratio between skilled and unskilled workers. Therefore, technology adoption differs across countries.

According to Zeira (2006), such a scenario leads not only to the adoption of endogenous technology, but also to endogenous determination of trade patterns. Developed countries with many skilled workers adopt all new technologies, while less developed countries with fewer skilled workers do not adopt all available technologies. This argument contradicts Wood's (1994) assumption that countries across the North and the South have access to identical technology in the sense that even if technology is available, it might not be adopted by all countries. Hence countries specialize in different intermediate goods, leading to international trade. While technical progress and trade liberalization are assumed to be independent, the patterns of trade are clearly endogenous and are affected by technical progress.

The results of the model show that in less developed countries, technical progress increases wage inequality but trade liberalization reduces it. Another interesting set of results refers to the emergence of productivity differences between countries. These differences are a result of differences in human capital, but are also amplified by endogenous technology adoption. Thus, countries with more skilled workers produce more intermediate goods by use of skilled technologies, which are more labour saving. Hence such countries have higher productivity. Another interesting result is that international trade can amplify productivity differences across countries, for a reasonable set of parameters. Trade leads to specialization in skill in developed countries and as skilled production is more labour-saving than unskilled production, the gap between countries increases. (Zeira 2006: 2–3)

Global Outsourcing or Production Sharing

Global production sharing or outsourcing is a fourth macro hypothesis to explain the rising skill premium and demand for skilled labour. In recent years, as globalization proceeds, the development of workers' skills has become a critical strategic issue for governments and firms in both the developed and developing countries (OECD 1997). With ever-accelerating technological change and innovation, the acquisition, accumulation and diffusion of knowledge and skills have become even more important in helping firms and countries to become competitive (World Bank 1998). The globalized production processes change the nature of skills required of the country's work force, which may in turn generate new demands for continuous upgradation of skills and for acquiring new skills.

On similar lines, Feenstra and Hanson (1996, 2003) argue that trade and investment liberalization in the developing countries allows the transfer of production of intermediate goods and services from the developed ones. As these activities are skill-intensive, they result in a greater demand for and returns to skilled labour in the developing countries. Therefore, trade liberalization and foreign direct investment that promotes trade-in manufactures and services can benefit skilled workers. They provide empirical evidence for this from Mexico.

Quality Upgrading by Firms

The fifth hypothesis explaining the demand for skilled workers and skill premiums is a micro one at the level of the firm. Globalized production processes are making firms de facto institutions for developing the necessary skills to improve productivity and competitiveness. This is largely because the knowledge and skills required for today's production activities are becoming increasingly tacit, hard to obtain and expensive to transfer between firms, making them more specific, often even firm-specific (Najmabadi and Lall 1995). The investment of firms in training to generate and diffuse knowledge and skills can create 'competitive assets' (Amsden 1995). Thus the role of firms as places of 'learning' may have become critical in receiving knowledge and ideas from abroad, and transferring and diffusing them internally and to other firms. Little is known, so far, about how globalization processes have changed the pattern of skill development for workers in domestic firms, and small firms in particular, in the developing countries, and the factors that have motivated firms to develop their workers' skills.

Sargeant and Mathews (1997) argue that transnational corporations (TNCs) can be significant contributors to the development of skills in the developing world (UNCTAD, 1994). Skilled workers contribute to the human capital capability of a developing country's work force, and can aid in efforts to achieve advanced industrialization and economic growth. While it is generally accepted that many TNCs teach useful skills to their developing country employees, it is much more difficult to identify the TNCs most likely to make significant contributions to skill development. Empirical evidence for the 1970s and 1980s shows that TNCs operating in Mexico as maquiladoras were regularly criticized for not transferring useful skills to a significant number of employees (Bustamente 1983; Fernandez-Kelley 1983). Similar experiences have been reported from other parts of the developing world.

Upgradation of technology and skills

Firms also need to upgrade their technology and the quality of their production process to be globally competitive. This is also considered a mechanism whereby the demand for and returns to skilled labour can increase in the developing countries. There is substantial evidence in the literature to suggest that an increased use of integrated manufacturing (IM) has very positive consequences for skill development (Cappelli and Rogovsky 1994; Lall 1992) and for an increase in the demand for skilled labour in developing countries.

There exists a significant body of research that points to a link between the uses of computer-controlled production machinery and skill development. Wilson (1992) found that maquilas using a substantial degree of computer-controlled machinery were more likely to implement practices that would result in a worker being multi-skilled and participating in problem diagnosis, machine maintenance and quality control, than firms not using these technologies. Similarly, Kaplinsky (1995) found that individual techniques can be applied successfully with a work force where the majority of employees had completed only five to six years of formal education. The need for formal education may grow, however, as a firm attempts to systematically implement the full Just-In-Time and Total Quality Management (JIT/TQM) model. Successful implementation of these techniques is to a large extent dependent upon the availability of training. This is largely because training is widely regarded as the primary means by which firms impart skills to their workers. Finally, a firm's adoption of a wide variety of JIT/TQM practices creates a need for multi-skilled employees. According to Kaplinsky (1995: 64), 'this multi-skilling necessarily applies across a broad range of workers rather than only among the elite of the skilled workers'. Unskilled labour basically needs to be transformed into semi-skilled or skilled labour for JIT/TQM to function properly. If this is in fact the case, then firms wanting to enjoy the benefits of JIT/TQM need to substantially increase their skill development activities.

Sargeant and Mathews (1997) argue that increasing the human capital capabilities of lower-level employees in developing countries is critically important, and that TNCs can make substantial contributions towards this. Their study empirically confirms that TNCs that have implemented intensive TQM programmes are more likely to help increase skill development than TNCs that do not have these programmes. While Mexico may serve as an appropriate model for other developing countries in diffusing TQM methods, there is still at least one critical weakness in the Mexican example. There is no evidence in the Sargeant and Mathews study to suggest that a production-level employee with outstanding performance in a firm using TQM (or other IM practices) will receive greater monetary compensation than a production worker with mediocre performance in the same firm or at a TNC not using TQM.

Doubts were raised in the 1970s as to whether such upgradation of technology actually led to skill development in the developing countries. Braverman (1974) argued that the introduction of advanced technology results in 'deskilling', not 'upskilling'. Technology then was considered skill-replacing and not skill-enhancing. Numerically controlled machinery and other forms of advanced automation often serves to replace skilled workers. In a survey of Brazilian industry, the majority of managers indicated that the knowledge required by unskilled workers after the introduction of IM was either unchanged (31 per cent) or had decreased (29 per cent) (Rush and Ferraz 1993).

It is possible that while the use of all or parts of IM results in increased employment and skill development for technical and managerial employees, semi-skilled and unskilled employees remain unaffected or are negatively affected by these changes. The introduction of IM can result in upskilling, deskilling or skill displacement (that is, the skills required prior to the introduction of the new technology are no longer needed and workers have to learn an entirely new set of skills). It is also argued that technology does not determine the level of skill needed in the modern work place

(Wilkinson 1983). Through job design, managers and workers can make conscious decisions to determine the level of skill required for a particular job.

Workers' Investments in Education and Skills

The sixth is again a micro hypothesis based on the notion that own investment in education and skills can increase productivity and incomes, and also contribute to the economic growth of the nation. Wage differentials are explained by differences in levels of education and training. The original Mincerian function is now used to break down the wage gap among skilled and unskilled workers into the impact of distribution of skilled workers and the rise in the wage of skilled workers. This helped in understanding the extent to which improvements in incomes can be obtained through investments in education at the individual level.

Rising Skill Premium in India

The possible causes for the rise of skill premium has been presented above in the form of six hypotheses, with international evidence for each. Following Chamarbagwala (2006), the first five hypotheses may be clubbed together and called a SET hypothesis, or Skill Enhancing Trade set. These include the macro trade-related hypotheses, skill-biased technological change, combining the trade and technology explanations and global outsourcing, and the micro hypothesis related to quality upgrading by firms. There are very few studies that directly address the issue of rising skill premium in India, and even fewer studies that do so using rigorous empirical and econometric techniques. The few very recent studies that we did find all address this question using the above mentioned hypotheses, sometimes framed slightly differently. We review below a few studies that broadly argue that the SET hypothesis is a relatively convincing argument for the rise in skill premiums in India.

Evidence of India's widening skill–wage gap, or the wage premium to skilled workers, is documented for the period 1983–2000 by Chamarbagwala (2006). Using the non-parametric methodology developed by Katz and Murphy (1992), she tests hypothesis 1, on the impact of trade liberalization on the increasing skill levels of the work force and rising wage premium. While she was not able to separately test for the other three macro views of technological change and outsourcing, she notes that the finding of within-sector wage and demand shifts for skilled men and women rejects hypothesis 1 with regard to the trade impact but overall supports the SET hypothesis. There was a deepening of skills in the Indian economy in the early reform period of 1987–94 for manufacturing, and later, during 1993–

2000, for services, which was generated not solely by increased trade liberalization but by other changes. Some of the reforms she lists are domestic sector reforms such as deregulation, delicensing of industries and privatization.

Berman, Somanathan and Tan (2005) (quoted in Harrison 2008) also test for hypothesis 2, that is, the possibility of skill-biased technological change in India. They use three-digit industry-level data on the employment and wage bill shares of non-manual workers and find that skill-biased technological change did arrive in India in the 1990s, following the fall in demand for skill in the late 1980s. They find that increased output and capital–skill complementarity are the best explanations, with increased output alone predicting almost half of the acceleration in skill upgrading between the 1980s and 1990s. This raises the possibility that adjustment costs in labour or capital prevented significant skill upgrading in sectors where output was not growing. However, skill upgrading did not occur in the same set of industries in India as it did in other countries, suggesting that it might not have been due to international diffusion of recent vintages of skill-biased technologies.

Rising wage inequality since the economic reforms of 1991 has been noted by Kijima (2006). The wage inequality in urban India has been growing at an increasing rate since 1983, especially in the higher (above median) wage groups. Kijima tries to find the causes for the increase in wage inequality using hypothesis 6 at the individual level. The individual wage equations reveal not only the distribution of skills, but also changes in the skill price. Using the Juhn *et al.*, (1993) method and estimating the Mincerian wage equation, Kijima constructed two hypothetical wage distributions: one, keeping the components (skill distribution, skill price, residual distribution) fixed over time, and two, allowing both observable skill returns and quantities to vary over time with the residual distribution held fixed. The results of this break down revealed that after 1991, the component of skill prices accounted for the dominant portion of increase in wage differentials. Therefore, it was the increase in individual skill wages rather than the distribution of skills that explained the increasing wage gap after the economic reforms, or, there was a skill premium attached to the skilled jobs.

Kijima (2006) further investigates the reasons for the increase in skill wage premium using hypotheses 2 and 1 – skill-biased technological change and trade liberalization effects. Following the Autor *et al.* (1998) method, he constructs a demand shift index for skilled and unskilled labour and finds that the increase in wages of tertiary educated individuals rose in the post-1991 period largely due to relative demand shifts rather than supply shifts. He uses the Autor *et al.* method to decompose the change in skilled workers and their wage bill over time into within and between industry shifts, and finds that the change in skilled workers is primarily accounted for within industry shifts. This implies that skill-biased techno-logical change (hypothesis 2) had a greater impact than trade reforms (hypo-thesis 1).

A study of the ICT industry in India and Brazil using firm-level and individual-level data addresses hypothesis 5 (Harrison 2008). It studies the impact of the adoption of ICT technology by a firm on the demand for skilled workers and on their wages. The study uses both employment shares and wage bill shares as the dependent variables. Two empirical approaches were adopted. First, detailed information on the adoption of ICT by firms and the educational composition of their work force, at two points in time, used to estimate skill-share equations in levels and log differences. The results are strongly suggestive of skill-biased ICT adoption, with ICT being able to explain up to a third of the average increase in the share of skilled workers in Brazil and up to one half in India. These results are robust to differencing in order to eliminate unobserved firm fixed effects. However, concerns remain over the possible simultaneity of firms' decisions about technology choice and factor mix, so a second approach used exogenous variation in the relative supply of skilled workers across states within each country to identify the skill bias of ICT. The log relative wage of skilled workers by state was used as the main measure of the relative supply of skilled labour, supplemented by direct measures of education levels across states. The results are again consistent with skill bias in both countries, and are robust to various methods of controlling for unobserved heterogeneity across states.

The Book
The major evidence from the studies presented above is that the SET hypothesis holds for India from 1991, since the advent of economic reforms and trade liberalization. That is, skill-enhancing trade is the major cause for the widening wage gaps between skilled and unskilled workers. It has never been so clear that skills are at a premium in this era of global markets.

Chapter 2 of the book presents the multilayered structure of the manufacturing sector in India. It analyses the differential impact of reforms on growth with quality employment in the various industry groups within the manufacturing sector. It looks at whether workers have benefited from this growth process, and which industry groups have done so. The chapter also presents evidence of sub-contracting linkages between the formal and informal sectors through the labour market, product market and technol-ogy transfer.

Chapter 3 addresses the hypothesis of skill-biased technological change as an explanation for the rise in wage premiums of skilled workers and discusses the skill profile of the work force. It presents a simple framework to analyse this issue. The hypothesis of skill-biased technological change is tested for the one-digit industry groups of India.

Chapter 4 addresses the hypothesis of the combined impact of trade and technology on skill premiums in the manufacturing sector. The industry groups in the manufacturing sector are categorized by user groups and trade categories in order to analyse the impact of technological change on skilled workers and their wage premiums.

Chapter 5 focuses on technology and skill transfer in small and informal enterprises. It addresses two main issues: one, whether there has been any transfer of skills and technology from large or medium firms to small and informal firms; two, whether the small and informal firms have gained or improved their capabilities, both in terms of technology and skills, under the global competitive forces.

Chapter 6 deals with the aspect of skill content in a particular sector, that is, the auto component sector. It explores how skill formation takes place in that sector and what it means across different processes.

Chapter 7 presents the Japanese model of the 'Keiretsu' system or sub-contracting relationships between large and small firms. While much of this system has changed, we outline the lessons to be learnt from the model regarding the benefits of transfer of technology to small firms and to the process of skill formation among workers.

Chapter 8 summarizes the main arguments in the book and presents the policy relevance of the study, suggesting some broad issues for policy-making considerations.

CHAPTER TWO

Growth and Informality
in the Manufacturing Sector

The reasons behind the contemporary concern with informality, or the unorganized sector, in both developing and developed countries are to be found in their changing economic structure. Over the last two decades, there has been a trend towards informal contracts and weaker employer–employee relations, made possible both by developments in technology and by the emergence of new structures of governance and contract. It has become technically feasible to work from home and for multiple employers, because of the new ICT structures. There is also probably a benefit to employers, in terms of reducing their fixed costs by contracting out wherever possible. The result is a much more complex structure of employment.

The process of globalization, besides creating an environment for technological change and upgrading the skill content of the work force, brings in its wake a twin process of informalization of the work force. This has been documented for both developed and developing countries. While the initial processes of informalization in developed and developing countries were different, as suggested earlier, types of informal work in both informal enterprises and in the formal sector have grown. In India, and many South Asian countries, the informal sector and informal work have always engaged the majority of the work force. Even in African countries, where the concept of the informal sector was first discovered only in the 1970s, informal work has become the norm.

Based on the broad hypotheses presented in the last chapter, here we focus on skill-biased technological change and the impact of outsourcing on the entry of new technologies and skills, presenting evidence on these from both a macro and a micro perspective. The latter is mainly based on a survey of enterprises in the autocomponents industry, which has had a large inflow of new technologies in the wake of the liberalization policies in India since 1991.

Before we begin presenting the evidence on these two hypotheses, we discuss the broad structure of the Indian economy, emphasizing its dualistic or, rather, multisectoral nature. We then discuss the structure, size and changing nature of the overall work force in India in general, and of the manufacturing sector in particular, which has been largely affected by the reforms since the early 1990s in terms of formality and informality. Next, we analyse how this process has differentially affected the formal and informal sectors, and industry groups within them. We also examine the broad implications of this growth for workers in the manufacturing sector, in terms of growth of employment and an increase in wages. This is a descriptive analysis and does not introduce any econometric techniques. Finally, we present empirically the phenomenon of outsourcing or sub-contracting in the manufacturing sector as a backdrop against which the hypotheses of skill-biased technological change and outsourcing to small enterprises can be viewed.

The Multilayered Structure of India's Work Force

There has been an interesting debate at the international level on the concept of the informal sector and informal employment. Recognizing that the lack of a clear definition of the informal sector was the bane of this debate, in 1993, the International Conference of Labour Statisticians (ICLS) adopted a definition of the informal sector based on the nature of the enterprise. The importance of this definition is that it was accepted and incorporated into the System of National Accounts, 1993. However the debate continued on the basis of the argument that the enterprise-based definition of the informal sector did not capture certain segments of workers who are equally worse off whether they are in the formal or informal sectors, and that they remained invisible to the statistics if a sector definition was adopted. In 2002, the ICLS (ILO 2002) presented a framework to capture informal work or informal employment in the formal sector as well (for a discussion of these issues see Charmes and Unni 2001).

In a recent Report on Conditions of Work and Promotion of Livelihoods (GoI 2007), the National Commission for Enterprises in the Unorganized Sector discusses the changing nature of the structure of employment in the last decade. The Report presents both the definition and the size of employment in the informal sector and in informal employment. Of the 458 million workers in 2004–05, 395 million or 86 per cent were in the unorganized/informal sector.[1] While a majority of agricultural workers are informal, even in the non-agricultural sector 72 per cent of the workers were in the informal sector. This marked a 4 percentage point increase since

---

[1] In India, the informal sector has officially been termed as the unorganized sector. In this book we use the terms formal/organized, informal/unorganized, interchangeably.

TABLE 2.1   *Distribution of Formal and Informal Sector Workers by Industry and Status, 2004–05*

	Agriculture			Non-Agriculture			All		
	Formal	Informal	Total	Formal	Informal	Total	Formal	Informal	Total
Self-employed	38.1	64.8	64.2	5.1	62.8	46.4	8.3	64.1	56.5
Regular salaried	20.1	0.6	1.1	74.3	17.4	33.6	69.0	6.7	15.2
Casual	41.8	34.6	34.7	20.7	19.8	20.0	22.7	29.2	28.3
Total	100.0	100.0	100.0	100.0	100.0	100.0	100.0	100.0	100.0
Percentage to total	2.4	97.6	100.0	28.4	71.6	100.0	13.7	86.3	100.0

Source: GoI 2007.

TABLE 2.2   *Distribution of Enterprises and Workers in Organized and Unorganized Manufacturing (percentages)*

	1984–85	1989–90	1994–95	2000–01
Enterprises				
Organized Sector				
> 100 workers	0.2	–	0.3	0.1
10–100 workers	0.5	–	0.9	0.8
Total organized	0.7	–	1.2	0.9
Unorganized Sector				
DME	2.5	–	5.0	4.4
NDME	96.8	–	10.0	9.7
OAME		–	83.8	85.1
Total unorganized	99.3	–	98.8	99.0
Total	100.0	100.0	100.0	100.0
Workers				
Organized Sector				
> 100 workers	10.0	–	11.8	10.2
10–100 workers	15.0	–	18.4	16.3
Total organized	25.0	–	30.2	26.5
Unorganized Sector				
DME	9.7	–	12.8	14.1
NDME	65.2	–	9.2	10.4
OAME		–	47.9	49.0
Total unorganized	74.9	–	69.8	73.4
Total	100.0	100.0	100.0	100.0

Notes: OAME: Own account manufacturing enterprises, only family labour with no regular hired workers.

NDME: Non-directory manufacturing enterprises, with at least one hired worker and one to five total workers.

DME: Directory manufacturing enterprises, with at least one hired worker and six to nine total workers.

Source: *Annual Survey of Industries*, various issues. NSSO (1989), NSSO (1994a), NSSO (1994b), NSSO (1998a), NSSO (1998b), NSSO (1998c), NSSO (2002a), NSSO (2002b), NSSO (2002c).

1999–2000. The size of employment in the formal and informal sectors by agriculture and non-agriculture is presented in Table 2.1. Nearly two-thirds of the workers in the informal sector were self-employed, while 69 per cent in the formal sector were regular workers. Casual workers constituted 23 per cent of labourers in the formal sector and 29 per cent in the informal sector.

The Commission also empirically recorded the informalization of the formal sector. It estimated that the total number of informal workers, those without social security and other benefits, were 423 million in 2004–05, having increased from 362 million in 1999–2000. It showed that between 1999–2000 and 2004–05, employment in the formal sector grew from 54 million to 63 million. However, formal workers, or those with social security benefits, in the formal sector remained stagnant at about 34 million. That is, the entire increase in employment in the formal sector was accounted for by informal work.

Structure of the Manufacturing Sector

There is a multilayered structure of enterprises and workers even within the manufacturing sectors. There were 14.8 million enterprises in the manufacturing sector in 2000–01, employing 45.7 million workers. Of these, nearly 1 per cent of the enterprises and 26 per cent of the workers were in the organized sector (Table 2.2).[2] About 10 per cent of the total workers were in large organized enterprises more than 100 workers. The organized manufacturing sector grew till about 1994–95 and then began to decline, both in absolute number and proportion. In the first phase of liberalization, till the mid-1990s, the organized sector appeared to have an advantage (see Unni *et al.* 2001). In the later phase, however, the unorganized manufacturing sector found its feet and grew rapidly in terms of value added and employment (Rani and Unni 2004a).

The enterprises in the unorganized sector were further divided by size of employment. Own account manufacturing enterprises (OAME), consisting of enterprises based primarily on family labour, accounted for nearly 85 per cent of all organized and unorganized manufacturing enterprises, and 49 per cent of all workers in 2000–01 (Table 2.2). Non-directory manufacturing enterprises (NDME), enterprises with at least one hired worker

---

[2] The data on the organized sector is obtained from the Annual Survey of Industries (ASI). The ASI collects two separate sets of data: the Census Sector, referring to a census of enterprises with more than 100 workers, and the Factory Sector, referring to a sample survey of enterprises with 10–100 workers. We use both sets to show the structure of the industry, but in later, limited analysis of organized sector data, we use only the Factory Sector data.

and less than six total workers, constituted nearly 10 per cent of all enter-prises and workers. Directory manufacturing enterprises (DME), with at least one hired worker and more than ten total workers, constituted about 4 per cent of all enterprises and 14 per cent of all workers. While the proportion of enterprises in the larger units, DME and NDME, declined in the last period, the proportion of workers in all the three size-classes in the unorga-nized sector grew in comparison to the organized sector.

Share of employment within the unorganized sector

Within the unorganized manufacturing sector, nearly 67 per cent of the workers were in own account enterprises in 2001, more so in rural areas (Table 2.3). Less than 20 per cent of workers were in the larger unorganized enterprises with six to ten workers (DME), and about 14 per cent were in the NDME with less than six workers. Overall, workers were engaged in larger enterprises in urban areas, and over the period 1984 to 2001, the share of employment in the larger units increased marginally. Further, there was a slow shift of workers in unorganized manufacturing to urban areas.

Share of value added within the unorganized sector

While 67 per cent of employment in the unorganized manufactur-ing sector was in own account units, only 39 per cent of the value added was in these smaller family units (Table 2.4). At the other extreme, while nearly 20 per cent of the workers were in DME, about 37 per cent of the value added was produced in these larger units. There was also a shift of the share of value added towards the larger units from 29 to 37 per cent, during 1984–2001. The major shift, however, occurred in the pre-liberalization and early liberalization phase. After 1994, the share of value added by size of enterprises was more stable with a small increase in mid-sized enterprises.

While there was a process of urbanization of workers in the unorga-nized manufacturing enterprises, the share of value added did not shift as dramatically to urban areas. The shift in share of workers and value added to urban areas was again mainly in the mid-sized units after 1994.

The concentration of workers in own account units and the larger share of value added in the larger units obviously has implications for the low productivity of workers in the small units. The larger share of value added and smaller share of workers in urban areas implied that the units in urban areas had greater productivity per worker. It is perhaps the nature of the products produced in the type of units and in the urban areas that explained at least part of this difference by size and location.

TABLE 2.3 *Share of Workers in the Unorganized Manufacturing Sector by Size and Location*

	1984–85	1989–90	1994–95	2000–01
Total				
DME	12.9	17.3	18.3	19.2
NDME	87.1	13.0	13.2	14.1
OAME		69.6	68.5	66.7
Total	*100.0*	*100.0*	*100.0*	*100.0*
Urban				
DME	27.8 (56.4)	30.9 (51.1)	32.9 (54.8)	30.4 (53.6)
NDME	72.1 (21.8)	24.4 (10.0)	25.1 (11.2)	26.5 (13.8)
OAME		44.6 (18.3)	42.0 (18.7)	43.0 (22.4)
Total	*100.0 (26.3)*	*100.0 (28.6)*	*100.0 (30.5)*	*100.0 (34.7)*
Rural				
DME	7.7	11.9	11.9	13.2
NDME	92.3	8.5	7.9	7.5
OAME		79.6	80.1	79.2
Total	*100.0*	*100.0*	*100.0*	*100.0*

Note: Figures in parentheses are the share of urban workers in the total.
Source: NSSO (1989), NSSO (1994a), NSSO (1994b), NSSO (1998a), NSSO (1998b), NSSO (1998c), NSSO (2002a), NSSO (2002b), NSSO (2002c).

TABLE 2.4 *Share of Value Added in the Unorganized Manufacturing Sector by Size and Location*

	1984–85	1989–90	1994–95	2000–01
Total Value Added by Size				
DME	28.6	31.6	37.1	36.7
NDME	71.4	24.7	22.9	24.1
OAME		43.8	40.0	39.1
Total	*100.0*	*100.0*	*100.0*	*100.0*
Share of Value Added in Urban Areas				
DME	80.8	72.1	72.6	68.7
NDME	43.4	71.2	72.4	76.1
OAME		27.0	34.6	33.8
Total	*54.1*	*52.1*	*57.4*	*56.8*

Source: NSSO (1989), NSSO (1994a), NSSO (1994b), NSSO (1998a), NSSO (1998b), NSSO (1998c), NSSO (2002a), NSSO (2002b), NSSO (2002c).

Differential Impact of Reforms on Growth

The process of economic reform in India, including trade, industry and labour policies, had a major impact on the manufacturing sector (Appendix Chart A 2.1; for details see Rani and Unni 2004a). Within manufacturing, it led to a differential impact on the formal and informal sectors. We provide a descriptive analysis of this differential impact on growth during the two periods of reform – the early period from 1989 to 1994, and the later period of rapid reforms after 1994 – in the various industry groups in the two broad segments of the manufacturing sector, formal and informal.

Categorizing Growth

In the traditional literature on growth in the debate on globalization, growth is measured purely as value added or as gross domestic product (GDP). The creation of employment or any measure of growth in the demand for labour is not recognized as a goal of economic development. The standard assumption is that a rise in GDP will automatically lead to growth of productive employment, and, consequently, an increase in the wages and incomes of the majority of workers.

In our view, the growth of value added or employment creation alone in an industry group is not sufficient to ensure productive employment for the majority of workers. Since our primary concern is generation of productive employment, we will define growth and non-growth industries not only in terms of growth in value added, but also growth of employment and labour productivity. Rapid value-added growth is essential to ensure a positive growth impulse in the industry as a whole. Growth of employment is necessary to ensure that the benefits of this growth of value added percolate to the lower segment of workers. Finally, employment at low levels of income is not sufficient to ensure overall well-being of workers. It requires growth with increasing labour productivity or income per worker – that is, industrial growth generating quality employment. Using these three variables, we define seven groups of growth versus non-growth industries, and club them into three categories.[3]

The first category of industries, Category A, consists of growth industries with an improving quality of employment (Chart 2.1). There are two groups of industries within it, both with growing value added and labour productivity, but one having growing employment (A.1) and the other declining employment (A.2). The second, Category B, consists of growth industries with a declining quality of employment (labour productivity), despite growing value added. Category C consists of non-growth industries (declin-

---

[3] These growth categories are defined in an earlier paper; see Unni and Rani 2003.

CHART 2.1   *Categories of Growth versus Non-Growth Industry Groups*

Category A: Growth industries with quality employment
1.   Growing Value Added, Growing Employment, Growing Labour Productivity
2.   Growing Value Added, Declining Employment, Growing Labour Productivity

Category B: Growth industries with poor quality employment
3.   Growing Value Added, Growing Employment, Declining Labour Productivity
4.   Growing Value Added, Declining Employment, Declining Labour Productivity

Category C: Non-growth industries
5.   Declining Value Added, Growing Employment, Declining Labour Productivity
6.   Declining Value Added, Declining Employment, Growing Labour Productivity
7.   Declining Value Added, Declining Employment, Declining Labour Productivity

---

ing value added) with declining labour productivity or declining employment growth.[4]

In common parlance, an industry with growing value added over time is considered to be potentially dynamic and developing. By this criterion, the first four categories of industry groups with growing value added (Chart 2.1) should be considered as growth industries, in the broad Categories A and B. However, we give greater importance to growth of employment and, preferably, productive employment as being beneficial to the economy in the long run. By this logic, the first two industry groups (A.1 and A.2) are the best, followed by the third and fourth (B.1 and B.2). The latter three groups of industries with declining value added can be considered as non-growth performing industries, Category C.

We define these three categories as industries having a higher growth rate of value added, employment and labour productivity in one period over the previous period. We categorize the industries as growth and non-growth for two time periods, growth in 1989–90 to 1994–95 (the early reforms period) over the previous period of 1984–85 to 1989–90 (the partial reforms period), and growth in 1994–95 to 2000–01 (the rapid reforms period) over the previous period of 1989–90 to 1994–95 (the early reforms period).

Growth in the Organized Sector

The industrial policy reforms of the new policy regime in the early 1990s abolished investment licensing and simplified rules to facilitate private investment. Exclusive monopoly of the public sector over a number of

---

[4] Similar growth categories were defined by Sheila Bhalla (2003) to identify what she called sunrise industries. Her analysis was till the mid-1990s, and included the trade and service sectors.

industries was abandoned. This allowed domestic private investors to invest in capacity and production in a wide range of industries, including heavy industries and automobiles, which were earlier reserved for public sector (Chandrasekhar and Ghosh 2002).

The early 1990s brought about more comprehensive trade liberalization, which encompassed the abolition of non-tariff barriers, a reduction of peak tariff rates, and dispersion along with devaluation of the rupee (Das 2003). Tariff barriers and quantitative restrictions on foreign trade were sharply reduced. The average tariff was brought down from 123 per cent in 1987–88 to 58 per cent in 1994–95 (Nouroz 2001), and quantitative restrictions on trade were lifted except for consumer goods and agricultural commodities (Varshney 2001: 234). The dismantling of quantitative restrictions occurred in the first two years, when import licensing was virtually abolished for imports of industrial raw materials, intermediates, components and capital goods. However, restrictions on imports of consumer goods continued, which provided 'substantial and open-ended protection to all industrial consumer goods' (Ahluwalia 2001).

Further, foreign portfolio institutions were given entry and the rules for foreign direct investment were liberalized. The policy allowed automatic approval of foreign collaboration agreements in thirty-four priority industries, subject to certain guidelines; and foreign firms could hold up to 51 per cent equity in these industries if their requirement for capital imports was financed through foreign equity (Kathuria 1995). This allowed firms to enter into joint ventures with multinational enterprises (MNEs) more freely, import technology from MNEs, import capital goods and expand capacities, and introduce new products without obtaining an industrial license. The liberalization measure also made technology transfer easier as now firms could import technology against royalty and lumpsum payments. Liberalization of foreign direct investment (FDI) was expected to facilitate the formation of alliances for technology transfer and international marketing. The reforms reduced dependence on sub-optimal domestic inputs and technology by allowing freer imports of raw materials, intermediate goods and capital goods (Siddharthan and Lal 2003). To encourage private initiative, tax policies were also rationalized. During this period, no reforms were undertaken in areas related to the privatization of public sector enterprises and labour laws.

All these policies together appeared to have helped the organized sector, with growth in value added of 8.3 per cent, employment growth of 2.1 per cent and fixed capital growth of 13.6 per cent during 1989–95 (Rani and Unni 2004, Table 1). However, in the phase of later rapid reforms or the mid-1990s, the rate of growth of value added in the organized sector came down to 6.9 per cent and employment to 0.7 per cent, while fixed capital continued to grow at 12 per cent.

In the organized sector, a large number of industry groups were in growth category A.1, with growing value added, employment and productivity in the period 1989–95, the first phase of reforms (Chart 2.2 and Appendix Table A 2.1). During this period, the consumer goods industry dominated growth in the organized sector due to domestic protection and high levels of tariff (Nouroz 2001). Consumer durable industries like motor vehicles, radio, television and communications, medical, precision and optical instruments, watches and clocks, furniture and other manufacturing, and metal-based industries were in Category A.1; office accounting and computing machinery were in Category A.2. Consumer non-durables like other chemical products (pharmaceuticals), food and leather products were in Category A.1, and textiles in A.2.

While about half of these industry groups were able to retain their positive growth position in the next phase of reforms, the late 1990s, the rest moved to the lower growth category A.2 with declining employment growth. The industry groups that retained quality growth impetus in the last phase were products in food, textile, leather, chemicals, rubber, non-metallic mineral, fabricated metal and motor vehicles. The machinery industries continued to have high growth of value added but with declining growth of employment. Metal-based and machinery industries were earlier noted to benefit from reforms that allowed expansion of capacity and import of technology. These industries in the organized sector appeared to have followed a capital-intensive path to growth. The wearing apparel or garment industry had value added and employment growth in both periods but with declining labour productivity, Category B.3.

Growth in the Unorganized Sector

The opposite pattern was observed in the unorganized manufacturing sector. We found that in the first period of reforms, the early 1990s, very few industry groups were in Category A and, within that, in Group A.1 (Chart 2.3 and Appendix Table A 2.2). However, in the later period, the late 1990s, a large number of manufacturing industries in the unorganized sector grew with quality employment. Further, in the first phase of reforms, a large number of unorganized manufacturing industries were in Category C, but in the later reforms period most of the industry groups moved to higher growth categories.

The rapid economic reforms of the mid-1990s allowed small-scale industry (SSI) to expand through the de-reservation of products and by raising the ceiling of investment in plant and machinery from Rs 60 lakh to

CHART 2.2   *Growth and Non-Growth Industries in the Early and Rapid Reforms Phase in the Organized Sector*

Specification	Early Reforms 1989–95 over 1984–90	Rapid Reforms 1994–2001 over 1989–95
Category A		
1 Growing Value Added Growing Employment Growing Labour Productivity	Food Products Leather Products Chemical and Chemical Products Rubber and Plastic Products Other Non-Metallic Mineral Products Fabricated Metals Medical, Precision and Optical Instruments, Watches, Clocks Motor Vehicles Other Manufacturing Basic Metals Machinery and Equipment Electrical Machinery Communications Equipment Transport Equipment Publishing, Printing and Recording Media Tobacco Products	Food Products Leather Products Chemical and Chemical Products Rubber and Plastic Products Other Non-Metallic Mineral Products Fabricated Metals Medical, Precision and Optical Instruments, Watches, Clocks Motor Vehicles Other Manufacturing Textiles Cotton Ginning
2 Growing Value Added Declining Employment Growing Labour Productivity	Textiles Office, Accounting and Computing Machinery	Tobacco Products Basic Metals Publishing, Printing and Recording Media Transport Equipment Machinery and Equipment Electrical Machinery Communications Equipment
Category B		
3 Growing Value Added Growing Employment Declining Labour Productivity	Wearing Apparel, Dressing and Dyeing of Fur Paper Products	Wearing Apparel, Dressing and Dyeing of Fur
Category C		
5 Declining Value Added Growing Employment Declining Labour Productivity		Paper Products
7 Declining Value Added Declining Employment Declining Labour Productivity	Cotton Ginning Wood Products	Wood Products Office, Accounting and Computing Machinery

CHART 2.3   *Growth and Non-Growth Industries in the Early and Rapid Reforms Phase in the Unorganized Sector*

Specification	Early Reforms 1989–95 over 1984–90	Rapid Reforms 1994–2001 over 1989–95
Category A		
1 Growing Value Added Growing Employment Growing Labour Productivity	Fabricated Metals Office, Accounting and Computing Machinery	Fabricated Metals Food Products Paper Products Publishing, Printing and Repro- duction of Recorded Media Chemical and Chemical Products Basic Metals Other Non-Metallic Mineral Products Machinery and Equipment Electrical Machinery Radio, Television, Communication Equipment and Apparatus Motor Vehicles
2 Growing Value Added Declining Employment Growing Labour Productivity	Leather Products	Leather Products Textiles Transport Equipment Other Manufacturing
Category B		
3 Growing Value Added Growing Employment Declining Labour Productivity	Wearing Apparel, Dressing and Dyeing of Fur	Wearing Apparel, Dressing and Dyeing of Fur Tobacco Products Wood Products
Category C		
5 Declining Value Added Growing Employment Declining Labour Productivity	Food Products Basic Metals	–
6 Declining Value Added Declining Employment Growing Labour Productivity	Tobacco Products Radio, Television and Com- munications Equipment and Apparatus Transport Equipment	Cotton Ginning Medical, Precision and Optical Instruments, Watches and Clocks
7 Declining Value Added Declining Employment Declining Labour Productivity	Rubber and Plastic Products Other Non-Metallic Mineral Products Paper Products Cotton Ginning Textiles Wood Products Publishing, Printing and Repro- duction of Recorded Media Chemical and Chemical Products Machinery and Equipment Electrical Machinery Medical, Precision and Optical Instruments, Watches and Clocks Motor Vehicles Other Manufacturing	Rubber and Plastic Products Office, Accounting and Computing Machinery Leather Products

Note: *Wearing apparel excludes tailoring establishments.

Rs 3 crore, and for the tiny industries from Rs 5 to 25 lakh in 1996–97. The composite loan limit for SSI increased to Rs 2 lakh from Rs 50,000. The export promotion capital goods (EPCG) scheme at zero duty was extended to the small-scale engineering industry. Further, the ceiling for working capital was doubled for small-scale units from Rs 2 to Rs 4 crore, and small-scale units were exempted from excise duty.

All these reforms for the small-scale sector may have fuelled the growth of the unorganized sector, defined by size of employment. We had earlier noted an increase in the share of workers in mid-sized units with one to six regular workers. The value added grew rapidly in the unorganized manufacturing sector at 6.9 per cent in 1994–2001, compared to negative growth in the earlier periods, employment grew at 2.1 per cent and capital grew at 6.4 per cent.

This could mean that with the reforms, some of the growth-oriented industry in the organized sector spilled over to the unorganized sector, partly through sub-contracting linkages. Secondly, with the enhancement of the investment ceiling for plant and machinery in small-scale industries and other concessions accorded to this sector, the firms might have opted for better technology or technological upgradation, which helped to improve output. Thirdly, with liberalization and de-reservation of small-scale industries, the forces of competition were unleashed and there was reorganization or restructuring of the unorganized sector, which might also have led to improved output.

In the late 1990s, the industries in the unorganized sector that performed very well, Category A, were largely consumer non-durables consisting of food and paper; chemical industries including pharmaceuticals and cosmetics; consumer durables like radio, television and communications equipment; motor vehicles; and capital goods such as metal-based and machinery industries. Category B industries marked by growth with poor quality employment and declining labour productivity were consumer non-durable industries such as tobacco, wood products and garments. Garments had a phenomenal growth profile in terms of value added and employment but with declining labour productivity, in both the organized and unorganized sectors. And finally, there was a group of non-growth or non-performing industries in Category C, consisting of cotton-ginning, precision instruments, rubber and plastic products, and office, accounting and computing machinery. These latter industries were perhaps faced with stiff competition both internally and from imported goods.

The capital goods industry was liberalized in the early phase of reforms, allowing for the inflow of technology through import of capital and intermediary goods, and through FDI and other foreign investments. In the organized sector, industries such as fabricated metals, machinery and equipment, and electrical machinery were high-growth industries in the early reform period as well as in the later reform period. However, after 1994 they moved to Category A.2 with growth of labour productivity but no growth of employment. In the unorganized sector these industries were not high-growth industries prior to 1994, but after 1994 they entered the A.1 growth category with growth of employment and labour productivity. These industries appeared to have capital-intensive growth in the organized sector (shedding employment), while labour productivity grew along with labour absorption in the unorganized sector.

The autocomponents industry, a capital goods industry, witnessed major changes due to the liberalization measures that allowed inflow of technology and foreign investments in the motor vehicles sector. We make an attempt to look at this industry at the micro level in the later part of the book. The motor vehicles industry had grown with quality employment (Category A.1) in both the organized and unorganized manufacturing sectors in the late 1990s. The autocomponents industry is classified as such only in the three-digit level in the National Industrial Classification, but it consists of manufacturing of parts in fabricated metals, machinery and equipment, and electrical machinery industries. All these industry groups had growth with quality employment (A.1) in the late 1990s in the unorganized sector. This growth could be partly fuelled by outsourcing linkages between the formal motor vehicle industry and the informal autocomponents industry that we shall discuss later.

The economic reforms of the late 1990s were to a very large extent geared towards the small-scale sector, actually helping this sector to grow. Most of the industries in the unorganized sector had a positive growth in output, largely due to improved capacities and technological upgradation as reflected in capital growth (Rani and Unni 2004). The garment industry, which had high output and employment growth in the organized sector till the mid-1990s, slowed down in the late 1990s, and there was a growth in unorganized sector output and employment. This could mean that with the adoption of flexible production processes, large firms subcontracted to small firms, leading to this informal segment registering high growth in output, employment and capital.

Implication of Growth for the Well-Being of Workers

Workers can benefit from growth in industry in two ways: if there is a high growth of employment and/or if there is a growth in wages. We defined good quality growth as that which includes the growth of both employment and labour productivity. The assumption is that growing labour productivity can be transferred to the workers in terms of high wage growth. So far we have discussed the extent to which an increase in employment occurred in industries with high growth of value added and labour productivity. Now, we discuss whether these industries also had a high growth of wage earnings. In other words, did the workers in the unorganized sector gain from the growth in the industry? And, was the increase in the ranks of the unorganized sector due to pull or push factors?

Most of the industry groups in the unorganized sector had relatively high wage growth as compared to the organized sector. The average rate of growth per annum of wage earnings in the unorganized sector, 12 per cent, was much higher than that in the organized sector, which was 1 per cent (Table 2.5). The growth in wage earnings in the unorganized sector was more or less commensurate to the growth categories that indicated quality growth in the sector. That is, Category A had the highest growth of wage earnings and Category C.7 had negative growth. Thus, the benefit of growth in the unorganized sector was transferred to the workers based on the performance of the industry in this sector.

In the organized sector, the high growth in value added in the Category A.1 industries, 8.6 per cent, was accompanied by high growth of labour productivity, 6.7 per cent, but the growth of wage earnings of 1.4 per cent was not commensurate to this growth. Thus, in the organized manufacturing sector, even in the industries where there was rapid growth of value added and labour productivity, the workers did not benefit from high growth of either employment or wage earnings.

Within Category A.1, industries with high growth of value added and labour productivity, in both the organized and unorganized sectors, were chemicals, other non-metallic minerals, fabricated metal products and motor vehicles. However, while the growth of wage earnings in these industry groups was high in the unorganized sector, that in the organized sector was much lower. Other industries within the unorganized sector alone were electrical machinery, other machinery and equipment, and communication equipment. Employment growth in these industry groups was definitely due to pull factors, or efficiency considerations. The workers were able to benefit from the process of growth through the generation of employment and a rise in wage earnings, though to a much lower extent in the organized sector. As noted earlier, autocomponents parts were manufactured within the fabricated metal products, electrical machinery, and machinery and equipment industries. The workers in these industries did benefit from a growth of wage earnings.

Category A.2 industries were those with negative employment growth, but positive growth in labour productivity and wage earnings. In

TABLE 2.5   *Growth Rates of Value Added, Employment, Labour Productivity and Emoluments per Worker in Organized/Unorganized Manufacturing by Growth Category, 1994–95 to 2000–01*

Industry Group/ Category	Organized				Industry Group/ Category	Unorganized			
	VA	EMP	LP	EW		VA	EMP	LP	EW
Category A.1									
Cotton ginning	11.8	2.7	9.2	0.2	Basic metals	7.0	1.2	5.9	12.9
Food	4.3	1.6	2.7	2.4	Food	6.5	1.7	4.8	11.7
Textiles	2.9	0.2	2.6	–1.3	Paper	10.9	5.7	5.2	16.7
Leather	6.3	1.7	4.4	2.7	Printing, publishing	6.0	4.0	2.0	10.2
Chemicals	10.7	3.1	7.6	1.9	Chemicals	8.3	7.6	0.7	11.3
Rubber	11.9	0.3	11.6	1.4	Electrical machinery	21.7	18.6	3.1	9.1
Other non-metal	12.0	3.1	8.9	1.8	Other non-metal	13.4	2.7	10.7	22.2
Fabricated metal	10.8	3.7	7.1	2.2	Fabricated metal	8.4	4.3	4.1	7.1
Precision equipment	13.2	3.3	9.9	4.2	Machinery equipment	12.3	7.6	4.7	9.6
Motor vehicles	11.3	4.3	7.0	1.7	Motor vehicles	16.5	9.4	7.1	14.0
Other manufacturing	19.6	9.8	9.7	–1.5	Communication equipment	10.8	4.8	6.0	9.7
Sub-total	8.6	1.9	6.7	1.4		9.0	3.0	6.3	11.4
Category A.2									
Tobacco	7.7	–1.9	9.6	0.6	Textiles	6.3	–0.2	6.4	11.7
Printing, publishing	3.2	–6.4	1.9	–3.9	Leather	1.7	–2.6	4.4	13.1
Transport equipment	6.7	–10.1	16.7	3.2	Transport equipment	3.4	–0.5	3.9	11.1
Machinery equipment	6.4	–0.1	6.5	3.3	Other manufacturing	5.0	–3.4	8.4	12.5
Electrical machinery	5.3	–0.8	6.1	–0.3					
Communication equipment	3.6	–3.1	6.6	2.3					
Basic metals	7.2	0.0	7.3	1.3					
Sub-total	6.2	–2.1	8.3	1.5		5.7	–1.3	7.0	11.8
Category B.3									
Wearing apparel	2.2	3.7	–1.5	2.9	Wearing apparel	14.4	14.4	–0.1	10.1
					Tobacco	5.0	7.7	–2.7	–5.6
					Wood	1.2	2.4	–1.2	8.5
					Rubber	0.8	1.5	–0.6	5.1
Sub-total	2.2	3.7	–1.5	2.9		5.0	5.2	–0.2	7.4
Category C.5									
Paper	–0.9	1.7	–2.6	–0.1					
Sub-total	–0.9	1.7	–2.6	–0.1					
Category C.6									
					Cotton ginning	–1.5	–11.9	10.4	24.6
					Precision equipment	–1.3	–4.4	3.1	3.1
Sub-total						–1.3	–7.0	5.6	5.0

TABLE 2.5 *(contd)*

Industry Group/ Category	Organized				Industry Group/ Category	Unorganized			
	VA	EMP	LP	EW		VA	EMP	LP	EW
Category C.7									
Office machinery	−12.3	−6.1	−6.2	−1.7	Office machinery	−53.1	−30.8	−22.4	−1.9
Wood	−5.1	−4.8	−0.3	3.4					
Sub-total	−10.2	−5.2	−5.0	0.5		0.1	−1.0	−2.0	−1.9
Total	*6.9*	*0.7*	*6.2*	*1.2*	*Total*	*6.9*	*2.1*	*4.8*	*12.1*

Notes: VA: Value Added; EMP: Employment; LP: Output per Worker; EW: Emoluments per Worker.
Value added deflated by the GDP deflator; Wages deflated by the CPI for industrial workers at 1982 prices.
The organized sector data is for 1994–95 to 1999–2000.
Source: NSSO (1998a), NSSO (1998b), NSSO (2002a), NSSO (2002b), CSO (1990a), CSO (1995a), CSO (1995b), CSO (2002).

the unorganized sector these included textiles, leather products, transport equipment and other manufacturing. The workers in these industries gained in terms of higher earnings but not in terms of employment.

In Category B, wearing apparel was one industry in which employment grew with negative growth in labour productivity in both the organized and unorganized sectors. Surprisingly, there was high growth of wage earnings as well, more so in the unorganized sector. Efficiency considerations were not the reason for the positive effects on labour in this industry. It is possible that very high demand during this period contributed to gains for the workers in terms of employment and wages.

The other two industries in the unorganized sector where employment and wages grew without commensurate growth in labour productivity were wood and rubber products. There may have been crowding in these industry groups, though the wages still showed positive growth. The tobacco industry in the unorganized sector was a certain case of overcrowding with negative growth in labour productivity and wages, but high growth of employment. That is, workers in this industry were there more due to push factors than pull factors. Rolling of bidis (traditional cigarettes) forms part of this industry, with a large proportion of women engaged in it. This industry was also one where sub-contracting was the norm, as we note later.

Overall, we can safely assume that the growth of employment in the unorganized sector in the Category A.1 industry group was mainly due to pull factors. These were the dynamic growth industries in the late 1990s with positive growth impulses. Further, in these industries, the benefit of growth was transferred to workers in terms of growth of employment and high wages. In the rest of the categories where there was either negative growth of employment or inefficient growth of employment, push factors could have been operating.

Linkages between Formal and Informal Sectors: Benefit to Workers

One of the outcomes of globalization and liberalization is increased outsourcing from larger units to smaller ones. This process also fosters linkages between the formal and informal sectors. The negative features of this process, often discussed in the literature, are exploitation of smaller enterprises and workers in them through long working hours, low wages and poor working conditions, since they are often not in a position to bargain (Mazumdar 2007). The positive features include growth of employment and inflow of technology to smaller enterprises that can help to improve productivity and enhance skill-sets.

In this empirical review, we consider three types of linkages between the formal and informal sectors: through the labour market, the product market and technology. Besides the transfer of skills, labour market linkages develop through hiring contract labour. An increase in employment opportunities and transfer of skills are some of the possible outcomes of labour market linkages. The product market is linked by various types of sub-contracting arrangements. Forward linkages exist in the form of sub-contracting of output and backward linkages through input linkages. The workers in the informal sector benefit through increased employment opportunities. Market interaction between the sectors also occurs through the transfer of technology. The transfer of technology between firms could take various forms and this could benefit the workers through upgradation of skills. In what follows we analyse the market interaction between sectors through all the three market linkages to the extent permitted by the macro data, and discuss how the workers could benefit from such linkages.

Flexibility of the Labour Market in Organized Manufacturing

Labour market linkages between the formal and informal sectors are established through attempts at increasing labour flexibility in the organized or formal sector firms (Ramaswamy 1999). Numerical flexibility is part of the external flexibility to adjust the labour input, which is the focus of the classical labour market theory. This basically involves adjustment mechanisms of labour such as turnover, temporary layoff and recall, temporary work, part-time work, sub-contracted and home-based work, or flexible working time (that is, work shifts and overtime practices) without modifying the number of employees. All these constitute forms of linkages between organized sector firms and labour contractors who perform the role previously undertaken by the human resources departments (HRD) of large firms.

Temporary, part-time and home-based workers form a segment of the informal labour market, and may directly establish links with the formal sector firms. That is, the labour market linkages between the formal sector firms and informal workers can be mediated either through labour contractors or agencies, or directly with the workers. These linkages within the labour market could also take the form of wage flexibility.

An overall increase in flexibility in the labour market in organized manufacturing was observed with an increase in the hiring of workers through contractors, both among total employees and total workers, including managerial and professional workers (Table 2.6). This method of recruiting workers implied increasing flexibility for the firm since the workers' contracts were flexible and did not include all the benefits that permanent workers received.

Across the industry groups, there was an increase in the proportion of contract workers to total workers from 13 to 20 per cent at the all-India level. Among the eleven industries in Category A.1, or good quality growth category, in the organized sector, only four showed an increase above the national average in hiring contract workers. In the seven industries in Category A.2, with quality employment but no employment growth, three were increasingly hiring contract workers above the national average. However, of the three industries with poor growth performance in Category C, two were increasingly hiring workers through contractors. It appears that the industry groups with contract labour in the organized sector were not the top-quality growth industry groups, though some of them also engaged in this practice.

A large number of operations in these industries either involved assembly labour or certain repetitive jobs, and firms found it economical to outsource these activities to contractors, who hired workers on a piece-work or daily-wage basis to undertake these operations. This helped in improving productivity for both the firm and the workers. The practice of farming out or contracting out parts of the shop floor was widely prevalent in the consumer durable industries, motor vehicles, and dyeing and printing industries. It was also observed later in our study of the autocomponents industry. Outsourcing reduced the burden of managing workers for the enterprise, the firms then being able to concentrate on building customer contacts, customer care, expansion, research and development, apart from reducing costs tremendously.

The rise in flexibility in large firms was facilitated by the change in labour law legislations introduced in the latter half of the 1990s, which allowed firms with more than 100 workers to retrench. Most firms reduced their permanent workers and preferred to hire casual or contract labourers

TABLE 2.6   *Flexibility in the Organized Manufacturing Sector Labour Market,*
1995–2002

Industry	Proportion of Workers Employed through Contractors			
	To Total Employees		To Total Workers	
	1995–96	2001–02	1995–96	2001–02
14. Cotton-ginning, cleaning and baling	14.11	19.19	15.93	23.38
15. Food products	14.14	17.09	17.79	22.14
16. Tobacco products	11.31	56.01	11.34	59.69
17. Textiles	7.72	7.57	8.82	8.91
18. Garment industry	3.65	6.11	4.05	7.11
19. Leather products	8.51	10.39	9.90	12.40
20. Wood (except furniture)	4.25	8.91	5.16	11.93
21. Paper and Paper products	13.26	18.32	16.49	23.41
22. Publishing, Printing	1.92	4.66	2.85	7.55
23. Coke, Refined Petroleum	12.33	22.23	17.57	29.62
24. Chemical products	10.92	14.69	15.63	21.93
25. Rubber products	6.73	10.96	9.67	14.67
26. Other Non-Metallic Mineral products	25.14	8.78	30.09	10.96
27. Basic Metals	15.28	18.43	19.67	24.94
28. Fabricated Metal products	11.35	19.94	15.10	26.86
29. Machinery and Equipment	3.74	9.30	7.42	23.77
30. Office Accounting and Computing	11.87	23.80	23.19	37.84
31. Electrical Machinery	7.29	10.26	10.37	15.18
32. Radio, TV, Communications	2.36	7.10	3.29	11.15
33. Medical Precision, Optical	2.15	3.66	3.64	5.65
34. Motor Vehicles	7.79	12.40	10.19	17.15
35. Other Transport equipment	18.33	9.68	22.88	12.91
36. Furniture and Other Manufacturing	12.19	10.60	14.82	14.08
Total	*10.74*	*15.38*	*13.82*	*20.32*

Source: *Annual Survey of Industries, 1995–96*, Volume 1, Table 3: 109, Central Statistical
Organization, Department of Statistics and Programme Implementation, Ministry of
Planning and Programme Implementation, Calcutta: Government of India.
Annual Survey of Industries, 2001–02, Volume 1, Table 4: 306, Central Statistical
Organization, Department of Statistics and Programme Implementation, Ministry of
Planning and Programme Implementation, Calcutta: Government of India.

through sub-contractor agencies. This legislation also allowed many firms
to introduce automation or better technology, reducing their dependence
on workers. As a result, the labour-intensive processes were sub-contracted
out to small or informal firms, greatly minimizing labour costs and operations. The labour reforms thus created labour market flexibility as well as
encouraged inter-firm linkages in the product market through sub-contracting arrangements.

While the practice of hiring contract labour in the formal sector increased the employment opportunities for workers in the informal labour market, it is seen as one of the negative impacts of the economic reform. Jobs created by this form of linkage are poor quality ones with none of the social security benefits that would be available to the workers if they were permanent employees in the formal sector firms. In fact, the labour laws now allow firms to dodge their social responsibility and to place the onus of providing other benefits on the contractors. The contractors, in turn, are easily able to evade the provisions of the Contract Labour Act which require providing security cover to the contract workers hired by them.

Product Market Linkages in Unorganized Manufacturing

The Unorganized Manufacturing Sector Survey of 1994–95 had a direct question with regard to 'whether the enterprise was ancillary to the parent firm or not', whether there was a captive relationship between the parent and the ancillary unit. Only about 3.6 per cent of the firms reported that they were ancillary to the parent firm, and nearly 7 per cent of the large enterprises (DME) reported likewise (Appendix Table 2.3). Across the industry groups, ancillarization was found to be higher in wearing apparel, paper and paper products, chemicals, machinery and equipment, electrical machinery, and motor vehicles. In all these, labour-intensive tasks, machining and assembly activity were sub-contracted out to small firms run with family labour or hired labour. In the chemicals, paper, and machinery and equipment industries, over 20 per cent of own account enterprises (OAE) undertook sub-contracted work as ancillary units to the parent firm, while in the wearing apparel, electrical machinery and motor vehicle industries, 7 to 18 per cent of the medium (NDME) and large enterprises (DME) undertook sub-contracted work as ancillary units largely due to the nature of operations. However, it is very difficult to discern from this data the nature of the sub-contracting – whether it is 'vertical' or 'horizontal', and what kind of linkages existed between the parent and the ancillary firms.

The Unorganized Manufacturing Sector Survey of 2000–01 introduced a new question: 'Does the enterprise undertake any work on contract basis or not?' This lent a slightly broader interpretation to the question of sub-contracting and included firms that were not necessarily just ancillaries to the parent firm. The proportion of unorganized sector firms undertaking sub-contract work was 30.7 per cent, and higher among firms operating from home (36 per cent), compared to firms outside (18.5 per cent) (Table 2.7). Across the industry groups, more than 30 per cent of the firms in fourteen out of twenty-two industries were sub-contracting in production

TABLE 2.7   *Proportion and Distribution of Firms Sub-Contracting In by Location and Industry Group, 2000–01*

Industry	Proportion of Sub-Contracting Firms	Distribution of Sub-Contracting Firms by Location			
	Total	At Home	Outside	No Fixed Premises	Total
14. Cotton-ginning, cleaning and baling	8.3	6.9	93.1	0.0	100
15. Food products	3.6	71.1	23.5	5.4	100
16. Tobacco products	89.3	99.1	0.8	0.1	100
17. Textiles	55.5	89.7	10.3	0.1	100
18. Wearing apparel	17.4	70.5	29.4	0.1	100
19. Leather products	23.7	66.2	33.8	0.0	100
20. Wood (except furniture)	11.3	58.9	16.3	24.8	100
21. Paper and Paper products	42.0	80.2	19.8	0.1	100
22. Publishing, Printing	39.6	31.7	68.3	0.0	100
23. Coke, Refined Petroleum	0.3	0.0	100.0	0.0	100
24. Chemical products	66.8	95.9	4.1	0.0	100
25. Rubber products	42.6	59.0	40.9	0.0	100
26. Other Non-Metallic Mineral products	5.6	69.4	29.6	1.0	100
27. Basic Metals	36.5	36.9	63.1	0.0	100
28. Fabricated Metal products	22.1	39.8	59.7	0.4	100
29. Machinery and Equipment	22.0	25.2	73.9	0.9	100
30. Office Accounting and Computing	63.6	0.0	100.0	0.0	100
31. Electrical Machinery	32.0	57.0	43.0	0.0	100
32. Radio, TV, Communications	46.8	44.8	55.2	0.0	100
33. Medical Precision, Optical	37.7	33.5	66.5	0.0	100
34. Motor Vehicles	48.1	7.3	92.7	0.0	100
35. Other Transport Equipment	42.7	22.7	77.3	0.0	100
36. Furniture and Other Manufacturing	35.4	52.1	37.8	10.1	100
37. Recycling	44.2	61.0	39.0	0.0	100
Total	*30.7*	*82.0*	*15.3*	*2.6*	*100*

Source: NSSO Unorganized Manufacturing Sector Survey, 2000–01. Computed.

activity. Even industries with high growth of good quality employment, Category A.1, were engaged in sub-contracting activity.

The distribution of sub-contracting firms across locations showed that about 82 per cent of the firms operated from home, while 15 per cent operated from business places and 3 per cent had no fixed premises. Among the high growth (A.1) industries, 95 per cent of the sub-contracting firms in the manufacture of chemical products, and more than 50 per cent of the firms manufacturing other non-metallic mineral products and electrical machinery, did so from home. The growth industries have thus clearly penetrated the lowest segments of the informal labour market.

Market interaction through services

Besides sub-contracting production work, the firms were also linked through service contracting. The Unorganized Manufacturing Sector Survey captured the 'receipts from services provided to others including commission charges' which allowed us to estimate the sub-contracting in of services undertaken by the firms. About 67 per cent of the firms reported undertaking sub-contracted service activities, with the larger enterprises (DME) less likely to undertake these compared to the smaller ones (NDME and OAME) (Table 2.8). Such service contracts need not be a regular arrangement between two firms and were probably only an indicator of market interaction between firms in the product market. In the firms that undertook service sub-contracting work, such work, on average, amounted to 70 per cent of the receipts (Table 2.8). The proportions declined as the firm size increased, showing that the large firms were less dependent on such contracts. In the traditional sector, – tobacco products, garments and textile products, for instance – almost 90 per cent of the receipts were from sub-contracting work, while in the modern sector most of the industry groups received only around 60 per cent of their receipts from subcontracting.

The Survey also attempted to capture the service activity sub-contracted out through a question on 'service charges for work done by other concerns' (contract, sub-contract, legal, audit, advertising and other accounting services, warehousing expenses, commission expenses, and so on). About 13 per cent of the firms sub-contracted out services to other concerns, and it was quite high among the large firms (42 per cent) and quite low among the own account enterprises (10 per cent) (Table 2.9). Sub-contracting out of services among large firms was quite high in the modern sector and comparatively low in the traditional sector. However, the value of services sub-contracted out as a proportion of the total expenses was very small (7 per cent), and was almost the same across different sizes of firms, which could mean that very low labour-intensive tasks were being sub-contracted out.

Thus, besides sub-contracting of production activities, outsourcing of various service activities of firms was also quite prevalent. The general pattern of market interaction between firms was that small firms depended on the large ones for service orders, while large firms contracted out services, perhaps to reduce labour, equipment and administration costs. The smaller firms in the informal sector generated employment and incomes through

TABLE 2.8   *Sub-Contracting In Services by Enterprise Type, 2000–01*

	Firms Sub-Contracting In Work				Sub-Contracted Work in Total Receipts			
	OAME	NDME	DME	Total	OAME	NDME	DME	Total
14. Cotton-ginning, cleaning and baling	100.0	93.9	78.2	98.7	75.3	89.2	73.0	77.4
15. Food products	44.7	48.0	19.6	44.2	78.3	51.1	21.9	62.7
16. Tobacco products	96.5	31.2	10.8	95.1	98.9	98.4	40.9	97.2
17. Textiles	69.2	74.5	69.7	69.6	94.3	92.2	86.8	90.6
18. Wearing apparel	97.8	97.1	88.2	97.5	95.5	93.9	90.0	94.0
19. Leather products	54.5	47.1	44.2	52.8	33.9	52.6	82.7	52.4
20. Wood (except furniture)	42.1	77.5	65.5	43.8	84.5	48.8	17.3	55.9
21. Paper and Paper products	45.1	46.3	41.8	45.0	76.1	72.0	22.3	36.8
22. Publishing, Printing	86.0	79.8	82.5	82.6	86.1	72.6	52.5	65.4
23. Coke, Refined Petroleum	0.0	4.2	0.6	2.1	0.0	100.0	100.0	100.0
24. Chemical products	89.4	16.8	43.2	80.8	97.0	63.8	50.2	69.5
25. Rubber products	66.2	59.8	41.6	59.7	63.6	75.4	49.2	60.2
26. Other Non-Metallic Mineral products	5.6	12.0	4.4	5.9	61.4	43.4	65.8	57.6
27. Basic Metals	93.7	79.0	44.1	81.7	40.0	52.3	15.6	30.3
28. Fabricated Metal products	87.8	73.9	66.9	83.0	57.7	53.1	52.8	54.3
29. Machinery and Equipment	92.7	72.3	55.6	82.4	74.7	63.6	33.2	47.8
30. Office Accounting and Computing	–	82.9	56.7	76.2	0.0	0.9	3.6	2.9
31. Electrical Machinery	91.9	75.9	30.0	71.7	75.0	67.2	43.1	59.0
32. Radio, TV, Communications	68.1	67.6	76.1	71.5	41.7	77.3	68.8	68.6
33. Medical Precision, Optical	92.9	52.1	36.5	68.8	51.8	46.2	91.4	65.6
34. Motor Vehicles	52.4	87.1	70.9	73.6	60.4	80.5	56.2	62.7
35. Other Transport Equipment	84.5	76.8	52.1	73.8	49.9	54.6	74.1	62.8
36. Furniture and Other Manufacturing	77.8	82.8	78.7	78.6	59.4	55.3	64.8	59.3
37. Recycling	91.0	59.8	28.3	81.5	77.1	88.7	87.8	81.6
Total	67.1	71.1	49.8	66.8	80.9	66.5	57.4	69.7

Source: Same as Table 2.7.

sub-contracting in service activities from the larger firms in the informal and formal sectors. Workers in the informal sector thus benefited from the employment created in this process.

Technology Transfer Linkages

The nature of sub-contracting undertaken by a firm could be 'vertical' or 'horizontal'. In 'vertical' sub-contracting, the firm is fully dependent

TABLE 2.9   *Sub-Contracting Out Services by Enterprise Type, 2000-01*

	Firms Sub-Contracting Out Work				Sub-Contracted Work in Total Receipts			
	OAME	NDME	DME	Total	OAME	NDME	DME	Total
14. Cotton-ginning, cleaning and baling	1.4	0.0	21.1	1.5	25.7	0.0	2.4	2.6
15. Food products	13.7	14.4	28.5	14.3	4.2	1.9	0.6	2.1
16. Tobacco products	12.8	18.7	54.5	13.2	57.6	49.8	22.3	31.2
17. Textiles	16.3	36.7	47.3	19.7	24.3	8.1	7.3	8.8
18. Wearing apparel	8.8	22.0	34.5	10.9	15.6	14.3	11.3	12.3
19. Leather products	10.1	14.0	31.8	12.0	4.5	8.9	7.4	7.3
20. Wood (except furniture)	3.2	14.2	38.7	4.0	16.0	6.1	1.7	4.2
21. Paper and Paper products	3.6	29.2	55.6	11.9	13.8	3.4	2.9	3.1
22. Publishing, Printing	26.0	35.1	50.0	33.4	19.7	14.6	12.1	13.0
23. Coke, Refined Petroleum	0.0	62.9	65.3	37.7	0.0	0.6	0.5	0.6
24. Chemical products	1.5	31.5	40.5	7.0	10.0	2.1	2.2	2.2
25. Rubber products	2.8	29.7	54.9	20.5	3.1	1.3	2.6	2.4
26. Other Non-Metallic Mineral products	3.3	17.9	29.6	6.7	8.7	5.0	3.1	3.5
27. Basic Metals	8.3	21.9	52.3	19.1	4.5	1.2	0.4	0.5
28. Fabricated Metal products	3.8	14.6	40.9	8.8	16.5	3.6	5.3	5.3
29. Machinery and Equipment	4.9	38.3	70.6	22.4	6.5	7.8	5.2	5.9
30. Office Accounting and Computing	0.0	15.8	73.5	30.5	0.0	2.7	1.7	1.8
31. Electrical Machinery	8.2	14.1	65.0	24.4	6.6	2.3	9.3	9.3
32. Radio, TV, Communications	7.8	22.9	60.3	35.9	1.9	4.2	1.4	2.0
33. Medical Precision, Optical	3.8	32.6	67.5	24.8	8.7	2.3	4.1	3.4
34. Motor Vehicles	14.0	45.6	54.6	41.6	14.3	9.6	4.9	5.6
35. Other Transport Equipment	25.2	47.6	76.0	45.8	12.1	3.2	2.3	2.9
36. Furniture and Other Manufacturing	16.5	39.4	42.7	21.2	7.6	5.4	3.8	5.4
37. Recycling	6.4	42.5	53.2	15.0	11.4	2.4	0.7	1.6
Total	10.3	24.3	41.8	12.9	8.2	6.2	6.6	6.7

Source: Same as Table 2.7.

upon the parent firm, middleman or contractor to supply the raw material, design and equipment. While the literature generally regards such vertical linkages as exploitative, a positive feature is that it is a form of transfer of technology between firms. In 'horizontal' sub-contracting, the firm is independent and sources its raw material, design and equipment by itself (Watanabe 1983). A vertical sub-contractor is a dependent producer, while the horizontal sub-contractor is an independent producer. The Unorganized Manufacturing Sector Survey of 2000–01 asked entrepreneurs a series of questions about the type and nature of contracts, which helped us to categorize them into 'vertical' and 'horizontal' types.

Only about 1.3 per cent of the firms were independent producers with horizontal sub-contracting, and this was slightly higher among medium-sized firms, NDME (Appendix Table A 2.4). Across industry groups, horizontal sub-contracting was found in paper and paper products, publishing, rubber products, basic metals, office accounting and machinery, radio, television and communications, and motor vehicles. About 27 per cent of the firms were vertically subcontracted, and across different size categories, it was lower in medium-sized enterprises. Across industry groups, this kind of sub-contracting was observed in consumer goods such as tobacco products, textiles, paper and paper products and other chemical products; consumer durables such as radio, television and communications, watches and clocks, and motor vehicles. In the high-growth Category A.1 group, capital goods industries such as fabricated metals, machinery and equipment, and electrical machinery were vertically integrated through sub-contracting chains.

Vertical sub-contracting was in the nature of transfer of technology, since the sub-contracting firm supplied raw material and equipment, and sometimes the contractor specified the design. About 88 per cent of the dependent firms received raw material from the contractor and only 7 per cent of the firms were supplied with equipment (Appendix Table A 2.5). The design was specified by the contractor for 93 per cent of the firms. The proportions were almost the same across firms of different sizes in the case of both design specification and equipment supply, but there was a slight variation in the supply of raw material. A significantly higher proportion of own account enterprises received raw materials, compared to medium and large ones.

Vertical sub-contracting linkages were undertaken by a large proportion of firms in the high-growth industries. Linkages with large firms, perhaps in the organized sector, are also likely to have helped firms in the unorganized sector to grow. Linkages in the transfer of technology between large firms and subcontractors mainly occurred through specified raw materials and supply of design. Firms in fewer industry groups were supplied with equipment. Capital goods industries with high growth that obtained transfer of technology through the supply of equipment were fabricated metal, machinery and equipment, and electrical machinery. Consumer non-durable industries such as wearing apparel, leather goods, paper and chemical products, many of which were high-growth industries, also had a relatively large proportion of firms being supplied with equipment as part of the vertical linkages.

An important benefit of technology transfer through the specification of design is that it has to be implemented by the work force within the firm to a very large extent. This requires skill training, to ensure product quality and efficiency in the production process. Vertical sub-contracting of this kind is beneficial to workers since it enhances their skill levels. Industries that received a supply of equipment also saw benefits to workers through an upgradation of skills, since it was they who had to operate the machines ultimately. Therefore, over and above the creation of employment and wage increases, the sub-contracting linkages also improved the skills and hence the marketability of the work force.

Many of the changes initiated by the industrial and trade policy reforms allowed a large-scale transfer of technology and an increase in the size of firms. Increase in firm size also meant that more efficient technologies could be adopted in many industries. The direct benefits of these were opportunities for employment and enhanced wages, and the indirect benefit was skill upgradation. We will later study the case of skill formation in the autocomponents industry through the inflow of technology.

Conclusions

In the late 1990s, the informal or unorganized sector appeared to be a dynamic one. The policy changes of that decade, with a focus on the small-scale sector, facilitated the growth of the informal sector. The industrial policies of dismantling reservation for products and increasing the investment limits for the small-scale sector led to the growth of at least the larger enterprises in the informal sector. The trade policies of reducing tariffs and removing quota restrictions facilitated the inflow of technology, which encouraged the industry to reduce dependence on sub-optimal technology. All this also led to the expansion of both the domestic and foreign markets. In order to meet the demand for products and to have a flexible arrangement to adjust to changing volumes of production, the larger enterprises in the organized and unorganized sectors increasingly relied on sub-contracting out production and intermediate products to small firms in the informal sector. With large-scale sub-contracting to home-based units in addition, the formal sector was able to penetrate to the lowest segments of the informal sector.

In the late 1990s, the industries in the unorganized sector that performed very well, with high growth and quality employment, were largely consumer non-durables consisting of food and paper; chemical industries including pharmaceuticals and cosmetics; consumer durables like radio, television and communications equipment, and motor vehicles; and capital goods such as metal-based and fabricated metals, machinery and equipment, and electrical machinery. The benefits of the growth were transferred to the workers in the form of an increase in employment and wages in most of these industries. Many of the industries also engaged in vertical sub contracting for growth, and this helped in technology transfer through the supply of design, raw materials and, to a lesser extent, equipment.

For the workers, the impact of these policy changes and the consequent changes in organization of production was both positive and negative. On the positive side, the expansion of markets meant increased employment opportunities and growth of real wage earnings across almost all segments of the work force. There was also the growth of a skilled work force with increasing wage premiums, as we shall see in the next chapter. Inter-linkages between firms in the formal and informal sectors through sub-contracting and technology transfers led to an upgradation of skills in the work force, essential for improving the marketability of workers in the fast-changing labour market scenario. One of the negative outcomes of the policy changes was the increasing gap between various segments of workers, particularly between the skilled and the unskilled. We turn to these issues in the next chapter.

Appendix Chart

CHART A 2.1   *Economic Policies and their Impact in the Reforms Periods*

Policy	Impact
I. 1984–85 to 1989–90: Partial Liberalization Period	
Industrial Policy	
1 Dismantled internal controls	
– De-licensing of several industries	Expansion and diversification of some
– Easing of licensing restrictions	product groups: broad-banding
2 Flexibility of operation of domestic capital	Growth in the organized sector
– Ceiling limits on investment for big business houses raised	
3 No reforms on privatization of public sector	
Trade Policy	
1 Import liberalization	
– QR continued	Foreign competition increased
– Some QR replaced by tariffs	
– Some tariffs lowered	
Domestic protection reduced	
– Import of number of capital goods allowed on OGL	Slow down in machinery industry
– Import of intermediate goods on OGL	Slow down in metal-based industry in
• metal products	organized and unorganized sectors
• organic heavy chemicals	(high employment-intensive industries)
2 EPR of chemical industry remained high	
– Synthetic fibres	High growth of value added
– Soaps, cosmetics, glycerin	High capital intensity
– Pesticides	Low employment growth
– Inorganic heavy chemical	
3 EPR of consumer goods remained high	High growth in consumer goods
Labour Policy	
No reforms	No change
II. 1989–90 to 1994–95: Early Reforms Period	
Industrial Policy	
1 Encourage private investment	
– Abolished investment licensing	Allowed domestic industry to expand
– Simplified investment rules	capacity and production
– Monopoly of public sector abandoned	– Automobile industry
– Heavy industries	– Heavy industries
– Automobiles	
– Motor car delicensed in 1993–94	
– SSI investment limit in plant and machinery increased, Rs 2 to 5 lakhs	High positive growth in fixed capital in organized and unorganized sectors
– Abolished industrial licensing for all but 18 industries, 15 industries in 1993	
– Excise duty reduction on automobiles, 55 to 40 per cent	

CHART **A 2.1** (*contd*)

Policy	Impact
Excise and customs duty reduction in components of spare parts of automobiles in 1993–94	Entry of multinational companies: Ford, General Motors, Hyundai, Daewoo
2 No reforms in private sector of public sector enterprises	Absence of massive labour displacement

Trade Policy

1 QR abolished	
– Except consumer goods and agricultural commodities	
Reduced peak tariff rates and dispersion (123% in 1987–88 to 58% in 1994–95) Import licensing abolished	Reduced dependence on sub-optimal domestic inputs and technology
– Capital goods	– Growth of capital good industry
– Intermediate goods and raw materials	– Unorganized metal-based and machinery industry affected, organized sector recovered slightly
2 Allowed import of motor vehicle parts in 1992–93	Growth of automobile industry
3 Devaluation of rupee	Growth of exports
4 QR remained for	High growth of consumer goods industry Distortion of resource allocation to consumer goods away from basic and capital goods
– Consumer goods	
– Agricultural commodities	
5 Foreign investment encouraged	
– Foreign portfolio institutions allowed entry	
– Rules of FDI liberalized	
– Automatic approval of foreign collaboration	– Facilitates formation of alliances for technology transfer
• In 34 priority industries	– International marketing encouraged
– Foreign firms could hold up to 51% equity if capital imports financed through foreign equity	– Joint ventures with multinational enterprises
	– Import of technology from multinational enterprises
• In 34 priority industries	– Import capital goods
	– Expand capacities
	– Introduce new products without industrial license
– Import technology against royalty and lump-sum payments	– Technology transfer easy

Labour Policy

No reforms	Absence of massive labour displacement

III. 1994–95 to 2000–01: Rapid Economic Reforms

Industrial Policy

1 Public sector reforms	
– 'Disinvestments', sale of portion of government equity, government retains majority control	– General slow down in organised sector
	– Slow employment growth in the organized sector

CHART A 2.1 (contd)

Policy	Impact
– Push through privatization of public sector firms, 1998	
2 Industrial licensing for pharmaceuticals and cosmetics removed	– Growth of pharmaceutical and cosmetics etc. in organized and unorganized sectors
3 – De-reservation of SSI to allow larger firms to enter garments in 2001 – Investment ceiling of SSI in plant and machinery raised from Rs 5 to 25 lakhs – Ceiling on working capital for SSI doubled from Rs 2 to 4 crores	– High growth in the garments sector – Growth of unorganized sector
Trade Policy – Tariff rates further reduced, 52 to 41% • In consumer goods industry – Export Promotion Capital Goods (EPCG) scheme at zero duty extended to small-scale engineering industry	
Credit Policy Credit squeeze in 1996 – Based on quantity of credit rather than interest rate	Beginning of the recession
Labour Policy – Laws amended to allow firms with more than 100 workers to lay off labour	Decline in growth of employment in the organized sector

Notes: QR: Quantitative restrictions
       EPR: Effective Protection Rates
       SSI: Small Scale Industry
Source: Economic Survey, various years, Ministry of Finance and Company Affairs, New Delhi: Government of India.

Appendix Tables

TABLE A 2.1   *Growth Rates in Value Added, Employment and Labour Productivity in Organized Manufacturing by Two-Digit Industry Group*

Industry Groups	Value Added			Employment			Labour Productivity		
	1984–90	1989–95	1994–2000	1984–90	1989–95	1994–2000	1984–90	1989–95	1994–2000
Category A.1									
Cotton-ginning	6.65	–6.36	11.84	3.06	–0.93	2.66	3.59	–5.43	9.18
Textiles	5.91	6.41	2.86	–2.41	–0.34	0.21	8.33	6.75	2.65
Food products	10.52	5.82	4.31	1.79	2.30	1.65	8.74	3.52	2.66
Leather goods	5.18	11.05	6.26	6.49	3.79	1.68	–1.32	7.25	4.57
Chemical products	9.10	9.35	10.72	1.80	3.37	3.11	7.31	5.98	7.61
Rubber products	8.64	7.54	12.00	4.87	5.14	3.11	3.77	2.40	8.89
Other Non-Metallic Minerals	8.27	4.38	11.92	1.14	0.41	0.32	7.13	3.97	11.60
Fabricated Metals	4.67	6.93	10.83	2.52	2.07	3.74	2.15	4.86	7.09
Precision equipment	11.25	9.04	13.18	4.14	3.02	3.32	7.10	6.01	9.87
Motor Vehicles	5.25	9.11	11.30	1.89	3.50	4.31	3.36	5.61	6.99
Other Manufacturing	–1.68	22.16	19.57	1.33	8.44	9.83	–3.02	13.72	9.74
Sub-total	*7.90*	*7.50*	*8.63*	*0.67*	*1.73*	*1.92*	*7.23*	*5.77*	*6.71*
Category A.2									
Tobacco products	–0.58	5.08	9.58	–5.73	–5.21	–6.17	5.15	10.29	15.74
Publishing, Printing	1.32	10.85	3.19	–2.75	2.66	–6.43	4.07	8.19	9.63
Other Transport equipment	–1.38	7.31	6.66	–4.27	2.01	–10.08	2.90	5.30	16.75
Machinery and equipment	1.75	5.13	6.37	–0.69	0.86	–0.09	2.44	4.28	6.47
Electrical Machinery	3.51	9.71	5.31	2.28	2.53	–0.81	1.23	7.17	6.12
Communication equipment	17.93	13.18	3.56	6.73	2.91	–3.05	11.20	10.27	6.62
Basic Metals	5.20	10.02	7.22	–2.51	1.34	–0.03	7.71	8.67	7.25
Sub-total	*4.07*	*8.90*	*6.22*	*0.30*	*1.77*	*–2.07*	*3.78*	*7.13*	*8.29*
Category B.3									
Wearing Apparel	20.19	26.97	2.20	11.15	17.30	3.73	9.04	9.67	–1.53
Sub-total	*20.19*	*26.97*	*2.20*	*11.15*	*17.30*	*3.73*	*9.04*	*9.67*	*–1.53*
Category C.5									
Paper products	9.32	3.56	–0.88	0.36	3.57	1.75	8.96	–0.01	–2.63
Sub-total	*9.32*	*3.56*	*–0.88*	*0.36*	*3.57*	*1.75*	*8.96*	*–0.01*	*–2.63*
Category C.7									
Office, Accounting and Computing Machinery	7.98	10.67	–12.29	–4.23	–1.57	–6.12	12.21	12.24	–6.17
Wood products	2.10	–3.84	–5.11	–0.73	–0.17	–4.81	2.83	–3.67	–0.30
Sub-total	*5.28*	*5.75*	*–10.15*	*–1.79*	*–0.56*	*–5.16*	*7.08*	*6.31*	*–4.99*
All	**7.20**	**8.25**	**6.94**	**0.65**	**2.13**	**0.70**	**6.55**	**6.11**	**6.24**

Note: The last time period for the organized sector data is from 1994–95 to 1999–2000.

Source: CSO (1985a), CSO (1985b), CSO (1985c), CSO (1990a), CSO (1990b), CSO (1990c), CSO (1995a), CSO (1995b), CSO (2002).

TABLE A 2.2   *Growth Rates in Employment, Value Added and Labour Productivity in Unorganized Manufacturing by Two-Digit Industry Group*

Industry Group	Value Added			Employment			Labour Productivity		
	1984–90	1989–95	1994–01	1984–90	1989–95	1994–01	1984–90	1989–95	1994–01
Category A									
Food products	0.33	–1.52	6.52	–3.65	0.79	1.69	3.98	–2.30	4.83
Paper products	7.64	–3.95	10.91	10.21	–1.13	5.73	–2.57	–2.83	5.18
Publishing, Printing	12.25	–6.04	5.97	12.60	–2.16	3.99	–0.36	–3.89	1.98
Chemical products	10.83	–12.94	8.29	9.62	–9.39	7.63	1.21	–3.55	0.66
Other Non-Metals	6.15	1.34	13.43	2.03	–1.81	2.69	4.12	3.15	10.74
Fabricated Metals	–6.25	4.83	8.37	–0.31	2.38	4.27	–5.94	2.45	4.10
Machinery and equipment	11.21	–10.67	12.31	6.69	–2.55	7.56	4.53	–8.12	4.75
Electrical Machinery	–	–	21.72	9.10	–6.30	18.63			3.09
Radio, TV	2.23	–0.44	10.76	9.25	–1.52	4.77	–7.02	1.08	5.99
Motor Vehicles	–26.93	–1.84	16.54	8.38	3.00	9.40	–35.31	–4.84	7.14
Sub-total	*0.59*	*–0.68*	*9.30*	*–0.46*	*–0.36*	*3.01*	*1.05*	*–0.32*	*6.28*
Textiles	3.50	–2.88	6.26	–5.63	–2.43	–0.16	9.13	–0.45	6.42
Basic Metals	2.10	–3.82	7.02	–1.58	1.84	1.16	3.69	–5.66	5.86
Other Transport	–22.86	–3.10	3.43	5.25	–6.87	–0.45	–28.11	3.77	3.87
Other Manufacturing	10.66	5.38	4.99	5.80	1.35	–3.44	4.86	4.03	8.43
Sub-total	*4.07*	*0.19*	*5.70*	*–2.48*	*–1.12*	*–1.26*	*6.55*	*1.32*	*6.96*
Category B									
Tobacco products	7.24	–4.30	5.03	12.89	–8.80	7.73	–5.65	4.49	–2.70
Wearing Apparel	–29.52	6.24	14.40	–41.34	1.52	14.44	11.82	4.72	–0.05
Wood products	6.12	–7.31	1.20	7.53	–3.08	2.36	–1.40	–4.23	–1.17
Coke, Petroleum	–4.33	–6.73	0.16	3.11	–10.76	0.45	–7.44	4.03	–0.29
Sub-total	*–1.56*	*–4.93*	*5.01*	*0.57*	*–4.75*	*5.16*	*–2.14*	*–0.18*	*–0.15*
Category C									
Cotton-ginning	3.85	–20.83	–1.53	–16.08	–4.33	–11.93	19.93	–16.49	10.40
Medical Precision	26.31	–7.01	–1.31	7.76	–0.39	–4.36	18.54	–6.62	3.06
Sub-total	*19.81*	*–8.95*	*–1.33*	*–6.27*	*–2.04*	*–6.96*	*26.08*	*–6.90*	*5.63*
Rubber products	15.69	4.79	0.83	12.18	4.77	1.45	3.52	0.03	–0.63
Office Accounting	–1.60	19.91	–53.12	–12.41	5.91	–30.76	10.82	14.00	–22.36
Leather products	–16.50	8.24	1.71	–6.94	–1.65	–2.65	–9.56	9.89	4.36
Sub-total	*–3.43*	*6.92*	*0.12*	*–2.60*	*0.68*	*–1.02*	*–0.85*	*6.24*	*–2.02*
All *	0.99	–0.99	6.92	–0.95	–1.73	2.16	1.94	0.75	4.76

Note: The classification of industry groups is based on the last period's (1994–2001) growth categories. The last time period for the unorganized sector data is 2000–01.
Wearing apparel excludes tailoring establishments.

Source: NSSO (1989), NSSO (1994a), NSSO (1994b), NSSO (1998a), NSSO (1998b), NSSO (1998c), NSSO (2002a), NSSO (2002b), NSSO (2002c).

TABLE A 2.3   *Proportion of Unorganized Enterprises Ancillary to the Parent Firm, 1994–95*

Industry	OAME	NDME	DME	Total
14. Cotton-ginning, cleaning and baling	3.7	0.3	0.9	3.4
15. Food products	1.3	1.9	0.9	1.3
16. Tobacco products	6.7	8.2	1.4	6.6
17. Textiles	4.6	5.9	10.1	5.1
18. Wearing Apparel	8.8	17.4	7.3	11.1
19. Leather products	4.8	7.3	28.7	6.5
20. Wood (except furniture)	1.4	1.5	2.3	1.4
21. Paper and paper products	23.8	6.8	3.3	20.6
22. Publishing, Printing	5.1	3.2	3.2	4.0
23. Coke, Refined Petroleum	0.0	8.8	0.3	2.6
24. Chemical products	19.5	2.8	5.2	17.0
25. Rubber products	3.2	7.6	7.4	5.7
26. Other Non-Metallic Mineral products	2.2	3.5	3.2	2.4
27. Basic Metals	8.2	5.8	2.8	6.7
28. Fabricated Metal products	2.9	6.1	16.9	5.1
29. Machinery and equipment	20.7	9.7	16.3	17.3
30. Office Accounting and Computing		0.0	63.9	25.7
31. Electrical Machinery	4.7	12.0	14.9	11.0
32. Radio, TV, Communications	0.0	3.2	2.3	1.8
33. Medical Precision, Optical	3.6	4.1	43.6	9.4
34. Motor Vehicles	0.2	11.1	18.5	10.6
35. Other Transport equipment	1.3	4.9	5.5	3.4
36. Furniture and Other Manufacturing	2.2	1.8	3.2	2.2
Total	*3.3*	*4.3*	*6.7*	*3.6*

Source: NSSO Unorganized Manufacturing Sector Survey, 1994–95. Computed.

TABLE A 2.4   Proportion of Unorganized Sector Firms undertaking Sub-Contracting Activity by Industry Group and Enterprise Type, 2000–01

Industry Group	Undertaking Sub-contracting Work				Horizontal Sub-Contracting				Vertical Sub-Contracting			
	OAME	NDME	DME	Total	OAME	NDME	DME	Total	OAME	NDME	DME	Total
14. Cotton-ginning, cleaning and baling	2.6	37.9	46.6	8.3	1.9	30.3	0.0	5.8	0.7	7.7	46.6	2.5
15. Food products	3.4	4.9	3.7	3.6	1.2	1.9	1.5	1.3	2.2	3.0	2.2	2.3
16. Tobacco products	90.4	48.8	7.1	89.3	2.2	16.5	0.5	2.3	88.2	32.3	6.6	86.9
17. Textiles	54.6	61.2	60.6	55.5	4.0	8.0	10.9	4.8	50.6	53.2	49.7	50.7
18. Wearing Apparel	16.7	17.0	55.0	17.4	5.1	6.6	16.8	5.5	11.6	10.4	38.2	11.9
19. Leather products	18.3	39.7	56.6	23.7	4.3	13.4	20.6	6.6	14.0	26.3	36.0	17.1
20. Wood (except furniture)	10.5	25.5	23.7	11.3	1.9	7.7	8.0	2.2	8.6	17.7	15.7	9.1
21. Paper and paper products	43.1	43.4	30.5	42.0	10.5	10.4	12.8	10.7	32.6	33.1	17.7	31.3
22. Publishing, Printing	35.2	42.2	43.7	39.6	19.3	27.8	24.6	24.0	15.9	14.4	19.1	15.6
23. Coke, Refined Petroleum	0.0	0.4	0.7	0.3	0.0	0.4	0.4	0.2	0.0	0.0	0.3	0.0
24. Chemical products	76.5	11.5	14.6	66.8	2.8	7.2	4.7	3.2	73.7	4.4	10.0	63.6
25. Rubber products	41.9	46.1	39.3	42.6	6.0	10.1	14.4	8.8	35.9	36.0	24.9	33.9
26. Other Non-Metallic Mineral products	5.0	9.8	7.2	5.6	2.5	4.9	4.3	2.8	2.5	5.0	2.8	2.7
27. Basic Metals	27.1	54.8	24.8	36.5	9.5	13.6	5.4	10.4	17.6	41.2	19.4	26.1
28. Fabricated Metal products	16.1	33.6	42.7	22.1	3.9	10.7	13.8	6.3	12.2	22.8	28.9	15.9
29. Machinery and equipment	12.6	36.8	33.9	22.0	3.3	5.5	11.4	4.9	9.3	31.3	22.5	17.1
30. Office Accounting and Computing	0.0	82.9	7.1	63.6	0.0	82.9	7.1	63.6	0.0	0.0	0.0	0.0
31. Electrical Machinery	39.8	25.3	24.6	32.0	1.7	7.5	9.1	5.1	38.1	17.9	15.4	26.9
32. Radio, TV, Communications	31.3	39.1	60.6	46.8	12.7	3.4	24.8	15.0	18.6	35.8	35.8	31.8
33. Medical Precision, Optical	41.8	36.7	28.4	37.7	1.3	9.1	4.2	4.6	40.5	27.6	24.2	33.1
34. Motor Vehicles	16.7	58.8	55.5	48.1	6.4	4.3	13.6	8.0	10.3	54.5	42.0	40.1
35. Other Transport equipment	30.2	52.8	47.3	42.7	2.3	6.6	4.3	4.3	27.9	46.2	42.0	38.4
36. Furniture and Other Manufacturing	32.1	45.8	58.9	35.4	4.9	10.9	12.3	6.2	27.2	34.8	43.0	29.2
37. Recycling	47.4	28.0	37.4	44.2	1.9	30.3	0.0	5.8	35.6	24.0	46.6	32.8
Total	30.7	28.9	34.7	30.7	1.2	1.9	1.5	1.3	27.5	21.0	25.4	26.8

Source: NSSO Unorganized Manufacturing Sector Survey, 2000–01. Computed.

TABLE A 2.5   Proportion of Sub-Contracting Firms Receiving Technology Transfer by Industry Group and Enterprise Type, 2000–01

Industry Group	Undertaking Sub-Contracting Work				Horizontal Sub-Contracting				Vertical Sub-Contracting			
	OAME	NDME	DME	Total	OAME	NDME	DME	Total	OAME	NDME	DME	Total
14. Cotton-ginning, cleaning and baling	26.4	20.2	100.0	30.0	99.3	65.4	29.1	70.6	0.0	45.2	0.0	28.7
15. Food products	71.9	63.2	65.6	70.2	56.9	54.8	48.4	56.3	3.6	1.5	2.0	3.2
16. Tobacco products	97.6	66.3	92.8	97.4	93.5	46.5	77.8	93.3	2.2	15.6	28.3	2.3
17. Textiles	92.7	87.1	82.2	91.5	94.9	96.8	95.0	95.0	9.2	5.5	5.3	8.6
18. Wearing Apparel	72.1	61.7	69.8	70.7	92.9	90.9	97.8	92.9	11.8	7.0	10.7	11.2
19. Leather products	76.5	66.3	64.3	72.3	90.1	95.9	94.7	92.2	14.9	6.8	2.6	11.1
20. Wood (except furniture)	83.8	70.5	68.1	82.2	91.9	91.9	91.4	91.9	5.7	7.1	5.2	5.8
21. Paper and paper roducts	76.4	81.7	58.0	75.8	92.3	92.1	96.1	92.6	12.5	14.9	6.1	12.4
22. Publishing, Printing	45.3	34.2	43.8	39.5	93.7	95.6	95.9	95.0	3.7	3.6	5.3	3.9
23. Coke, Refined Petroleum	0.0	0.0	50.0	11.8	0.0	0.0	0.0	0.0	0.0	0.0	0.0	0.0
24. Chemical products	96.3	38.2	68.1	95.2	100.0	98.9	99.6	100.0	26.7	5.6	4.5	26.0
25. Rubber products	85.9	78.2	63.4	79.5	84.5	98.4	80.9	88.0	12.1	10.5	13.3	11.8
26. Other Non-Metallic Mineral products	60.6	51.3	40.0	56.5	85.8	89.8	86.1	86.5	9.1	3.7	1.7	7.3
27. Basic Metals	64.7	75.1	78.3	71.5	26.9	91.4	34.4	45.2	3.9	4.8	17.0	5.6
28. Fabricated Metal products	76.2	68.6	68.2	72.3	98.9	99.2	99.9	99.1	17.1	5.7	10.2	11.9
29. Machinery and equipment	75.1	85.2	66.8	78.3	79.0	87.0	86.8	84.3	16.6	8.6	4.7	10.5
30. Office Accounting and Computing	0.0	0.0	0.0	0.0	0.0	26.0	2.8	4.3	0.0	0.0	0.0	0.0
31. Electrical Machinery	96.5	70.7	62.9	84.4	87.6	78.0	85.4	85.1	12.4	11.5	14.6	12.7
32. Radio TV, Communications	59.3	91.5	59.2	67.9	98.8	76.5	99.9	93.4	0.0	2.1	52.4	30.6
33. Medical Precision, Optical	98.5	75.3	85.1	88.6	97.7	93.4	100.0	96.5	3.6	8.3	6.3	5.6
34. Motor Vehicles	61.7	93.1	75.6	83.5	100.0	95.7	96.9	96.5	0.2	3.7	8.6	5.4
35. Other Transport equipment	92.5	87.6	90.8	89.8	94.9	60.8	85.9	76.9	6.6	31.2	16.2	20.4
36. Furniture and Other Manufacturing	85.2	76.6	79.2	83.0	96.8	94.2	95.1	96.1	16.2	4.3	4.9	13.0
37. Recycling	75.1	86.1	72.2	75.7	98.7	84.1	90.0	97.1	25.4	35.4	22.8	26.0
Total	90.6	73.2	73.4	88.2	93.1	92.2	92.6	93.0	7.5	6.0	7.3	7.3

Source: Same as Table A 2.4.

CHAPTER THREE

Technical Change and the Indian Work Force
Skill-Biased Growth

In 2004–05, nearly half the work force in India was illiterate and another 30 per cent educated up to the primary or middle level of schooling. To meet the requirements of rapid economic growth and to meet the shortage of skilled manpower, an ambitious plan of expansion of technical education was undertaken. A three-tier system was adopted that included Industrial Training Institutes (ITI) offering vocational training to develop particular skills; polytechnics offering diploma programmes in advanced vocational and technical training for supervisory and middle-level executives in industry; and professional engineering colleges and technical departments in universities offering degree programmes to train professionals for skills at a higher level (Ramachandran 2002). A large increase in engineering colleges was witnessed in 1990–2000, the turn-out from undergraduate programmes increasing by 90 per cent. A boom in polytechnics was seen between 1980 to 1990. From 1981, the number of ITI and craft schools tripled, while enrolment in them more than doubled (Mathur and Mamgain 2002).

Traditional micro theory of demand and supply predicts that an increase in the supply of skilled workers leads to a fall in the price or the wages of skilled work. However, recent evidence from the United States and other countries shows a rise in skill premiums along with an increase in the skilled work force. In the introductory chapter we presented a review of the theory and the hypotheses in an attempt to explain this phenomenon. Here, we elaborate on the skill-biased technological change hypothesis in the context of the Indian work force. We provide a framework to analyse the links between technological change and the growth of skilled workers and wage premiums, and, further, explore these linkages empirically.

Skills of Workers and Technical Change: A Simple Framework
In most of mainstream economics, workers are considered a homogeneous group. So policy options regarding the creation of employment, as

discussed above, are also addressed in aggregate terms. The only level of disaggregation considered is by industry group or sector, and not by the quality of the work force. Without a disaggregated view of the work force one cannot devise appropriate policies to generate employment. It is essential that we know how the availability of different levels of skilled and unskilled labour, and changes in technology affect the demand for labour. The demand for various types of skilled labour is dependent upon the elasticity of substitution between skilled and unskilled labour. How does this elasticity of substitution vary across different sectors in the economy?

The awareness that workers constitute heterogeneous groups of non-production and production workers is reflected in the management literature. It is also reflected in the categorization of workers in the Annual Survey of Industries (ASI) related to the organized manufacturing sector. This follows, further, from the definition of 'workers' in the Factory Act as those directly engaged in the production process, with 'other than workers' referring to those not directly related to production.

Theories of the firm and industrial organization identify several variables to explain the variations and shifts in the ratio of non-production to production workers (NP/P). These include shifts in the production function, the scale and size of firms, capital intensity, and so on. The role of relative wages in determining the ratio of NP/P depends on the extent of substitutability between production and non-production workers. Given the magnitude of the elasticity of substitution, it will be advantageous for an enterprise to expand the employment of non-production workers and reduce the number of production workers when the wages of production workers rise faster than that of non-production workers (Seth and Aggarwal 2004). That is, if the two kinds of workers are perfectly substitutable, there is a negative relationship between the wages of non-production and production workers, and the ratio of the two kinds of workers. However, Seth and Aggarwal (2004) do not find this clear negative relationship in their analysis. This probably implies that the two are not perfectly substitutable in the context of organized manufacturing in India.

For our purposes, we visualize two categories of skilled and unskilled workers (H/L being the ratio between the two) to replace non-production and production workers. A negative relationship between the wages of skilled and unskilled labour, and the ratio of skilled to unskilled workers would imply that there is perfect substitution between the two categories.

A simple framework to link wages to the supply of skills and to the demand generated by the frontier of technological possibilities in an economy was presented by Daron Acemoglu (2002). There are two types of workers, skilled and unskilled, and the two are imperfect substitutes. Imperfect substitution between the two types of workers is important in understanding how a change in relative supply affects the skill premium.

Elasticity of substitution between skilled and unskilled workers is equal to $e = 1 / 1 - \rho$, where $\rho <= 1$

Skilled and unskilled workers are:

gross substitutes if $e > 1$, then skilled workers will replace unskilled workers using the new skill-biased or skill-using technologies (or $\rho > 0$)

gross complements if $e < 1$, then unskilled workers can replace skilled workers, or unskilled workers can be used to do the jobs of skilled workers (or $\rho < 0$).

If labour markets are competitive, as the fraction of skilled workers in the labour force increases, unskilled wages should increase. Similarly, everything else remaining constant, as skilled workers become more abundant, their wages should fall. Acemoglu (2002) defines skill premium as the wage of the skilled worker to the wage of the unskilled worker.

Skill premium: $W = W_H/W_L = (A_H/ A_L)^{e-1/e} (H/L)^{-1/e}$

where W_H = wages of skilled labour and W_L = wages of unskilled labour.

This skill premium is derived from a CES production function for the aggregate economy with inputs of skilled (H) and unskilled (L) labour, and factor-augmenting technology (A_H and A_L). The elasticity of substitution between skilled and unskilled labour (e) is important for the behaviour of the skill premium when supply changes. If the elasticity of substitution between skilled and unskilled work is greater than 1 (substitutability), then, as the H/L ratio increases, the skill premium increases.

Acemoglu (2002) shows that the tendency for the skill premium to fall with an increase in the supply of skilled workers could be countered by changes in technology. It is crucial to understand how skill premium responds to technology. The elasticity of substitution is again a crucial variable for the skill premium in the context of technical change. The conventional wisdom is that skill premium increases when skilled workers become more productive, or when the technology favours skilled work. This is captured in a ratio called technical change.

Technical change = $T = A_H/ A_L = (W_H.H / W_L.L)^{e/e-1} / H/L$

where A_H = technology used by skilled workers; A_L = technology used by unskilled workers; e = elasticity of substitution between skilled and unskilled labour; H and L are skilled and unskilled

FIGURE 3.1   *Skill Premium with Skill-Biased Technical Change*

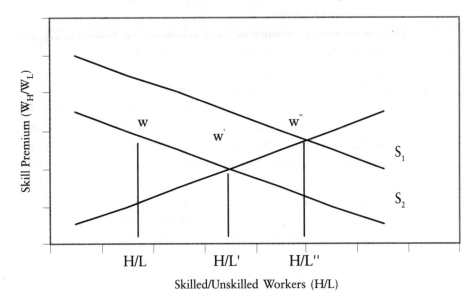

Skilled/Unskilled Workers (H/L)

labour respectively. An increase in T implies technical change measured by a rise in the relative productivity of skilled workers.

Figure 3.1 shows the downward-sloping relative demand for skills curve (S_1). On the X axis is the relative supply of skilled to unskilled workers, and on the Y axis is the skill premium or wages of skilled to unskilled work. An increase in the relative supply from H/L to H'/L' moves the equilibrium point down along the downward-sloping curve, and reduces the skill premium from w to w'.

However, if e > 1, then there is an improvement in the skill-complementary technology or skill-biased technical change, and an increase in the skill premium. This can be seen as a shift out of the relative demand curve for skills from S_1 to S_2, moving the skill premium from w' to w"; that is, the demand for skilled workers will increase.

The opposite is true if elasticity of substitution is less than 1, that is, e < 1. Then, skill-biased technology or an improvement in the productivity of skilled workers will lead to a shift inwards of the relative demand curve, or unskilled workers will replace the skilled workers. Therefore, the tendency for the skill premium to fall when the supply of skilled workers increases is countered by the changes in technology towards skill-using or skill-biased technology, or by increasing the relative productivity of skilled workers.

Measurement of Skills and Technology

Measurement of Skills

There is no direct measure of the level of skill of workers. The two ways by which skill can be identified is by occupational classification and by level of education. Both have their limitations. Occupational classification gives broad categories of non-production, professional, managerial–administrative, clerical, sales and service workers; and the rest are classified as production workers. The former, non-production workers, are assumed to be more skilled than the production workers. One can also consider only managerial and professional workers as skilled if one is interested in higher levels of skill.

The other method of identification of skill level is based on the level of formal education. In the United States, unskilled workers are defined as those with a high school diploma and skilled workers as those with college degrees. This may be appropriate for the United States, but most studies of other countries define skilled workers as high school graduates and those having an even higher level of education. We use this latter definition in the analysis of the relation between technical change and skill premium, and include all workers who have completed their education in higher secondary education and above as skilled workers, between 15 to 64 years of age. The rest of the workers in this age group are treated as unskilled workers (Unni and Rani 2004).

Defining skill by level of education has its limitations. A large proportion of workers in India are illiterate. However, they have various forms of skills acquired through informal training. In 2004–05, the National Sample Survey estimated that among the youth in the age group 15 to 29 years, while nearly 4 per cent received formal vocational training, nearly 8 per cent received training through non-formal sources. The proportion of informally trained workers is likely to be even larger if we take into account all workers, as we shall see later while discussing the autocomponents industry.

Measurement of Technology

Measurement of the level of use of technology in any industry group is an even more difficult proposition. We use two methods to measure technology.

Total factor productivity

Growth of total factor productivity (TFPG) is estimated for the manufacturing sector by using the growth accounting technique. TFPG is taken as the difference between the growth rate in value added and a weighted sum of growth rates of capital and labour:

$$TFPG = Y(t) - \alpha L(t) - (1-\alpha)K(t)$$

where Y, K and L are the growth rates of real value added, gross capital and labour respectively. The weights α and $(1-\alpha)$ are the share of labour[1] and capital respectively (Goldar and Mitra 1999).

The TFPG was estimated for four data points, as time-series data for the unorganized sector was not available. One limitation of this method of estimating TFPG using four data points is that the growth rates of Y, L and K are dependent on the two end-point years. The estimate of TFPG is then affected by the peculiarities or performance of the industries in those two years, unlike a time-series estimation where the growth is averaged out over the period of study.

A second limitation of using total factor productivity as an indicator of technology is that it captures growth in value added which is not accounted for by growth in inputs such as labour and capital. TFPG is a residual productivity growth and includes the effects of technological change, better utilization of capacities, skills and organization. Therefore it measures technological change in a broader sense than just physical technology.

Technical Change

Using the relative wage bills for skilled and unskilled workers, Acemoglu defined technical change, T, as follows:

$$T = \frac{Ah}{Al} = \frac{S_H^{e/(e-1)}}{H/L}$$

where $S_H = W_H . H / W_L . L$

The limitation of this indictor of technical change is that it is dependent on or is measured by the wage bill. The assumption is that wages are directly related to the productivity of the worker, which is also dependent on the use of technology. That is, when skilled workers are paid more or when there is an increase in skilled workers in the industry, this is due to an increase in the productivity of skilled workers, which in turn occurs due to a change in technology. While this assumption may hold for many activities in the manufacturing sector, it would not be true for the public sector enterprises or administration with protected wages, for certain service sectors such as trade and education, and for the construction industry. In public enterprises and these service sectors, the rise in wage bill for skilled workers might not be related to any increase in the productivity of the workers.

---

[1] Total emoluments (wages/salaries plus bonus) as a proportion of value added was used as the share of labour.

Levels of Skills in the Work Force

In 2004–05, about half the work force in India was illiterate or had below primary level education; 30 per cent had elementary education; 9 per cent had secondary education; and only 12 per cent were educated above the higher secondary level or had a graduate degree (Table 3.1) Further, less than 3 per cent of the work force had any form of technical training. As can be expected, there was a great variation in levels of education across industry groups. Workers in the service sectors, in business services, public administration, and health and education had the highest levels of formal education as well as technical training. Sectors where about 40 per cent of the workers had elementary education were manufacturing, trade, hotels and transport. Elementary reading and writing skills were perhaps a minimum requirement in these sectors. About 3–4 per cent of the workers in these sectors, except in transport, also had technical training. Of the workers engaged in agriculture, mining and quarrying, construction and work in private households, more than half were illiterate. About 2 per cent of the workers in the construction industry had some technical education.

The levels of formal and technical education among the work force

TABLE 3.1   *Formal Education and Vocational Technical Training among Workers by Industry (All Ages), 2004–05*

Industrial Category	Illiterate and Below Primary	Elementary	Secondary	Higher Secondary and Above	Total	Percentage of Workers with Technical Education
Agriculture	63.0	26.6	5.9	4.4	100.0	0.5
Mining and Quarrying	54.6	26.2	6.7	12.5	100.0	5.5
Manufacturing	37.7	38.2	10.9	13.3	100.0	4.3
Electricity, Gas, Water	12.3	27.5	22.1	38.1	100.0	17.5
Construction	50.7	36.8	6.6	5.9	100.0	2.0
Trade	27.0	35.6	16.4	21.0	100.0	3.1
Hotels and Restaurants	40.2	39.7	10.1	10.1	100.0	1.8
Transport Storage	30.0	37.2	14.9	17.9	100.0	4.4
Finance, Business Services	1.6	13.0	12.0	73.4	100.0	.12.8
Real Estate	9.0	17.4	11.9	61.7	100.0	23.4
Public Administration	11.3	20.5	17.1	51.1	100.0	9.7
Education	4.1	8.3	11.5	76.1	100.0	17.7
Health and Social Work	10.8	16.7	15.7	56.8	100.0	35.1
Other Services	44.9	32.8	10.2	12.0	100.0	2.6
Private Households	65.0	27.9	4.6	2.5	100.0	0.2
Total	49.8	29.3	8.6	12.2	100.0	2.8

Source: NSS 61st Round, 2004–05, Employment Unemployment Survey. Computed.

categorized by occupation are very revealing. The overall observation that non-production workers have higher levels of education and technical training than production workers is seen to be true. Thus, a broad measure of skill in terms of the ratio of non-production workers, used later in the analysis, is valid.

More than 80 per cent of professionals such as scientists, doctors, auditors, jurists, programmers and teachers were educated beyond the higher secondary level (Table 3.2). Clerical workers like stenographers and computer operators also had high levels of education. Additionally, a large proportion of these workers had technical training. Two other occupation groups where half to three-fourths of the workers had such high levels of education were business services and accounts. Other professionals, administrative and managerial workers, clerical, trade and service workers, and workers in production-related activities such as electrical and machine fitters had the next highest levels of education and technical skill training.

Growth of Skilled Occupations

In the later analysis we shall see that there was an overall rise in the skill content of the work force by the measures of a both formal education and occupational groups, in the period between 1993–94 to 1999–2000. Further, during 1999–2000 to 2004–2005 there was a sharp growth in some skilled occupational groups. While the overall growth of workers was less than 3 per cent, more than 10 per cent growth was observed in skilled occupations like programming professionals, computer operators, business services, sales workers, tailors and others engaged in the garment sector, and workers in the construction sector (Table 3.3). More than 5 per cent growth in skilled professionals was noted among teachers, artists and journalists and other professionals, administrators, managers and proprietors. Housekeepers, cooks, waiters in the hospitality industry, maids and domestic workers in households, hairdressers and beauticians, and carpenters, painters and other production workers also recorded 5 per cent growth.

Skill-Based Work Force and Skill Premium

The simple framework outlined above helps us to analyse the links between relative wages and relative supply of skilled labour and the demand generated by technical change in the various one-digit industry groups in the economy. We compute the elasticity of substitution between skilled and unskilled workers since it is an important variable in understanding how changes in relative supply affect skill premium. Two types of workers, skilled and unskilled, are defined for the period 1993–94 to 1999–2000, when the Indian economy went through a phase of rapid reforms, using the

TABLE 3.2   Education and Vocational Technical Education by Occupation (All Ages), 2004–05

Occupational Category	Illiterate and Below Primary	Elementary	Secondary	Higher Secondary and Above	Total	Percentage of Workers with Technical Education
Scientists, Architects, Engineers	–	–	–	88.3	100.0	73.6
Physicians, Surgeons, Scientific Medical, Paramedical	–	–	–	86.7	100.0	64.8
Nurses, Health Technicians	9.1	14.1	19.9	56.8	100.0	30.9
Mathematicians, Statisticians, Programmers	–	–	–	98.9	100.0	61.8
Economists, Auditors, Social Scientists, Jurists	1.3	4.0	6.5	88.2	100.0	23.1
Teachers	0.9	4.5	11.3	83.3	100.0	19.3
The Arts, Journalists	23.7	23.8	13.2	39.4	100.0	10.5
Professional Workers, Others	20.7	39.0	18.8	21.5	100.0	6.4
Administrative, Managerial, Proprietorship	18.9	27.9	14.6	38.7	100.0	8.9
Clerical Related, Village Officials	5.3	20.4	18.6	55.7	100.0	5.8
Stenographers, Typists, Card and Tape-punching Operators	–	–	–	90.3	100.0	30.0
Book Keepers, Cashiers	–	–	15.0	74.3	100.0	11.2
Computing, Machine Operators	–	–	–	95.7	100.0	48.2
Wholesale/Retail Trade, Manufacturers, Agents, Technical Salesmen, Commercial Travellers, Sales Workers (Other)	25.9	32.6	17.3	24.2	100.0	2.8
Salesmen, Shop Assistants (includes Street Vendors)	32.5	40.2	13.9	13.4	100.0	1.7
Insurance, Real Estate, Securities, Business Service Salesmen, Auctioneers	6.9	18.8	19.3	55.0	100.0	7.1
Hotel, Restaurant Keepers	41.7	40.2	9.7	8.4	100.0	0.4
Housekeepers, Matrons, Stewards, Cooks, Waiters, Bartenders	44.6	39.7	9.4	6.3	100.0	1.6
Maids, Related House-keeping Service (Others, includes Domestic Servants)	68.3	25.0	4.4	2.3	100.0	0.8
Building Caretakers, Sweepers, Cleaners	55.0	38.1	5.8	1.2	100.0	0.2
Launderers, Dry Cleaners, Ironing men	68.4	22.3	5.5	3.8	100.0	0.9
Hairdressers, Barbers, Beauticians	37.5	44.4	9.7	8.4	100.0	1.8

TABLE 3.2 (contd)

Occupational Category	Illiterate and Below Primary	Elementary	Secondary	Higher Secondary and Above	Total	Percentage of Workers with Technical Education
Protective Service Worker, Service Worker	18.8	33.5	22.4	25.3	100.0	2.2
Agriculture and Allied Activities	63.0	26.7	5.9	4.4	100.0	0.5
Miners, Quarrymen, Drillers	64.5	24.0	4.6	6.8	100.0	2.5
Metal, Wood and Chemical Preparers, Processors, Paper Makers	33.2	35.7	16.2	14.8	100.0	7.8
Spinners, Weavers, Knitters	44.7	42.1	8.5	4.6	100.0	0.7
Food Beverage Processors	45.1	38.9	10.1	5.9	100.0	1.1
Tobacco preparers, Tobacco product makers	67.7	28.7	2.3	1.3	100.0	0.3
Tailors, Dressmakers, Serving, Upholsterers	29.0	47.9	13.5	9.7	100.0	2.5
Carpenters, Cabinet-related Wood work	32.1	52.7	11.1	4.1	100.0	1.0
Blacksmiths, Tool Makers, Machine Tool Operators	35.5	36.7	13.6	14.3	100.0	6.2
Machine Fitters, Machine Assembly, Precision Instrument Makers	20.4	41.7	16.0	22.0	100.0	13.8
Electrical Fitters, Related Electrical and Electronic work	10.0	37.6	22.6	29.8	100.0	18.8
Plumbers, Welders, Sheet Metal, Structural, Metal Preparers, Erectors	25.5	45.5	16.2	12.8	100.0	7.1
Jewellery, Precious Metal, Metal Engravers (includes Gems)	20.8	52.2	15.2	11.8	100.0	1.2
Glass Formers, Potters	64.6	27.0	–	–	100.0	0.6
Painting	30.9	53.8	10.0	5.4	100.0	1.7
Production, Related (Others)	42.2	37.2	10.4	10.2	100.0	2.8
Construction Workers, Stone Cutters	53.2	37.4	6.1	3.3	100.0	0.4
Stationary Engines, Equipment Operators, Material Handling, Loaders	46.0	39.0	8.9	6.1	100.0	1.6
Transport Equipment Operators (includes Drivers)	35.3	42.7	14.3	7.7	100.0	2.4
Labourers (Others)	61.7	30.9	4.8	2.6	100.0	0.4
All	49.8	29.3	8.6	12.2	100.0	2.8

Source: NSS 61st Round, 2004–05, Employment Unemployment Survey. Computed.

TABLE 3.3   Growth Rate of Workers by Occupational Group, by Gender

Occupational Category	1999–2000/2004–2005			Percentage share to total workers	
	Male	Female	Total	1999–2000	2004–2005
Scientists, Architects, Engineers	-1.7		-1.4	0.5	0.4
Physicians, Surgeons, Scientific Medical, Paramedical	2.5	10.0	3.5	0.3	0.3
Nurses, Health Technicians	5.8	0.9	3.4	0.3	0.3
Mathematicians, Statisticians, Programmers	14.4		15.5	0.0	0.1
Economists, Auditors, Social Scientists, Jurists	2.0		2.7	0.4	0.4
Teachers	4.6	7.2	5.7	1.9	2.1
The Arts, Journalists	6.6		6.0	0.2	0.2
Professional Workers, Others	8.6		8.7	0.2	0.3
Administrative, Managerial, Proprietorship	6.0	5.2	5.9	3.0	3.5
Clerical Related, Village Officials	-1.1	2.8	-0.6	2.3	1.9
Stenographers, Typists, Card and Tape punching Operators	-3.5		-5.2	0.1	0.1
Book Keepers, Cashiers	4.5		4.4	0.3	0.3
Computing, Machine Operators	10.1		11.3	0.1	0.1
Wholesale/Retail Trade, Manufacturers Agents, Technical Salesmen, Commercial Travellers, Sales Workers (Other)	3.4	4.1	3.5	4.8	5.0
Salesmen, Shop Assistants (includes Street Vendors)	10.5	13.7	10.9	1.8	2.6
Insurance, Real Estate, Securities, Business Service Salesmen, Auctioneers	13.2		13.7	0.2	0.3
Hotel/Restaurant Keepers	3.7	5.7	4.2	0.4	0.4
Housekeepers, Matrons, Stewards, Cooks, Waiters, Bartenders	5.5	8.3	6.1	0.5	0.6
Maids, Related House-keeping Service (Others, includes Domestic Servants)	0.0	8.2	7.2	0.7	0.9
Building Caretakers, Sweepers, Cleaners	2.4	4.0	3.0	0.5	0.5
Launderers, Dry Cleaners, Ironing men	1.5	-4.1	-1.0	0.6	0.5
Hairdressers, Barbers, Beauticians	4.5	13.1	5.3	0.4	0.5

TABLE 3.3 (contd)

Occupational Category	1999–2000/2004–2005			Percentage share to total workers	
	Male	Female	Total	1999–2000	2004–2005
Protective Service Workers, Service Workers	0.8	4.0	0.9	0.9	0.8
Agriculture and Allied Activities	1.0	3.5	2.0	58.8	56.3
Miners, Quarrymen, Drillers	2.8		3.2	0.3	0.3
Metal, Wood and Chemical Preparers, Processors, Paper Makers	-3.5		-3.3	0.4	0.3
Spinners, Weavers, Knitters	2.2	2.4	2.3	1.5	1.4
Food Beverage Processors	-0.8	-0.6	-0.7	0.8	0.6
Tobacco preparers, Tobacco product makers	4.0	0.5	1.2	1.1	1.0
Tailors, Dressmakers, Sewing, Upholsterers	6.5	15.7	10.0	1.5	2.0
Carpenters, Cabinet-related Wood work	5.5		5.3	0.7	0.8
Blacksmiths, Tool Makers, Machine Tool Operators	1.1		1.1	0.4	0.4
Machine Fitters, Machine Assembly, Precision Instrument Makers	0.5		0.8	1.0	0.9
Electrical Fitters, Related Electrical and Electronic work	3.3		3.0	0.7	0.7
Plumbers, Welders, Sheet Metal, Structural, Metal Preparers, Erectors	4.6		4.3	0.3	0.4
Jewellery, Precious Metal, Metal Engravers (includes Gems)	2.9		3.4	0.4	0.4
Glass Formers, Potters	4.9	1.4	3.7	0.3	0.3
Painting	6.6		6.1	0.3	0.3
Production, Related (Others)	5.1	8.2	6.1	1.3	1.5
Construction Workers, Stone Cutters	9.5	8.5	9.4	2.7	4.7
Stationary Engines, Equipment Operators, Material Handling, Loaders	8.9	11.1	9.1	0.6	1.1
Transport Equipment Operators (includes Drivers)	5.6		5.6	2.3	2.6
Labourers (Others)	-0.2	-0.6	-0.3	3.0	2.5
All	2.5	3.8	2.9	100.0	100.0

Note: Occupational groups with negligible shares are not presented.
Source: NSS 61ˢᵗ Round, 2004–05, Employment Unemployment Survey. Computed.

National Sample Survey Employment–Unemployment data. The liberalization process allowed for the rapid entry of technology into various sectors of the economy (Rani and Unni 2004). Therefore, it would be interesting to study the impact of technical change on the demand for a skill-based work force.

As noted earlier, the skill content of the work force was the highest in the services sector and in utilities, followed by the manufacturing, trade and transport sectors. The ratio of skilled to unskilled workers in the years 1993–94 and 1999–2000 showed an increase for all workers, implying a movement towards skilled workers (Table 3.4). This was true for all the one-digit industry groups. The growth of the work force in the latter period of reforms was indeed skill-based growth.

The skill premium, or the ratio of skilled to unskilled wage rates, showed a decline for all workers (aggregate), and for the electricity, gas, water and construction industries (Table 3.4). This was similar to the expectation discussed earlier, that, given a perfect substitution between skilled and unskilled workers, there would be a negative relationship between the ratio of skilled–unskilled workers and the ratio of their wages. There was a positive relation, however, in manufacturing and other service sectors, and for the agricultural and mining sectors. In these sectors, when there was a rise in the ratio of skilled to unskilled workers, their wages, or skill premium, was also seen as rising. This could imply that skilled and unskilled workers were not substitutable in many of the industry groups, though in the aggregate they appeared to be perfect substitutes.

By Status and Gender

When all workers were disaggregated by status of employment, regular or casual (Table 3.4), a shift towards skilled workers and a rise in wage premiums were observed for both. However, the differentials were larger among regular workers as compared to casual workers. Among regular workers, it was more noticeable in manufacturing, hotels, communication and services. When all workers were disaggregated according to gender (Table 3.5), an increase was observed in the male skilled work force, whereas skills were more or less constant within the female work force. The skill premium, however, did not increase for either. Increase in skill premium for male workers in manufacturing, hotels, trade, communication and the services sector was accompanied by technical change. When workers were disaggregated by location, rural or urban (Table 3.6), a shift towards skilled workers was observed in all the industry groups. An increase in skilled workers and skill premium for urban workers was observed in manufacturing, hotels, trade, communication and the services sector.

TABLE 3.4   *Skilled–Unskilled Workers by Level of Education, Skill Premium (W) and Technical Change (T), All, Regular and Casual, 1993–94 and 1999–2000*

Industry	Skilled/Unskilled		W_H/W_L		Technical Change (T)	
	1993–94	1999–2000	1993–94	1999–2000	1993–94	1999–2000
All Workers						
Agriculture, Forestry and Fishing	0.03	0.04	1.56	1.72	0.63	0.82
Mining and Quarrying	0.19	0.20	2.27	2.33	35.14	29.57
Manufacturing	0.36	0.48	2.38	2.42	2.40	2.40
Electricity, Gas and Water	1.00	1.42	1.67	1.55	1.12	0.85
Construction	0.08	0.11	2.20	1.69	0.29	0.24
Trade	0.46	0.59	1.79	1.79	1.21	1.97
Hotels and Restaurants	0.17	0.28	1.62	1.94	0.62	1.24
Transport, Storage and Communication	0.43	0.57	1.85	1.94	1.55	2.10
Finance and Real Estate	–	–	2.87	2.41	0.18	0.25
Services	1.45	1.58	2.41	2.61	12.22	16.60
Total	0.22	0.25	3.50	3.37	2.71	2.93
Regular Workers						
Agriculture, Forestry and Fishing	0.08	0.16	2.92	2.37	2.57	2.19
Mining and Quarrying	0.53	0.61	1.30	1.33	3.28	2.21
Manufacturing	0.64	0.78	1.94	2.20	2.03	2.45
Electricity, Gas and Water	1.14	1.52	1.56	1.48	1.00	0.79
Construction	0.59	0.58	2.26	1.94	0.17	0.71
Trade	0.63	0.84	1.74	1.73	1.94	2.86
Hotels and Restaurants	0.22	0.40	1.57	1.94	1.01	1.75
Transport, Storage and Communication	0.67	0.91	1.57	1.66	1.62	2.08
Finance and Real Estate	–	–	2.54	2.24	0.15	0.22
Services	1.93	2.25	2.07	2.13	3.20	3.49
Total	0.99	1.17	2.10	2.16	3.28	3.79
Casual Workers						
Agriculture, Forestry and Fishing	0.02	0.04	1.22	1.28	0.41	0.51
Mining and Quarrying	0.02	0.05	0.96	1.19	1.00	1.23
Manufacturing	0.09	0.13	1.20	1.25	1.78	1.71
Electricity, Gas and Water	0.21	0.58	0.99	1.22	2.40	1.48
Construction	0.05	0.09	1.12	1.19	0.14	0.24
Trade	0.15	0.21	1.10	1.16	0.04	0.09
Hotels and Restaurants	–	–	0.93	1.29	0.00	0.00
Transport, Storage and Communication	0.09	0.13	1.06	1.09	0.22	0.31
Finance *and* Real Estate	–	–	1.22	0.94	1.34	1.03
Services	0.07	0.08	1.27	3.09	0.02	0.30
Total	0.03	0.06	1.25	1.37	0.42	0.56

Note: Skilled workers are those who completed education of secondary school level and above. W_H: wages of skilled workers; W_L: wages of unskilled workers.

Source: Computed using the individual records of National Sample Survey Organization, Employment–Unemployment Survey, 1993–94 (50th Round) and 1999–2000 (55th Round).

TABLE 3.5   *Skilled–Unskilled Workers by Level of Education, Skill Premium (W) and Technical Change (T), Male and Female, 1993–94 and 1999–2000*

Industry	Skilled/Unskilled		W_H/W_L		Technical Change (T)	
	1993–94	1999–2000	1993–94	1999–2000	1993–94	1999–2000
Male Workers						
Agriculture, Forestry and Fishing	0.04	0.06	1.37	1.52	0.68	0.87
Mining and Quarrying	0.23	0.24	2.04	2.11	9.51	8.33
Manufacturing	0.43	0.54	2.14	2.26	2.11	2.32
Electricity, Gas and Water	1.00	1.41	1.64	1.53	1.15	0.89
Construction	0.10	0.13	2.05	1.59	0.24	0.20
Trade	0.45	0.58	1.76	1.78	1.13	1.86
Hotels and Restaurants	0.18	0.30	1.55	1.88	0.66	1.28
Transport, Storage and Communication	0.42	0.55	1.84	1.92	1.48	2.00
Finance and Real Estate	5.94	4.15	2.84	2.35	0.23	0.31
Services	1.67	1.85	2.08	2.25	5.28	6.51
Total	0.27	0.32	3.00	2.91	2.49	2.72
Female Workers						
Agriculture, Forestry and Fishing	0.01	0.01	1.38	1.56	0.45	0.63
Mining and Quarrying	0.04	0.01	3.47	3.03	2.64	1.87
Manufacturing	0.13	0.18	3.51	2.93	5.60	4.20
Electricity, Gas and Water	1.05	1.83	3.08	2.06	0.52	0.28
Construction	0.01	0.02	4.10	3.42	0.67	0.68
Trade	0.61	0.76	2.92	2.21	19.85	12.62
Hotels and Restaurants	0.11	0.11	4.40	3.82	0.00	0.00
Transport, Storage and Communication	0.92	2.03	2.56	2.18	2.46	2.03
Finance and Real Estate	18.09	10.12	5.53	3.25	0.03	0.06
Services	0.96	1.05	3.62	3.78	51.12	71.04
Total	0.10	0.11	5.33	4.95	2.92	2.98

Source: Computed using the individual records of National Sample Survey Organization, Employment–Unemployment Survey, 1993–94 (50th Round) and 1999–2000 (55th Round).

Skill-Biased Technical Change

According to Acemoglu (2002), it is difficult to compute the elasticity of substitution (e) between skilled and unskilled workers, and the few estimates that exist find e to be between 1 and 2. In fact, he used a study by Autor *et al.* (1998), who arrived at an elasticity of substitution of 1.4 and 2.0 using workers with some college, college graduates and college equivalents.

We have used simple two-point growth rates to arrive at the elasticity of substitution between skilled and unskilled workers. We obtained an

TABLE 3.6   *Skilled–Unskilled Workers by Level of Education, Skill Premium (W) and Technical Change (T), Rural and Urban, 1993–94 and 1999–2000*

Industry	Skilled/Unskilled		W_H/W_L		Technical Change (T)	
	1993–94	1999–2000	1993–94	1999–2000	1993–94	1999–2000
Rural Workers						
Agriculture, Forestry and Fishing	0.03	0.04	1.42	1.65	0.51	0.73
Mining and Quarrying	0.08	0.10	1.94	2.02	5.70	5.22
Manufacturing	0.19	0.26	2.00	1.71	2.08	1.77
Electricity, Gas and Water	0.55	0.76	1.29	1.43	1.34	1.42
Construction	0.06	0.10	1.80	1.34	0.26	0.22
Trade	0.37	0.52	1.30	1.26	0.53	0.75
Hotels and Restaurants	0.09	0.17	1.40	1.50	0.32	0.57
Transport, Storage and Communication	0.30	0.38	1.69	1.59	0.61	0.76
Finance and Real Estate	4.48	1.93	2.36	1.48	0.45	0.70
Services	1.25	1.33	2.34	2.50	42.61	64.39
Total	0.10	0.13	3.07	2.81	1.36	1.37
Urban Workers						
Agriculture, Forestry and Fishing	0.04	0.07	3.30	2.32	5.36	3.55
Mining and Quarrying	0.48	0.47	1.65	1.69	0.01	0.01
Manufacturing	0.53	0.69	2.19	2.43	2.17	2.35
Electricity, Gas and Water	1.48	2.60	1.79	1.50	0.66	0.37
Construction	0.12	0.14	2.36	1.98	0.22	0.19
Trade	0.49	0.61	1.89	1.92	1.59	2.75
Hotels and Restaurants	0.21	0.34	1.60	2.04	0.78	1.60
Transport, Storage and Communication	0.54	0.77	1.85	1.97	1.85	2.13
Finance and Real Estate	7.58	6.70	2.94	2.62	0.05	0.06
Services	1.61	1.81	2.40	2.62	6.16	7.78
Total	0.67	0.78	2.59	2.71	3.84	4.66

Source: Computed using the individual records of National Sample Survey Organization, Employment–Unemployment Survey, 1993–94 (50th Round) and 1999–2000 (55th Round).

estimate of e = 2.1 for all workers, which is quite close to the values discussed in the literature mentioned above. The estimates ranged from (–)16.3 to 4.5, however, for the various industry groups, with manufacturing having the lowest and agriculture the largest substitution possibilities between skilled and unskilled workers. These elasticities, computed by industry groups separately for all workers, and by location (rural/urban), gender (male/female) and status (regular/casual), were then used to compute the technical change ratio (T).

The technical change ratio (T) for all workers rose from 2.71 to

2.93 in the period 1993–94 to 1999–2000, which implied that the productivity of skilled workers had risen (Table 3.4). During the period of rapid economic reforms in the late 1990s, the growth of the skill-based work force was due to skill-biased technical change for the economy as a whole.

For the country as a whole, most of the one-digit industry groups had similar results except for more or less constant ratios in manufacturing and declining ratios in electricity, gas and water, and construction industries (Table 3.4). Thus, in the aggregate, it was the services sector that had skill-biased technical change and an increase in the demand for skilled labour. Utilities and the construction industry did not have technical change biased towards skilled labour, and also did not show an increase in the demand for skilled workers. In the manufacturing industry, technical change in the aggregate was constant and did not show a bias towards greater skill.

By Status and Gender

Disaggregation by status of work, regular and casual workers (Table 3.4), showed that both groups experienced skill-biased technical change and demand for skilled workers, though more prominently among regular workers. In disaggregation by industry group, the manufacturing sector showed an increase in skill-biased technical change among regular workers, but a decline among casual workers. This is interesting in that the relatively new technology-intensive activities are likely to be undertaken by regular workers with more stable contracts and greater benefits, while the more manual activities in manufacturing are relegated to casual workers. In the service industries, both technical change and the demand for skilled workers appeared to grow for both regular and casual workers, although the absolute values for the indices were much larger for the regular workers.

The results of disaggregating by gender are revealing, with almost constant technical change for female workers and rising indices for male workers (Table 3.5). Here again, activities undertaken by men seemed to attract more technical change and greater demand for skills. Of course, the possibility exists that the introduction of technology leads to men taking over tasks previously undertaken by women, although there is no way to prove this using cross-section secondary data. When disaggregated by industry groups, skill-biased technical change and an increase in demand for skilled workers among male employees was seen mainly in manufacturing and in all the service sectors.

No skill-biased technical change was observed in the rural areas when all workers were disaggregated by location (Table 3.6). However, there was a distinctive increase in skill-biased technical change and a clear increase in the demand for skilled workers in urban areas. Further, disaggregation by industry group showed interesting results for urban manufacturing, and the services industries of trade, transport and storage, and social and personal services. The ratio of technical change showed a rise or a shift towards skill-biased technology.

Conclusion

We have presented a simple framework to analyse the impact of technical change on the rise observed in skilled workers and skill premium. We have evaluated the hypothesis of skill-biased technological change, one of the macro explanations for the phenomenon discussed in the introductory chapter. Overall, we have found support for this hypothesis of skill-biased technological change in the period of rapid reforms in the late 1990s. However, the process was more pronounced in certain sectors and segments of the work force.

The skill content of the various industrial sectors showed high skill in the services sectors and moderate levels of skill in industrial sectors such as manufacturing. The most recent period, till 2005, has also witnessed high growth of certain professional workers, service sector workers and production-related workers.

While there is hardly any rise in the skilled work force or in the wage premium in the aggregate, individual sectors presented a diverse picture. Overall, the manufacturing and services industries, urban workers and male workers showed a greater shift to a skilled work force with an increasing wage premium.

There was an inflow of technology in the country as a whole, and services appeared to have had greater technical change as measured by the wage bills. However, this has to be weighed against the limitation of this measure of technical change. Technical change was observed in the manufacturing sector in urban areas and among male workers. Activities undertaken by regular workers in manufacturing were more likely to have had skill-biased technical change. The most revealing result was that women were less likely to be engaged in activities that had skill-biased technical change than men.

By way of caution it is necessary to remember that the definition of a skilled worker was based on the level of education, so that persons who had education below the higher secondary level were treated as unskilled. This might have affected the results of skill-biased technical change measured by the wage bill, in certain sectors. In the construction sector, for example, skilled workers operating certain machines may be illiterate or have low levels of education and hence this industry did not show technical change by our measure.

CHAPTER FOUR

Trade, Technology and Skills in the Manufacturing Sector

In the early nineteenth century, the major technological changes were skill-replacing or non-skill-biased. That is, the effort was to make the activities undertaken by skilled workers so simple that unskilled workers could do them too. Recent technological changes, however, have favoured the skilled work force and are skill-biased. It has been argued that the growth of an educated work force was the reason for this form of technical development. For example, if we look at the development of the advanced scanner for use by unskilled workers as opposed to advanced computer-assisted machines to be operated by skilled workers, it is the latter in which technological development has rapidly taken place, leading to an increase in the demand for skilled labour.

In the last chapter, we analysed the hypothesis of skill-biased technological change and found that it had, indeed, occurred in many Indian industries, particularly in the services, trade and manufacturing sectors, in the late 1990s. The economic reform policies of the government since 1991, including liberalization of trade and deregulation of industries (documented in Rani and Unni 2004), affected the manufacturing sector to a large extent by allowing the inflow of technology. Another hypothesis discussed in the introductory chapter was the combined effect of trade and technology on skill premiums. In this chapter we analyse the extent to which this hypothesis can be applied to the manufacturing sector in India.

In order to study the impact of liberalization of trade and industry policies on specific industries in the manufacturing sector, we have categorized and grouped the industries in two ways: at the three-digit industry group level by trade category (export–import-oriented, etc.), and by user group (basic–capital–intermediate–consumer goods). We study technical change as measured by the growth of total factor productivity (TFPG) and using the wage bill criterion, as discussed in the previous chapter. We further examine whether the changes in technology have led to the use of more skilled labour and, if so, whether there was a skill premium attached to it.

Industry Groups Classified by Trade and User Group Categories

The macro reform policies of the early 1990s, including trade liberalization measures, made technology transfer relatively easy, and facilitated alliances with foreign firms and the inflow of foreign direct investment (FDI). Import licenses were abolished in the capital and intermediate goods industries in the late 1990s. The export promotion capital goods scheme with zero duty was extended to the small engineering goods industry, which helped the machinery and equipment industries to grow.

To study technical change resulting from trade policies in these industry groups, we categorize them by trade based on the value of export and import in two years, 1993–94 and 1999–2000. We further categorize the industries by user group.

Trade Categories

The following five trade groups were distinguished:

Category I: Export-Oriented – if the value of export was greater than the value of import in both years.

Category II: Import-Competing – if the value of import was greater than the value of export in both years.

Category III: Import-Competing to Export-Oriented – if the value of import was greater in the first year and the value of export was greater in the second year.

Category IV: Export-Oriented to Import-Competing – if the value of export was greater in the first year and the value of import was greater in the second year.

Category V: No Trade – if there was neither export nor import in the industry group.

User Group Categories

The manufacturing industries were categorized by use into five groups:

I: Basic goods including basic metals and chemicals;

II: Intermediate goods including wood, newsprint, leather goods, rubber and plastics, metal products, and non-metallic mineral products;

III: Capital goods including fabricated metal, machinery and equipment, electrical machinery, and transport equipment;

IV: Consumer durables including furniture, office equipment, electrical appliances, motor vehicles and electrical appliances;

V: Consumer non-durable goods including food, textile, paper products, footwear, etc.

The three-digit industry groups included in these trade and user group categories were constructed for the years 1993–94 and 1999–2000 using the National Industrial Classification (NIC) 1998. A concordance table was constructed to match the NIC 1987 classification used in NSS 1993–94, and NIC 1998 used in NSS 1999–2000 (Appendix Chart A 4.1).

The user group classification is presented in Chart 4.1, and the three-digit industry groups categorized by trade in Chart 4.2. The trade categories

CHART **4.1**   *User Group Classification of Industries*

User Groups	Industry Groups
Basic Goods	271, 272, 273 – Manufacture of basic metals 241 – Manufacture of basic chemicals 269 – Manufacture of non-metallic mineral products n.e.c
Intermediate Goods	201, 202 – Manufacture of wood and of products of wood and cork, except furniture; manufacture of articles of straw and plating materials 191 – Tanning and dressing of leather; manufacture of luggage and handbags 243 – Manufacture of man-made fibres 251, 252 – Manufacture of rubber and plastic products 281 – Manufacture of structural metal products, tanks, reservoirs and steam generators 314 – Manufacture of accumulators, primary cells and primary batteries 222 – Publishing, printing and reproduction of recorded media 231, 232, 233 – Manufacture of coke, refined petroleum products and nuclear fuel
Capital Goods	289 – Manufacture of other fabricated metal products; metal-working service activities 291, 292, 293 – Manufacture of machinery and equipment n.e.c 311, 312, 313, 315 – Manufacture of electrical machinery and apparatus n.e.c 342, 343, 351, 352, 353 – Manufacture of other transport equipment
Consumer Durables	361 – Manufacture of furniture 300 – Manufacture of office, accounting and computing machinery 319 – Manufacture of other electrical equipment n.e.c. 321, 322, 323 – Manufacture of radio, television and communication equipment and apparatus 341 – Manufacture of motor vehicles, motor cars 359 – Manufacture of transport equipment n.e.c 331, 333 – Medical instruments, watches and clocks
Consumer Non-Durables	151–155, 160 – Manufacture of food products, beverages and tobacco 171, 172, 173, 181, 182 – Manufacture of textiles and wearing apparel 210 – Manufacture of paper and paper products 192 – Manufacture of footwear 242 – Manufacture of other chemical products (pharmaceuticals) 261 – Manufacture of glass and glass products 332 – Manufacture of optical instruments and photographic equipment 369 – Manufacturing n.e.c

Note: Based on National Industrial Classification (NIC) 1998.

CHART 4.2   *Trade Category and User Group Classification of Industries*

User Groups	
	Category I: Export Oriented
Basic Goods	269. Non-metallic mineral products n.e.c
Intermediate Goods	191. Tanning and dressing of leather; manufacture of luggage and handbags
	251, 252. Rubber and plastic products
	281. Structural metal products, tanks, reservoirs and steam generators
	233. Nuclear fuel
Capital Goods	289. Other fabricated metal products; metal-working service activities
	342. Other transport equipment
Consumer Durables	319. Other electrical equipment n.e.c.
	341. Motor vehicles and motor cars
	359. Transport equipment n.e.c
	361. Furniture
	333. Watches and clocks
Consumer Non-Durables	151–155, 160. Food products, beverages and tobacco products
	171, 172. Spinning, weaving, finishing, and other textiles
	181–182. Wearing apparel
	192. Footwear
	242. Other chemical products (pharmaceuticals)
	369. Manufacturing (jewellery, sports) n.e.c
	Category II: Import-Competing
Basic Goods	241. Basic chemicals
	272. Non-ferrous metals
Intermediate Goods	201, 202. Wood and products of wood and cork, except furniture; manufacture of articles of straw and plating materials
	222. Publishing, printing and reproduction of recorded media
	231, 232. Coke, refined petroleum products
	314. Accumulators, primary cells and primary batteries
Capital Goods	291, 292, 293. General and special purpose machinery, domestic appliances
	311, 312, 315 Electric motors, generators, transformers, electricity distribution, electric lamps
	351, 353. Ships and boats, space craft and aircraft
Consumer Durables	300. Office, accounting and computing machinery
	321, 322, 323. Radio, television and communication equipment and apparatus, television, radio receivers
	331. Medical instruments
Consumer Non-Durables	210. Paper and paper products
	332. Optical instruments and photographic equipment
	Category III: Import-Competing to Export-Oriented
Basic Goods	271. Basic iron and steel
Intermediate Goods	243. Man-made fibres
Capital Goods	313. Insulated wire and cable
	343. Autocomponents: parts and accessories
Consumer Non-Durables	153–154. Grain, mill and other food products.
	261. Glass and glass products.
	Category IV: Export-Oriented to Import-Competing
Capital Goods	352. Transport equipment: railways and tramways
Consumer Non-Durables	152. Dairy products
	173. Knitted and crocheted products
	Category V: No Trade
Basic Goods	273. Casting Metals

Note: Based on National Industrial Classification (NIC) 1998.

are further divided into industries by user group. We found that almost all the industries were affected by the trade policies. At the three-digit level, only the metal-casting industry had neither export nor import and was a 'no trade' industry in both 1993–94 and 1999–2000. Similarly, very few industries shifted from export-oriented to import-competing: railway and tramway equipment, dairy products, and knitted and crocheted products. A majority of the industries were either export-oriented (metal products, motor vehicles, wearing apparel, pharmaceuticals) or import-competing (basic chemicals, machinery, electric motors, generators, office accounting and computing machinery, radio, television and communication equipment, medical instruments). Some industry groups also showed a movement from import-competing to export orientation: capital goods, especially autocomponent parts and accessories.

Later in the book we shall discuss a micro-level study of the auto-components industry. With the liberalization policies, the motor vehicles industry and the autocomponents industry saw the entry of new foreign companies and new technologies. In our classification we found that the manufacture of motor vehicles belonged to the export-oriented trade group, while the autocomponents industry shifted from import-competing to ex-port orientation by early 2000. In Chapter Two we noted that the auto-mobile industry was a major beneficiary of the trade policy reforms that allowed the inflow of foreign competition and technology. This apparently helped the automobile and autocomponents industries to grow into an export-oriented sector.

Technical Change in the Manufacturing Industry

The manufacturing sector showed an overall increase in technical change by the criterion of occupation, but there was no increase by the wage bill criterion using education to indicate skill content. Within the trade categories, technical change measured by the wage bill, using the crite-ria of both education and occupation, showed an increase in the export-oriented industry group (Table 4.1). Technical change measured by the TFPG index for the same period showed an increase in the unorganized sector but a decline in organized manufacturing.

The export oriented industries and those that moved from import to export orientation showed an increase in technical change in the unorga-nized sector. Liberalization of trade and industrial policies seems to have favoured the inflow of technology into export-oriented industries as a whole and those moving towards an export orientation, in the unorganized sector during this period. In the earlier review of policies in Chapter Two, we

TABLE 4.1   Skill Premium and Skill-Biased Technical Change by Trade Category and User Group, All Workers

Industry	Technical Change						Skill Premium (Education)				Skill Premium (Occupation)			
	Education		Occupation		TFPG		H/L		WH/WL		H/L		WH/WL	
	1993–94	1999–2000	1993–94	1999–2000	Org.	Unorg.	1993–94	1999–2000	1993–94	1999–2000	1993–94	1999–2000	1993–94	1999–2000
Trade Categories														
Category I: Export-Oriented	1.89	2.21	5.01	6.06	−2.60	3.84	0.32	0.40	2.1	2.3	0.03	0.04	4.0	5.2
Category II: Import-Competing	0.00	0.00	31.26	23.77	−4.93	−0.31	0.85	0.85	2.2	2.4	0.16	0.14	2.6	3.4
Category III: Import-Competing to Export-Oriented	2.71	2.17	4.79	3.86	−1.49	4.46	0.30	0.50	2.5	2.2	0.05	0.07	4.2	3.4
Category IV: Export-Oriented to Import-Competing	0.00	0.00	–	–	2.26	−4.05	1.00	0.99	1.5	1.3	0.03	0.03	3.3	3.8
Category V: No Trade					1.16	15.94								
Total	2.40	2.40	3.36	4.01	−2.69	1.59	0.36	0.48	2.4	2.4	0.05	0.06	3.7	4.4
User Categories														
Basic Goods	2.18	4.79	2.25	2.94	−0.93	3.33	0.37	0.39	2.5	3.1	0.06	0.08	3.7	4.3
Intermediate Goods	1.59	2.13	–	–	−7.71	0.62	0.49	0.52	2.0	2.0	0.06	0.06	3.2	3.7
Capital Goods	3.76	6.25	1.07	2.01	−1.35	2.69	1.21	1.29	1.9	2.5	0.17	0.19	2.3	3.1
Consumer Durables	2.86	6.32	6.09	7.84	−4.13	3.38	0.92	1.04	2.2	3.9	0.14	0.13	2.9	7.1
Consumer Non-Durables	2.87	2.18	1.13	8.49	−2.75	3.42	0.24	0.37	2.2	1.9	0.03	0.04	4.0	3.1
Total	2.40	2.40	3.36	4.01	−2.69	1.59	0.36	0.48	2.4	2.4	0.05	0.06	3.7	4.4

Source: National Sample Survey Organization, Employment–Unemployment Survey, 1993–94 (50th Round) and 1999–2000 (55th Round), Unorganized Sector Survey, 1994–95 (51st Round) and 2000–01 (56th Round). Computed.

noted that the reforms in the period after 1994 were favourable to the unorganized sector, and that appeared to surge ahead. A large number of industries witnessed growth of value added, as well as of employment and labour productivity. Sub-contracting linkages with larger firms and the inflow of technology could have helped the growth process in many of these industries.

In the user group classification, technical change measured by the criteria of education and occupation showed an increase in the basic, intermediate, capital goods and consumer durables industries, without reference to the trade categories. TFP growth in the unorganized sector was also higher in these industries and in the capital goods industries, as compared to the organized sector. In the early 1990s, trade liberalization allowed the inflow of technology in the intermediate and capital goods sectors, while domestic protection to the consumer industry was lifted in the mid 1990s.

Within the export-oriented industries, it was mainly the basic and intermediate goods and consumer durables that witnessed an inflow of technology, and not the consumer non-durable industries (Table 4.2). Non-metallic mineral products among basic goods, structural metal, rubber and plastic goods among intermediate goods and motor vehicle and transport equipment industries among durables had an inflow of technology. All of them had higher TFP growth in the unorganized sector. By the TFPG criterion, capital goods such as fabricated metal products also showed much higher technological change in the unorganized sector. As we noted above, the trade liberalization measures were particularly directed at the intermediate and capital goods sectors (Unni and Rani 2005).

Among the export-oriented consumer non-durable industries, wearing apparel showed technical change by both measures of education and occupation. The chemical products or pharmaceuticals industry showed a decline in technical change by the same criteria. In both the industry groups, TFP growth was higher in the unorganized segments.

While import-competing industries did not indicate overall technical change, among them, basic goods and capital goods showed an increase in the technical change indicator. Technical change using the TFPG measure was also positive in these industry groups in the unorganized sector. Within capital goods, it was manufacture of machinery and electrical machinery that recorded high growth with good quality employment in the unorganized sector after 1994. They were also found to have vertical sub-contracting linkages, including the supply of design specifications, raw materials and equipment (Chapter Two).

TABLE 4.2   Skill Premium and Skill-Biased Technical Change by Trade and User Group Categories, All Workers

Industry	Technical Change						Skill Premium (Education)				Skill Premium (Occupation)			
	Education		Occupation		TPG		H/L		WH/WL		H/L		WH/WL	
	1993 –94	1999– 2000	1993 –94	1999– 2000	Org.	Unorg.	1993 –94	1999– 2000	1993 –94	1999– 2000	1993 –94	1999– 2000	1993 –94	1999– 2000
Category I: Export-Oriented														
Basic Goods	8.38	11.05	0.57	0.54	1.83	3.46	0.16	0.14	2.3	2.1	0.02	0.02	4.1	3.6
Intermediate Goods	5.27	7.66	0.00	0.00	0.08	6.30	0.60	0.64	1.9	1.9	0.05	0.06	3.5	3.2
Capital Goods					-1.30	2.68								
Consumer Durables	2.26	7.17	0.00	7.14	-3.39	4.43	0.58	0.74	2.1	4.5	0.07	0.07	2.9	12.9
Non-Durables	2.34	2.03	13.39	10.17	-3.28	3.26	0.28	0.38	2.0	1.8	0.02	0.03	4.1	3.4
Sub-total	1.89	2.21	5.01	6.06	-2.60	3.84	0.32	0.40	2.1	2.3	0.03	0.04	4.0	5.2
Category II: Import-Competing														
Basic Goods	1.42	1.71	2.26	2.53	-4.10	0.39	1.23	1.34	2.0	2.8	0.24	0.38	2.2	2.5
Intermediate Goods	0.45	0.64	44.05	46.82	-13.00	-2.35	0.35	0.37	2.1	2.1	0.08	0.06	3.0	4.5
Capital Goods	3.76	6.25	1.07	2.01	-0.66	4.57	1.21	1.29	1.9	2.5	0.17	0.19	2.3	3.1
Consumer Durables	0.17	0.11	1.49	3.39	-5.29	-4.69	3.14	4.27	2.4	2.6	0.42	0.43	2.7	2.1
Non-Durables	1.62	1.37	2.05	3.24	4.21	5.36	0.44	0.81	1.5	1.4	0.14	0.04	1.4	1.8
Sub-total	0.00	0.00	31.26	23.77	-4.93	-0.31	0.85	0.85	2.2	2.4	0.16	0.14	2.6	3.4
Category III: Import-Competing to Export-Oriented														
Basic Goods	1.74	1.53	3.78	3.75	-0.61	-3.23	0.63	1.06	1.9	2.3	0.10	0.14	2.9	3.1
Intermediate Goods					0.86	79.71								
Capital Goods					-4.79	-1.66								
Non-Durables	2.93	1.95	5.10	2.50	-5.75	5.00	0.20	0.34	2.5	1.7	0.02	0.04	4.8	2.3
Sub-total	2.71	2.17	4.79	3.86	-1.49	4.46	0.30	0.50	2.5	2.2	0.05	0.07	4.2	3.4

TABLE 4.2 (contd)

Industry	Technical Change						Skill Premium (Education)				Skill Premium (Occupation)			
	Education		Occupation		TFPG		H/L		WH/WL		H/L		WH/WL	
	1993–94	1999–2000	1993–94	1999–2000	Org.	Unorg.	1993–94	1999–2000	1993–94	1999–2000	1993–94	1999–2000	1993–94	1999–2000
Category IV: Export-Oriented to Import-Competing														
Capital Goods	0.00	0.00	–	–	6.70	–11.30	1.00	0.99	1.5	1.3	0.03	0.03	3.3	3.8
Non-Durables	0.00	0.00	–	–	0.78	–3.93	1.00	0.99	1.5	1.3	0.03	0.03	3.3	3.8
Sub-total					2.26	–4.05								
Category V: No Trade														
Basic Goods					1.16	15.94								
Sub-total					1.16	15.94								
Total	**2.40**	**2.40**	**3.36**	**4.01**	**–2.69**	**1.59**	**0.36**	**0.48**	**2.4**	**2.4**	**0.05**	**0.06**	**3.7**	**4.4**

Source: Same as Table 4.1.

Skilled Workers and Wage Premium

In the late 1990s, there was more rapid growth of skilled workers as compared to unskilled workers in most of the industry groups in the manufacturing sector. This was reflected in the increase in ratio of skilled to unskilled workers as a whole in the manufacturing sector. The wage premium of skilled workers defined by the level of education remained constant, while it rose when defined by occupation (Table 4.1).

When viewed by trade category, there was an increase in skilled workers in export-oriented industries and in industries that moved from import to export orientation. The skill premium, however, rose only for the export-oriented industries. This fits our theoretical framework, since it was only the export oriented industries that had opted for skill-intensive technical change. The export industries were also those that gained or adapted the most to the trade liberalization policies. Therefore, the hypothesis of the positive effect of trade and technical change on skill premium is validated by this empirical evidence.

When looked at in terms of user groups, all the groups showed an increase in skilled workers, and nearly all except consumer non-durables had an increase in the wage premium of skilled workers. This, again, validated our prediction, as there was skill-biased technical change in these industries and no such technical change in the consumer non-durable industry group.

Among the export-oriented industries classified by user group, it was only the consumer durables sector, including the motor vehicles industry, that had an increase in skilled workers with an increase in skill wage premium (Table 4.2). The other two industry groups that had technical change, basic and intermediate goods, had neither an increase in skilled workers nor an increase in skill premium. They were able to manage the changes in technology with their existent work force. The consumer industries were protected from foreign competition till the mid-1990s. But once competitive forces were unleashed, the consumer durable group was able to upgrade its technology and skilled work force, reaping benefits for itself in terms of high growth and for its workers in terms of an increase in wage premiums.

The import-competing industries were equally affected by the trade reforms. Among them, the basic and capital goods industries recorded technical change. These industries also saw an increase in skilled workers and skill wage premiums by measures of both skill, and education and occupation. As noted above, among the import-competing capital goods industries it was manufacture of machinery and electrical machinery that showed an increase in skilled workers and wage premiums.

Technical Change, Skill and Wage Premium by Gender

The assumption in the measure of technical change, T, is that the increase in the wage bill reflects the increase in marginal productivity of the workers, and hence the impact of technological change in that industry. T measured by the wage bill allows us to distinguish between technical change that favours male and female labour.

The impact of technical change by gender presents on interesting picture (Tables 4.3 and 4.4). Technical change is clearly seen in male occupations both at the aggregate level and, as we have seen, for all workers in the export-oriented industries. Similarly, the positive relationship of an increase in skilled workers with an increase in wage premium of these workers was observed at the aggregate level and for export industries. Women workers did not benefit from any of these changes in the aggregate or even in the export-oriented industries.

Among the export-oriented industries, we had observed that though consumer non-durables as a whole did not show technical change or the positive relation of skill and wage premiums, the wearing apparel industry did so. Since wearing apparel has a large proportion of women workers, we looked for this relationship by gender. The interesting result is that technical change was seen for women but not for men. Increase in skilled workers and wage premium was also observed for female and not for male workers. This is perhaps the one industry where women workers have benefited from the economic policies favouring the sector.

When technical change and skill are measured by occupation, however, we find that the proportion of managerial and professional women in the garment industry is negligible. Therefore, the technical change is probably based on changes in production techniques in the industry, which favour the employment of educated female production workers.

Conclusions

Trade liberalization in the 1990s led to the opening up of the Indian economy to an inflow of FDI, technology, and capital and intermediary goods. In this chapter, we have tested the hypothesis of the combined impact of trade and the inflow of technology on the skills of workers and their wage premiums.

The impact of trade liberalization on technology upgradation was most prominently noted in export-oriented industries such as basic, intermediate and capital goods, and consumer durables. Liberalization of trade and industrial policies seems to have favoured the inflow of technology into export-oriented industries as a whole. It also favoured technical change in industries moving towards export orientation during this period, in the

TABLE 4.3 *Skill Premium and Skill-Biased Technical Change by Trade Category and User Group, Male Workers*

Industry	Technical Change				Skill Premium (Education)				Skill Premium (Occupation)			
	Education		Occupation		H/L		WH/WL		H/L		WH/WL	
	1993–94	1999–2000	1993–94	1999–2000	1993–94	1999–2000	1993–94	1999–2000	1993–94	1999–2000	1993–94	1999–2000
Trade Categories												
Category I: Export-Oriented	1.91	2.16	1.81	2.95	0.34	0.44	2.0	2.2	0.04	0.05	3.3	4.6
Category II: Import-Competing	–	–	28.68	23.84	0.84	0.85	2.1	2.4	0.15	0.4	2.6	3.4
Category III: Import-Competing to Export-Oriented	2.36	2.00	4.18	3.32	0.37	0.58	2.2	2.1	0.05	0.08	3.8	3.0
Category IV: Export-Oriented to Import-Competing	–	–	0.16	0.18	1.01	1.02	1.6	1.3	0.03	0.05	3.3	2.7
Category V: No Trade	–	–										
Total	2.11	2.28	1.25	1.87	0.43	0.54	2.1	2.3	0.06	0.07	3.3	4.0
User Categories												
Basic Goods	2.26	3.34	2.71	3.29	0.42	0.46	2.3	2.9	0.07	0.09	3.3	3.8
Intermediate Goods	1.47	1.70	63.77	88.58	0.49	0.53	2.0	1.9	0.07	0.05	3.0	3.5
Capital Goods	2.06	2.72	1.72	2.60	1.17	1.35	1.9	2.5	0.14	0.13	2.6	3.2
Consumer Durables	2.37	4.49	8.50	8.15	0.87	1.00	2.2	4.0	0.13	0.12	2.8	7.3
Consumer Non-Durables	2.25	1.87	4.73	3.91	0.30	0.43	1.9	1.7	0.04	0.05	3.2	2.7
Total	2.11	2.28	1.25	1.87	0.43	0.54	2.1	2.3	0.06	0.07	3.3	4.0

Source: Same as Table 4.1.

TABLE 4.4   Skill Premium and Skill-Biased Technical Change by Trade Category and User Group, Female Workers

| Industry | Technical Change | | | | Skill Premium (Education) | | | | Skill Premium (Occupation) | | | |
| | Education | | Occupation | | H/L | | WH/WL | | H/L | | WH/WL | |
	1993–94	1999–2000	1993–94	1999–2000	1993–94	1999–2000	1993–94	1999–2000	1993–94	1999–2000	1993–94	1999–2000
Trade Categories												
Category I: Export-Oriented	7.24	5.39	529.5	404.14	0.09	0.13	2.9	2.4	0.00	0.01	6.3	4.8
Category II: Import-Competing	0.91	1.18		4.41	0.94	0.75	3.2	3.0		0.23		5.7
Category III: Import-Competing to Export-Oriented	5.33	2.73	6.21	4.40	0.05	0.15	3.6	2.1	0.01	0.01	6.9	5.2
Category IV: Export-Oriented to Import-Competing					0.00	0.68		2.2	0.00	0.00		
Category V: No Trade												
Total	5.60	4.20	100.7	72.65	0.13	0.18	3.5	2.9	0.02	0.02	6.1	7.2
User Categories												
Basic Goods	–	–	37.41	43.86	0.09	0.09	5.7	3.7	0.02	0.01	9.5	5.6
Intermediate Goods	2.01	2.61	7.88	10.27	0.52	0.41	2.8	4.4	0.01	0.15	6.7	10.6
Capital Goods	0.94	1.51	2.27	1.49	1.88	0.69	2.5	1.6	0.55	0.28	2.2	1.6
Consumer Durables	0.13	0.23	4.69	4.98	2.25	1.53	2.7	3.1	0.24	0.13	5.1	3.7
Consumer Non-Durables	6.98	4.29	–	–	0.07	0.14	2.8	2.1	0.0	0.0	5.1	5.6
Total	5.60	4.20	100.7	72.65	0.13	0.18	3.5	2.9	0.02	0.02	6.1	7.2

Source: Same as Table 4.1.

unorganized sector. One such was the autocomponents industry, which we shall discuss later as a micro case study.

The flow of technology into export-oriented industries and those moving towards an export orientation during the 1990s led to an increase in the skill content of the work force in both these groups. However, the wage premium of skilled workers registered an increase mainly in industries that were export-oriented over a longer period and not in those that had recently moved towards an export orientation. It is possible that there is a time lag before the benefits of the inflow of technology and skills actually reach the workers in the form of a wage rise. This is a hypothesis that is worth testing. Further, even within the export-oriented industries classified by user group, it was mainly the consumer durable industries that had wage premiums for skilled workers. The motor vehicles industry was one such. Capital goods industries within the import-competing industry group also reaped the benefits of technical change, an increase in the skilled work force and wage premiums.

When the technology, skill content and wage premium were studied by gender, it was observed it is mainly male workers who benefit from these changes. The only export-oriented industry where women workers benefit from technical change, skilled work force and wage premium, was the wearing apparel industry. However, even here, the skills appeared to be concentrated among the production workers and it was not a movement towards the professionalization of workers in the garment industry.

Appendix Chart

CHART A 4.1   *Concordance Table for the Manufacturing Sector, NIC 1998 with NIC 1987*

Industry Group Two-digit	NIC 1998 three-digit	NIC 1998 Three-digit	NIC 1998 (55th Round, 1999–2000) Five-digit	NIC 1987 (50th Round, 1993–94) Three-digit
20. Food	Meat, fish, fruits, vegetables, oil and fats	151	15111 to 15118+15121 to 15127+ 15131 to 15139+ 15141+15142+15143+ 15144+15145+15146+15147	200+202+203+210+211+212
	Dairy products	152	15201+15202+15203+15204+15205+15209	201
	Grain mill	153	15311+15312+15313+15314+15315+15316+ 15317+15319+15321+15323+15324+15325 15326+15331+15332+15339	204+217+218
	Food products	154	15411+15412+15419+15421+15422 15423+15424+15425+15426+15427 15428+15429+15431+15432+15433 15434+15435+15440+15491+15492+15493+ 15494+15495+15490+15497+15499	205+206+207+209+ 213+214+215+219
21. Beverages and Tobacco	Beverages	155	15511+15512+15520+15531+15532+ 15533+15541+15542+15543+ 15544+15549	216+220+221+222+223
	Tobacco	160	16001+16002+16003+16004+16005+ 16006+16007+16008+16009	225+226+227+228+229
22. Textiles	Spinning, weaving, finishing	171	17111+17112+17113+17114+17115+17116 17117+17118+17119+17121+17122+17124 17125	231+232+233+234+235+240+241+242 244+245+247+250+251+ 252+253+254+255+256+236+ 243+246+248+257+258+259
	Other textiles	172	17211 to 17219+17211 to 17229+ 17231 to 17239+17291 to 17299 17301+17302+17303+17309	261+262+263+264+267+268+269+260
	Wearing apparel	181	18101+18102+18103+18104+18109 18201+18202+18203+18304+18205+18209	265+266+292+964 294+295+296

Industry Group Two-digit	NIC 1998 three-digit	NIC 1998 Three-digit	NIC 1998 (55th Round, 1999–2000) Five-digit	NIC 1987 (50th Round, 1993–94) Three-digit
23. Leather, Wood, Paper	Leather products	191	19111+19112+19113+19114+19115+19116+ 19119+19121+19122+19123+19129	290+293+299
	Footwear	192	19201+19202	291+311
	Wood	201	20101+20102+20103+ 20211+20212+20213+20219+20221+ 20222+20231+20232+20233 20239+20291+20292+20293+ 20294+20295+20296+20298+20297+20299	270+ 271+272+273+274+275+ 277+279
	Paper and paper products	210	21011+21012+21013+21014+21015 21016+21017+21019+21021+21022 21028+21029+21091+21092+21093 21094+21095+21096+21097+21098 21099	280+281+282+283
	Publishing and Recording	221	22110+22121+22122+22130+22190 22211+22212+22213+22219+22221+22222 2230	284+285+286+287+288+289
30. Chemicals	Petroleum products and Fuel	231	23101+23109 23201+23202+23203+23209 23300	318+319 314+315+316 317
	Chemicals, Fertilizer	241	24111 to 24119+24121+24122+24123+ 24124+24129+24131+24132 24133+24134+24139	300+301+302
	Pesticides, Paints Pharmaceuticals	242	24211+24219+24221+24222+24223+ 24224+24229+24231+24232+24233 24234+24235+24236+24239 24241+24242+24243+24244 24245+24246+24247+24248+24249+24291 +24292+24293 24294+24295+24296+24297 24298+24299	208+303+304+305+307+308+309

Industry Group Two-digit	NIC 1998 three-digit	NIC 1998 Three-digit	NIC 1998 (55th Round, 1999–2000) Five-digit	NIC 1987 (50th Round, 1993–94) Three-digit
31. Rubber, Plastic Fibres and Glass	Man-made fibres	243	24301+24302+24304+24305+24306	306
	Rubber products	251	25111+25112+25113+25114+25119+ 25191+25192+25193+25194+25199	310–312
	Plastic products	252	25201+25202+25203+25204+25205 25206+25207+25208+25209	313
	Glass products	261	26101+26102+26103+26104+26105 26106+26107+26109	321
32. Non-Metal Mineral products	Non-Metal Mineral products	269	26911+26912+26913+26914+26915+ 26916+26919+26921+26922+26931 26932+26933+26939+26941+ 26942+26943+26944+26945+26951 26952+26953+26954+26955+26956 26957+26959+26960+26991+26992+ 26993+26994+26999	320+321+322+323+324+ 325+326+327+329
33. Metal products	Metal	271	27101 to 27109+ 27201+27202+27203+27204+27205+27209 27310+27320	330+331+332+ 333+334+335+336+338+339 337
	Metal products	281	28111 to 28113+28121+28122+28123+ 28129+28131+28132+28123+ 28910+28920+28931+28932+28933+ 28939+28991 to 28999	340+341+352 343+344+345+346+ 349
34. Machinery	Machinery	291	29111+29112+29113+29119+29120 29130+29141+29142+29150+29191 to 29199+29111+29112+29113+29119+29120+ 29221+29222+29223+29224+29225 29230+29241+29242+29243 29244+29245+29246+29248	356+391+354+359 393+397+399 350+351+353+357 390+392
	Domestic appliances	293	29301 to 29309	355+364+388

Industry Group Two-digit	NIC 1998 three-digit	NIC 1998 Three-digit	NIC 1998 (55th Round, 1999–2000) Five-digit	NIC 1987 (50th Round, 1993–94) Three-digit
	Office Equipment	300	30001 to 30009	358+367
	Electrical Machinery	311	31101+31102+32203+31104+31109+31200	360+395
			31300	361
			31400	362
			31501 to 31506	363
			31901 to 31909	369
	TV, Radio, Video	321	32101 to 32109	368
			32201+32202+32203+32204+32205	365+396
			32209	366
			32301 to 32309	
	Medical	331	33111+33112+33113+33114+33115+	380
			33116+33119+33121+33122+33123+	
			33124+33125+33126+33127	
			33129+33130	
	Optical/Photography	332	33201 to 33209	381
	Watches and Clocks	333	33301+33302+33309	382
35. Transport	Motor Vehicles	341	34101 to 34107+34201+34202+34203	373+374
			34300	
	Ships, Rail, Air	351	35111 to 35117+35121 to 35123	370
			35201+35202+35203+35204	371+372
			35301 to 35303	377
	Motor Cycle-Carts	359	35911+35912+35913+35921+	375+376+378+379
			35922+35923+35929+35991	
			35992	
36. Other Manu-facturing	Furniture	361	36101 to 36109	276+277+342
	Other Manufacturing	369	36911+36912+36913+36920+36931	383+384+385+386+
			36932+36933+36934+36935+	387+389
			36939+36941+36942+36991 to 36999+	
	Recycling		37100+	
			37200	

CHAPTER FIVE

Sub-Contracting Relationships in the Autocomponents Sector

Do Small Firms and Informal Enterprises Benefit?

Economic organizations are transforming with the changing environment of international trade, finance and information. Flexible production systems with increased outsourcing and sub-contracting arrangements are becoming more dominant as firms adopt cost-cutting strategies to survive and compete in the market. There have been a large number of studies on sub-contracting arrangements across the world which empirically demonstrate the existence of different forms of sub-contracting, often specific to either an industry or a country. These studies explain the phenomenon on grounds of 'efficiency' or 'exploitation'. Global production-sharing or outsourcing also leads to an inflow of technology and a continuous upgradation of the work force, as observed in Chapter One.

Most of the research on sub-contracting relates to the relations between large and small firms or between assemblers and their suppliers, which are often medium and small-sized firms. In Chapter Two, we noted that a very small proportion of unorganized (or unregistered), small firms are ancillaries to a parent firm or purely in an assembler–supplier relationship with a large firm. The linkages between formal (large) and informal (including small) firms were studied in the 1970s and the 1980s, with the focus on the exploitative elements of such linkages. A few studies, however, did show that the relationships were mutually beneficial and led to the growth of small firms.

These flexible production systems have been widely prevalent in the automobile sector across the globe and it is argued that the divisible production processes work efficiently. In India, the flexible production system in the automobile sector began with the arrival of Suzuki Motor Company (SMC), a Japanese firm, which entered into a collaboration with Government of India in 1982. For many years, vertically integrated production processes in the autocomponents sector were restricted to this manufacturing firm, as the older domestic companies preferred in house manufacture of components. However, with the opening up of the economy from the beginning of 1990s, there was fierce competition in the automobile industry, with a number of international companies setting up their base in India. The trend was largely to capture the internal market demand, and also to exploit the low labour and capital costs for sourcing components to other markets. This brought about competitiveness among domestic firms and resulted in changes in the production processes for reasons of survival. It also led to the older Indian automobile companies like Tata Motors and Bajaj moving towards flexible production processes and developing their vendors in order to retain their market shares.

Early studies on sub-contracting approached the problem through the 'parent' assemblers, which reinforced the view that small firms were appendages of large firms. In this chapter, we study sub-contracting relationships of large and medium firms with small firms and informal enterprises, from the point of view of the latter. At the outset, it must be mentioned that we are defining informal enterprises and small firms here on the basis of size of employment. Enterprises having less than ten workers are defined as informal, and those having eleven to thirty workers are defined as small. We address three main issues. One, has there been any transfer of skills and technology from large and medium to small and informal enterprises? Two, have small and informal firms gained or improved their capabilities, both in terms of technology and skills, under the global competitive forces? Three, is there any potential for growth for small firms and informal enterprises through sub-contracting in the present competitive environment?

A lot of the research on sub-contracting focuses on vertically integrated production processes, and the horizontal relations that exist between firms, especially small and informal enterprises, have hardly been documented. A second major contribution of this study is our analysis of the horizontal flow of work in the supply chain to see if there is any potential for the development of 'skill concentration networks', and if there is scope for innovations among small and informal enterprises. The concept of skill concentration networks was developed in the case of Japanese small firms (Whittaker 1997). It referred to the movement away of small firms from 'volume or mass production sub-contracting' networks to 'skill concentration' networks in which a variety of low-volume products, often customized, were produced in operations that are difficult to automate. In these networks there are extensive trading links between small factories, all of which are not necessarily product makers but specialize in certain operations. In addition, there is informal or neighbourly cooperation between the firms, which ranges from lending tools and workers to consultation on technical matters.

We begin our discussion with a brief review of the literature on sub-contracting and the macro policies relating to the automobile industry which led to the development of the autocomponents sector. After a brief account of the characteristics of the study regions and sample enterprises, we look at whether the vertical sub-contracting relationships led to a diffusion of technology and skills, and helped the growth of small firms. Next, the horizontal flow of work among the informal enterprises and small firms is examined to see whether there is potential for skill concentration networks in the region. Finally, we discuss whether all these factors of technology and skill enhancement through linkages between firms had an impact on the growth of the firms.

A Brief Review of the Literature

Coase (1937), in his seminal work *Nature of the Firm* put forth the idea that certain activities would be outsourced where the perceived costs of using the market were less than that of undertaking the activity in-house. This would mean that for any input into the production process, a firm has two options: to produce the input in its own factories or to purchase it from other firms via the free market. Profit-maximizing firms are presumed to choose the least cost method of these two alternatives. However, between the two extremes of internal organization (in-house production) and free market transactions lies a spectrum of intermediate inter-firm arrangements, including production through a subsidiary or affiliate or sub-contracting (Sheard 1983: 51 in Holmes 1986).

Williamson (1975) argued that the choice of in-house production and sub-contracting is determined not only by production cost differences, but also by the costs of setting up and maintaining a sub-contracting relationship. Reve (1990) introduced the element of competence along with transaction cost for sub-contracting to occur. He distinguished between skill levels and argued that while 'core skills of high assets specificity could be internally governed and complementary skills of medium asset specificity can be more efficiently obtained through strategic alliances, governed bilaterally, the low specificity assets could be most efficiently contracted in the market' (ibid.: 142).

Becker and Murphy (1992) brought forth other factors, like the costs of 'coordinating' specialized workers and the amount of general knowledge available, to explain sub-contracting. They argued that coordination failures might also lead to the sub-contracting of work to smaller plants where labour organizations are weak. Empirical evidence on the automotive industry in different countries showed that decentralized production processes were adopted due to unionization in large plants, such as in northern Italy in the 1970s (Amin 1985; Murray 1983). In both North America and

Western Europe, a strategy of multisourcing parts was adopted to ensure uninterrupted supply when faced with strikes (Friedman 1977: 122).

In developing economies, where there is excess and heterogeneous supply of labour, labour can be purchased at differential prices, and if the wage differentials between large and small firms are relatively large, there is a tendency to sub-contract the most labour-intensive parts of the production process (Rubery and Wilkinson 1981; Sabel 1982; Scott 1983). The large and small firms can also draw from the various segments in the labour market, thus reducing costs for the same quality of labour. A number of simpler components or machining processes, which were earlier available in-house, have been sub-contracted to small firms in order to take advantage of their low costs of production (Papola and Mathur 1978; Lal 1980; Harriss 1982; Nagaraj 1984; Gupta and Goldar 1995; Holmstrom 1998; Chaudhury 1999).

Most of the empirical literature of the 1980s on sub-contracting or inter-firm linkages argued that the relationship was exploitative (Bose 1978; Harriss 1982; Banerjee 1988), though there was some evidence that showed the growth of small firms through sub-contracting (Nagaraj 1984, Holmstrom 1998). However, there seems to be a very thin line between 'exploitation' and 'efficiency' in sub-contracting, since the large firms become 'efficient' largely by exploiting the low labour and capital costs of the small firms.

The more recent literature on the flexible or divisible production process argues that the strategy of sub-contracting production processes to small firms helps large firms reduce their involvement in manufacturing, allowing them to focus more on product definition, programme management and brand identity, efficient assemblies, marketing of brands, and superior customer interface (Sahay, Saxena and Kumar 2004). The ability of large firms to make rapid adjustments to new circumstances, both in R&D and production activities, not only brings about dynamism in flexibility but also helps the small firms to grow as new techniques or skills get diffused. The incentive for the small firm in this world of competitiveness is that of an assured market for the product; if it is able to deliver in time and with the specified quality, then it would get more products to manufacture, which would allow it to expand and thrive. Large firms also expect their sub-contractors to improve efficiencies constantly by undertaking modifications in products, processes and practices (Basant and Chandra 2002; Helseley and Strange 2002; Morris and Basant 2004). Thus in this more recent literature it is argued that sub-contracting is an efficient form of production organization, though there is implicit mention of the attendant exploitation of labour.

It is against this background of diverse views that we examine whether small and informal firms within sub-contracting relationships are able to grow, and whether there is any diffusion of technology and skill from the larger to the smaller firms that enhances capabilities.

Policies for the Automobile Industry and Autocomponents Sector

We examine here the various policies that led to the ancillarization of autocomponent firms and later to their technological improvement, as the automobile industry was restructured. The policies towards the automobile sector immediately after Indian independence were protective[1] and 'reserved for firms willing to manufacture components and complete vehicles with a phased manufacturing programme' (Pingle 2000: 89). The state, apart from protecting, also regulated domestic competition through its licensing system and control over foreign exchange allocation, as all firms depended on imports of components.[2]

The Jha Committee, which was appointed to look into the poor quality and high prices that plagued the automobile industry under the protected regime, recommended that these could be brought under control through the development of the ancillary segment, which would increase competition and ensure better quality at lower prices. The protectionist and inward-oriented policies of the government reserved a part of components production for the small-scale sector, which led to the ancillarization of the components industry. However, the production of parts and components was very limited and geared towards the spare market, as large firms preferred to rely on components made in-house since the ancillary industry was underdeveloped (D'Costa 1995).

Though the policy led to the proliferation of the components sector, the issue of quality continued to be a problem. This was largely because the policy limited the ability of components manufacturers to innovate and upgrade technology. Little, Mazumdar and Page (1987), analysing the autocomponents sector, argued that the manufacturers often used worn-out machine tools without basic jigs and fixtures, which made it difficult for them to meet quality and standardization requirements despite impressive skills within the labour force.

The Industrial Policy Statements of 1977 and 1980 had a major impact on the automobile industry as the state loosened its grip by 'relaxing

---

[1] This led to the exit of the foreign automobile assemblers General Motors and Ford, while Indian assemblers like Hindustan Motors and Premier Automobile Limited entered the passenger car segment along with Mahindra and Mahindra, Ashok Motors and TELCO.

[2] The control strategy actually helped the state to influence the production rates of the firm.

regulations governing production licenses, foreign collaboration, asset size, limits on capacity and the scope of industrial operations' (D'Costa 1995: 487). These facilitated the joint venture in 1982 of Suzuki Motor Corporation (SMC) and Maruti Udyog Limited (MUL) of the Government of India to manufacture cars, and this was also the beginning of the process of restructuring in the Indian automobile industry.

The foreign collaborations of the 1980s were based on a 'phased manufacturing programme' wherein firms had to attain 90 per cent local content in the product within five years of signing the MoU (memorandum of understanding). The mandatory requirement of local content and the favourable government policy towards small-scale industries further encouraged the development of the automotive ancillary industry (D'Costa 1995). The Japanese collaboration further emphasized sub-contracting. This apparently led to the entry of an organized components sector into the market in the 1980s, with about 300 large and medium firms, and over 800 small-scale firms (Kathuria 1990 in D'Costa 1995). The emphasis of the Japanese collaboration on 'quality and sub-contracting combined with the Indian Government's decree on local content encouraged the development of technologically modern domestic suppliers' (D'Costa 1995: 493).

A major policy measure towards liberalization of the automobile industry was the introduction of 'broad banding' in 1985, permitting vehicle manufacturers to produce different kinds of vehicles instead of one kind as decreed by the industrial license. The abolition of the product license allowed component manufacturers to produce a wide range of parts and related products, and vehicle manufacturers to produce scooters, motor cycles, and three and four wheelers. The government also recognized the importance of economies of scale and hence permitted companies to raise their annual capacity. The auto ancillary industry was also delicensed in 1985, and it was allowed to expand capacity or set up new units. The mid-1980s, further, saw the introduction of more liberal policies for importing capital equipment for replacement.

The liberalization policy of 1991 delicensed all segments of the automobile industry except for motor cars, which was delicensed later in 1993–94, allowing a number of international automobile companies to set up their own plants or enter into joint ventures. The phased manufacturing programmes, which were being run on an administrative, case-by-case basis, were discontinued for all units (Gokarn and Vaidya 2001). The excise duty on automobiles was reduced from 55 to 40 per cent; the duty on various components and spare parts was also reduced. The policy allowed the import of capital goods and automotive components under open general license (OGL). Both the industrial and trade policies favoured the industry, allowing it access to sophisticated and second-hand machinery from abroad to compete in the global market.

The entry of international global companies into the economy increased competitiveness and with the development of flexible production systems, especially sub-contracting, the older domestic companies were forced to restructure their production processes to retain their market share. The changes in the automotive industry also generated a momentum in the autocomponents segment by propelling modernization and increasing production capacities. This was largely achieved due to policy changes, which included increasing the investment levels in plant and machinery from Rs 60 lakh to Rs 3 crore; these limits were raised even for the tiny sector. The composite loan limit for small-scale units was also increased from Rs 50,000 to Rs 2 lakh. As noted in Chapter Two, the export promotion capital goods (EPCG) scheme at zero duty was extended to a number of small-scale engineering industries, which helped the autocomponents sector. The working capital ceiling for small-scale units was doubled from the existing Rs 2 crore to Rs 4 crore and they were also exempted from excise duty (Rani and Unni 2004a). All these concessions led to the expansion and growth of small-scale units at least in the automotive segment, with most of them being vertically linked.

Characteristics of the Autocomponents Sector in Four Regions

A survey of 101 autocomponent[3] firms was conducted in four different regions of the country where autocomponent clusters were coming up. The regions covered were the National Capital Region (NCR, including NOIDA, Gurgaon and Faridabad in the outskirts of Delhi), Chennai and Coimbatore, Pune (Pimpri–Bhosari–Chinchwad), and Ahmedabad and Rajkot, from July 2004 to February 2005. The primary field survey addressed the issues of levels of technology use, the nature of linkages between large and small firms as production organizations were undergoing change, and whether there was any diffusion of technology and skills in small and informal enterprises as a result of the opening up of the economy. The entry of foreign direct investment (FDI) in 1997–98 and the easing of investment

---

[3] Automotive components can be classified into the following major segments. Engine and engine parts—pistons, piston rings, piston pins, gaskets, carburettors, fuel injection pumps, etc. Drive transmission and steering parts—transmission gears, steering gears, crown wheels and pinions, axles, wheels and similar parts. Suspension and braking parts—leaf springs, shock absorbers, brake assemblies, etc. Electrical—spark plugs, starter motors, generators, distributors, voltage regulators, flywheel magnetos, ignition coils and the like. Equipment—dashboard instruments, headlights, horns, wipers, etc. Others—fan belts, sheet-metal parts, plastic mouldings and like parts.

caps had led to growth in the small-scale sector in recent years (Rani and Unni 2004a), as observed in Chapter Two.

The four regions were chosen due to the specific characteristics of the growth of the autocomponents sector in them, as discussed below. The NCR had seen phenomenal growth and mushrooming of small autocomponent firms after the setting up of Maruti Udyog Limited in 1984. Since then a number of foreign collaborators including Japanese firms have entered the automobile sector. The Chennai region, which was an old autocomponents hub, had declined in the 1980s with the closure of Standard Motors, though the two-wheel segment continued to thrive in this area. The region revived and began to grow with the entry of Hyundai, giving small entrepreneurs an opportunity to set up business. There was major diversification into the autocomponents sector in Coimbatore, which was earlier known for its machine-tool industry. This diversification was largely because the entrepreneurs in the region saw potential for growth as various concessions were being provided by the government to this sector. It was the presence of foreign collaborators in the NCR and Chennai–Coimbatore region that triggered the growth of the autocomponents sector.

In contrast, the Pune region was an old automobile hub, with the presence of the Indian auto giants Bajaj and Telco. The survey aimed to explore how firms in this region had adapted to flexible practices in production organization, and their impact on small and informal enterprises.

The pilot-testing of the survey was done in the Ahmedabad and Rajkot region, where small firms had entered the autocomponents sector largely in the replacement markets. Rajkot had a very good machine-tool base, and had earlier diversified first into diesel engines and later into autocomponents. The diversification into the autocomponents sector was for certain specified products in both the domestic and export markets. We also observed that these four regions operated at different levels of technology and skill intensity of workers, as we shall discuss below.

Basic Characteristics of Autocomponent Firms
Size of the Firms

Out of the 101 autocomponent firms surveyed, 30 per cent were in the NCR, 28 per cent in Chennai–Coimbatore, 33 per cent in Pune, and 10 per cent in the Ahmedabad and Rajkot region. About 25 per cent of the surveyed units had less than 10 workers; 43 per cent had 10 to 30 workers; 15 per cent had 31 to 60 workers; 5 per cent had 61 to 100 workers; and 13 per cent had more than 100 workers employed in their units. The bias in the sample towards informal enterprises (with less than 10 workers) and small enterprises (10 to 30 workers) was deliberate, as we were interested in look-

TABLE 5.1　　　　*Basic Characteristics of Autocomponent Firms in Different Regions of India*

	NCR	Chennai	Pune	Ahmedabad–Rajkot	All Firms
Firm Size by Number of Workers					
Less than 10	13.3	28.6	39.4	0.0	24.8
10–30	40.0	39.3	45.5	50.0	42.6
31–60	23.3	14.3	9.1	10.0	14.9
61–100	3.3	10.7	0.0	10.0	5.0
More than 100	20.0	7.1	6.1	30.0	12.9
All sizes	29.7	27.7	32.7	9.9	100.0
Number of firms in each region	30	28	33	10	101
Registration Status					
SSI	83.3	82.1	54.5	90.0	74.3
ASI	10.0	3.6	3.0	10.0	5.9
Unregistered	6.7	14.3	42.4	0.0	19.8
Market Orientation					
Replacement markets	56.7	14.3	0.0	70.0	27.7
OEM	80.0	92.9	100.0	50.0	87.1
Exports	26.7	10.7	9.1	100.0	23.8
Age of the Enterprise					
Less than 5 years	16.7	14.3	33.3	0.0	19.8
5 to 10 years	20.0	25.0	24.2	20.0	22.8
More than 10 years	63.3	60.7	42.4	80.0	57.4
Sales Turnover (in lakhs)					
Less than 5	3.3	21.4	36.4	0.0	18.8
5–20	16.7	28.6	21.2	0.0	19.8
21–50	23.3	17.9	15.2	20.0	18.8
51–100	16.7	7.1	9.1	10.0	10.9
101–500	20.0	17.9	15.2	30.0	18.8
501–1000	0.0	3.6	0.0	10.0	2.0
Proportion of firms having growth of sales turnover during 2000 to 2004	86.7	82.1	84.8	90.0	85.1
Education Level of Entrepreneur					
Below Class 12	6.7	28.6	54.5	10.0	28.7
Graduate and others	53.3	28.6	9.1	70.0	33.7
ITI/DME	20.0	21.4	27.3	10.0	21.8
Engineering	20.0	21.4	9.1	10.0	15.8

Source: Autocomponents Survey, July 2004–February 2005, Gujarat Institute of Development Research.

ing at the technological capabilities and linkage aspects (both technology and skill) of such enterprises. We were able to capture a larger proportion of informal enterprises in the Pune and Chennai regions than in the other regions largely because these firms were clustered close to the State Industrial Development Corporations and were easy to identify. (See Table 5.1.)

Registration Status

The extent of formality and informality in firms is generally reflected by the extent to which they comply with certain norms. There is a substantial grey area, where firms comply with certain of the norms and not necessarily to the same degree with others. One such norm is registration. Using registration status to define formality and informality, we found that 20 per cent of the firms in the sample were unregistered. A majority of these were in Pune, which could be due to better capturing of such informal enterprises in the region. About 74 per cent of the firms had SSI registration, which was much higher in Chennai and the NCR region, and 6 per cent had ASI registration under the Indian Factories Act. If we classify registration status by firm size, then the unregistered firms were largely in the category of less than 10 workers. Being registered did not imply that the firms provided labour benefits to all its workers. Many of the firms engaged workers on a contract basis or as casual labour to undertake the various operations, had irregular work conditions, high turnover and low rates of remuneration. (See Table 5.1.)

Sales Turnover

The sales turnover in about 85 per cent of the firms grew over the period 2000–04, and this growth was observed in all the regions. Overall, about 19 per cent of the firms had a turnover less than Rs 5 lakh. This was quite high in the Pune region, which could be due to the firms there undertaking job work or machining, but not manufacture of any part or component with material. About 20 per cent of the firms had a sales turnover of about Rs 5 to 10 lakh, and this was much higher in the Chennai–Coimbatore region. Most of these firms were undertaking sub-contracting work with material. About 30 per cent of the firms had a sales turnover between Rs 21 lakh and Rs 1 crore. This was seen largely in the NCR, where most of the firms were undertaking work with material and catering to domestic and export replacement markets. About 11 per cent of the firms had an annual sales turnover of more than Rs 10 crore, largely in the NCR, and Rajkot and Ahmedabad region, dealing in the export replacement markets. (See Table 5.1.)

Markets

The larger turnover was mainly due to the market orientation of the firms, as 27 per cent of them exported autocomponents, largely from the NCR, Rajkot and Ahmedabad, to the replacement markets in Europe, the USA, Japan, Kenya and the Middle East. A further 28 per cent of the firms in these regions cater to the domestic replacement market, possibly with lower turnovers. The firms operating in the replacement markets were able to exploit the booming automobile market and establish their own niche, by either imitating or through reverse engineering. This was largely made possible due to the considerable diversity in products produced by the different firms and in their quality. Firms were able to invade the market and produce products with an affordable margin of profit. About 87 per cent of them supplied components to the original equipment manufacturers (OEMs). This was largely in the Pune and Chennai regions, and they were part of the supplier chain in the automobile industry.

The autocomponents market was booming only in the NCR and Chennai–Coimbatore region since the mid-1990s, and not in the Pune region. In Pune, most entrepreneurs experienced a slowdown during the late 1990s, and a spurt in the growth of the automobile industry was observed only in the last three to four years. The small and informal enterprises in Pune cater to the large firms in the region, and not to other markets either within India or abroad. This dependence makes them very vulnerable, especially to local situations. Pune experienced a slowdown in the late 1990s due to the failure of two ventures. Tata's first car, 'Indica', had technical problems and it was pulled out of the market. Bajaj's motorcycle could not take off as it faced stiff competition from Honda's model. In both these cases quality was the main issue. This meant that both the auto giants had to restructure their production organization to compete in the market. This had a direct impact on the sub-contracting firms that were completely dependent on these companies. However, after the restructuring process there was growth, and the present spurt in growth is mainly a result of this change. (See Table 5.1.)

The 'Integrated Market' View

The restructuring of the automobile industry in the early 1990s from in-house to flexible production processes led to a tiered structure of this industry. Production became hierarchical, integrating large firms with medium and small firms, and small and medium firms with informal enterprises, to improve efficiency. During the process of restructuring, a number of skilled workers in the formal enterprises were given an opportunity to opt out of the formal labour market and set up their own small workshops to undertake certain production processes. There were a number of reasons for the shift within the industry. First, there was wage rigidity; and though the skilled workers had permanent formal jobs with various benefits, there was no upward mobility. Many of them looked at the possibility of setting up an enterprise as a new opportunity and were willing to take the risk. They were assured of markets or the supply of sub-contracted work, and many were also provided with machines at a concessional rate to set up their enterprises. Second, in the period before restructuring, there were major lockouts or closure of enterprises. The lockouts often resulted in loss of days of work and pay for some workers, while wages were not paid on time to others. Third, many of the workers feared retrenchment in the process of restructuring and so decided to opt out of the labour market while they still had the contacts to establish their own enterprises. Fourth, some workers were very clear that they had enough contacts within the industry and could exploit the situation to their benefit as the automobile market was growing. So they exited from the formal labour market and set up small workshops which were registered later. Most of the firms that we interviewed had started as sweatshops with one machine and slowly expanded by adding more machines. Most of the owner–managers also reported that the income they earned from their informal enterprises were initially equal to the wages they had earlier earned in their formal jobs, and that, after a period of six months, they were able to earn more as they began to expand.

A very large proportion of the firms that were set up in this way employed workers not on a permanent basis but on a contractual or casual basis; that is, they employed informal workers. The jobs that these informal firms offered were equally valued by the workers, as they gained an opportunity to learn new skills while being paid, thereby improving their welfare. The informal firms provided an entry point to the labour market and a partial remedy to deficient or obsolete skills through on-the-job training to unskilled and inexperienced workers. This aspect is dealt with in greater detail in the next chapter.

A large proportion of the firms (58 per cent) in all the regions were set up before 1995. Many of them were set up in the mid-1980s, largely to supply parts or components or to undertake machining processes for automobile suppliers and assemblers. About 23 per cent were set up in the late 1990s, and about 20 per cent in the last five years. Pune is the only region that has showed a considerable increase in the proportion of small and informal firms entering the autocomponents sector in the last five years.

This is largely because this region experienced the restructuring process with the adoption of flexible practices in production organization in the mid-1990s, while the process had begun earlier in the other regions.

We first present the hierarchical structure of the automobile industry, which includes the autocomponents sector, and then list out the processes undertaken by different tiers and size class of firms. The automobile industry is vertically integrated with the assemblers at the top, followed by Tier 1, Tier 2 and Tier 3 suppliers (Figure 5.1). The process of shifting part of the assembly, i.e. sourcing assemblies or systems instead of individual components, down the supply chain results in the tiered structure. The Tier 1 supplier is the closest in the supply chain to the vehicle manufacturer, and undertakes the responsibility of integrating and supplying complete systems. Tier 2 and Tier 3 suppliers comprise the sub-assemblers and component manufacturers who supply to Tier 1 or Tier 2 suppliers. Tier 2 and Tier 3 suppliers also undertake certain core processes like forging, casting, pressure die-casting, aluminum die-casting, etc.

FIGURE 5.1   *Structure of the Automobile Industry*

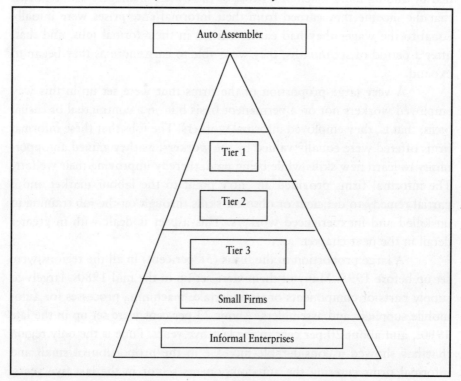

The small firms supply components to Tier 1 or 2 or 3 firms, depending upon the parts they manufacture. The informal enterprises do not generally produce the full part or component but undertake the machining of components, which could involve turning, tapping, milling or grinding operations, or making press components. Some of the informal enterprises also undertake processes like hardening, plating, powder-coating or anodizing of the components. They are authorized by the Tier 1 or 2 or 3 subcontractors to undertake these processes. There exists a very clear integration of the autocomponents industry down the assembly line. The flexible production processes also bring about some kind of continuum between the formal and informal sectors. This tiered structure, with its close association with the autocomponents sector, constitutes the 'integrated market' view of the automobile industry.

Though there is integration of the different tiers in the production process, their response to markets, both domestic and global, is quite different. The response of Tier 1 firms to the markets would be very different from that of firms in other tiers, as emphasis on quality parameters dominates. Similarly, labour conditions are different and are said to improve in the upper tiers. However, this is debatable in the present context as firms prefer to hire contractual workers due to the rapidly changing market situation. Efforts like zero inventory and lean management practices tie firms down the tiers to worse contractual relations, which has implications for labour.

Technical and Entrepreneurial Capabilities in the Firm
We document here the technological levels and capabilities in the firm, including both physical capital and those embodied in the worker, and the entrepreneurial capability of the owner–manager. The capability of the owner–manager includes his ability to get the workers trained, and to get critical and complicated tasks done; and his innovativeness in expanding and taking advantage of opportunities for the growth of the enterprise.

Technological Levels and Capabilities
The technological capability of a firm is its most important capability. It includes the kind of machines the enterprise owns, whether they are conventional manual, semi-automatic, automatic, pneumatic controls or computerized numerical controls; new or second-hand; branded, locally made or imported. The standard form of measuring technological capability in a firm is by the value of investment in plant and machinery. However, we have developed a technology index to measure technological capability

by assigning values to the machines and taking into consideration the criticality of the machine in undertaking an operation.

The technology index has been computed by taking into consideration three criteria: the type of machine, whether the machine is new or second-hand, and whether the machine is made locally or imported. Within each of these criteria we have assigned values, and every machine in the enterprise is assigned these values. Then, for each firm or enterprise these values are added up to constitute the technology index.

The first criterion is the type of machines that the firm possesses: manual, semi-automatic, automatic, programme logit control (PLC), numeric control (NC) and computer numeric control (CNC). The different machines take values from 1 to 10. We have been quite cautious while assigning these values to the machines. We came across different kinds of conventional lathe machines, like simple manual, Herbert 2D Capstan and Gee Dee Weiller lathe machines. Gee Dee Weiller lathe machines are categorized as manual, but their function and the operations they perform are multiple and similar to the operation of CNC. The value that this machine takes is slightly higher than that of a semi-automatic one. Similarly, caution has been taken to assign values to multi-function and single-function machines, and special-purpose machinery.

The second criterion is whether the machine is new or second-hand, and the assigned values are 5 and 3 respectively. The third criterion we have taken into consideration is whether the machine is locally made or imported, depending upon which the assigned values range from 8 to 1. Locally made machines are split into three categories: those manufactured in Chennai, Coimbatore, Bangalore and Pune (of the best quality); in Ludhiana and Rajkot (of average quality); and in other regions (of above-average quality). This classification was adopted because the firm owners often specified different quality characteristics for machines made in different regions. We assume that the higher the technology index, the better would be the technological capability of the firm both for innovation and expansion.

Almost all the enterprises, irrespective of size, operated manual machines.[4] Manual machines were used in the informal enterprises largely

---

[4] The manual machines used were turning lathes, grinding machines (cylindrical, centre-less and surface), traub machines, threading, tapping, boring, milling, drilling machines, mechanical and hydraulic presses, and special-purpose machinery. Some of the manual machines which the supplier sub-contracting firms possessed were branded and belonged to HMT, BFW (Bharat Fraser Works), G D Weiller, Herbert 2D Capstan or were imported from abroad. Some of the mechanical press machines, of 0.5 to 1.5 tonnes and not available in India were imported from Switzerland. However, a significant proportion of the informal enterprises sourced their manual machines from Rajkot or Ludhiana as they were cheap and easily available.

TABLE 5.2 *Levels of Technology of the Firms*

Technology Index	NCR	Chennai	Pune	Ahmedabad–Rajkot	All Firms
Minimum Index					
Less than 10	48	24	18	–	18
10 to 30	44	24	49	48	24
31 to 60	65	158	100	122	65
61 to 100	461	76		485	76
More than 100	80	216	154	186	80
Total	44	24	18	48	18
Maximum Index					
Less than 10	106	123	64	231	123
10 to 30	248	379	289	122	379
31 to 60	905	348	212	485	905
61 to 100	461	470			485
more than 100	1306	282	157	781	1306
Total	1306	470	289	781	1306

Source: Same as Table 5.1.

for 'job work' or machining, though some of them were innovative to develop parts and components also using such simple manual machines. The use of semi-automatic[5] and automatic machines[6] was restricted to a small number of firms. A very small proportion of firms had numeric control (NC) and computer numeric control (CNC)[7] machines, and these were mostly supplier sub-contracting firms. The technology index across firm sizes in the different regions is presented in Table 5.2. We have presented the minimum and maximum index of the firm across different sizes and different regions. This helps us get an idea of the levels of technology by firm size and region.

[5] The semi-automatic machines were turning lathes, radial drilling machines, surface grinding and milling machines. Reputed machine manufacturers like HMT, Praga Tools and Batliboi manufactured some of these machines. It was interesting to find some of the informal enterprises having second-hand branded machines.

[6] The automatic machines included milling machines, hobbing, broaching, grinding machines, R5 harbour machines which could undertake five different operations, and 'retrofitted' numerically controlled lathe machines. Most of these were branded HMT or BFW, or imported from abroad.

[7] The numeric control (NC) and computer numeric control machines (CNC) were largely to undertake the production process, and also to develop tools, dies, jigs or fixtures. Most of these machines were from Bharat Fraser Works (BFW), Lakshmi Machine Works (LMW), Electronica (Pune and Bangalore), Technofab and Miyano. Some of them were also imported from Germany. There were also some programme logit control (PLC) moulding machines and injection moulding machines that were made with specifications within the country, or imported from Germany and Taiwan.

Overall, we find the lowest technology index of a firm to be 18, which means that the firm is operating with the simplest manual lathe machines, locally made, and undertaking 'job work' or machining operations. The highest technology index is 1306 and this firm has a number of CNC and other sophisticated machines, many of which are imported. The highest technology index is in the NCR region. As a word of caution, one should mention that there were certain exceptional cases of firms in the NCR, which increased the technology index in that region.

Broadly speaking, the technology index was seen to increase with an increase in firm size. The technology index in both the NCR and the Ahmedabad–Rajkot region is better because a large proportion of the firms are small or large, cater to the replacement market, and undertake more of specialization and component sub-contracting than just 'job work' or machining. The technology index is the lowest in the Chennai and Pune regions, since a large proportion of firms there are informal, and undertake 'job work' or machining which requires manual conventional lathes or grinding machines.

Skills Embodied in a Worker

The skills embodied in a worker or owner–manager also helps improve the technical capability of a firm. If the owner–manager possesses the skill to fabricate machines or the capability to get special-purpose machinery made as per certain specifications, then the technological level of firm improves considerably. This is a very important asset for small firms and informal enterprises as these machines are not easily accessible due to high costs. For the sub-contracting firms, this was often made possible by the visits of owner–managers of small firms and informal enterprises to large firms. They would carefully observe the machines or new techniques or special-purpose machinery, and note down the details or drawings. They would then copy and develop the machines in-house either through their own expertise or through consultation with tool-room experts. Thus fabrication of machines or manufacturing special-purpose machinery to undertake certain critical operations according to the customer's requirement becomes very important for these small and informal enterprises. We found that about 32 per cent of the firms either fabricated machines or developed special-purpose machinery. This was seen to be much higher in the NCR, and in Rajkot and Ahmedabad (Table 5.3), which largely catered to the replacement markets. Obviously, such manufacture of machines or innovation of parts of machines requires exceptionally enterprising people. In both these regions more than half the entrepreneurs were graduates (Table 5.1).

Good technical knowledge about not only the machine but also the

TABLE 5.3   *Capabilities of the Firms*

	NCR	Chennai	Pune	Ahmedabad–Rajkot	All Firms
Fabrication of machines	40.0	28.6	24.2	40.0	31.7
Developing dies/jigs/fixtures	46.7	42.9	48.5	30.0	44.6
Continuous improvement in processes to reduce costs and improve productivity	30.0	50.0	33.3	20.0	35.6
Drawing Capabilities					
Undertaking component and process drawing	3.3	10.7	15.2	0.0	8.9
CAD/CAM	33.3	35.7	15.2	0.0	24.8
Manual	23.3	7.1	12.1	70.0	19.8
Rough drawings	0.0	7.1	24.2	10.0	10.9
No process drawings	3.3	35.7	33.3	0.0	21.8
No drawings	36.7	3.6	0.0	20.0	13.9

Source: Same as Table 5.1.

dies and tools on the part of the owner–manager and workers is an important capability. This knowledge helps them to understand the drawings and develop dies, tools, jigs and fixtures for the component. The capability level of a firm increases if it also has a tool room. In normal parlance, a tool room in a firm or enterprise consists of a vertical milling machine, surface grinding machine, vertical and horizontal bandsaw machines, lathe, drilling machines, bench grinder, wire cut machine, and measuring instruments and equipment like height masters, test indicators and slip gauges. Since the firms or enterprises that we interviewed were largely informal or small, we have classified firms as having tool rooms even if they had some of the machines listed above for developing either special tools or jigs and fixtures.

The tool room in a firm or enterprise helps the workers to repair worn or damaged manufacturing tools to serviceable condition in a short time. It can assist to develop special parts for the machine, especially when there is a breakdown. It can fabricate new manufacturing tools for production use or modify existing tools to improve the initial design or rectify the fault. It can fabricate machines or develop special-purpose machinery, and it helps in in-house development of jigs, fixtures, dies or moulds.

Firms or enterprises having a tool room facility are thus considered to be capable of developing their own dies and tools. Sub-contractors often prefer such firms for outsourcing parts or components. About 45 per cent of the firms surveyed had the knowledge to develop their own dies, jigs and fixtures for the parts or components they manufactured or the process they undertook. These proportions were much higher in the Pune and Chennai–

Coimbatore regions (Table 5.3). For instance, in Chennai–Coimbatore, one of the parent firms had initially asked the sub-contracting firm to undertake a particular process in seven operations so that the quality could be maintained. This was not cost-effective for the sub-contracting firm and it suggested that it could undertake the process in four operations. As it had good knowledge of tools, jigs and fixtures, it was able to reduce the number of operations, maintaining the quality at the same time. The parent firm finally agreed to the sub-contracting firm's suggestion once they saw that the process was as per the requirement. Similarly, a firm in the Pune region develops special tools and jaws for the component it makes, which is a complicated and difficult operation. Due to its expertise in tool-making for that particular component, it is the sole supplier and the component manufacturing will remain with him.

Technical knowledge of the machines and tools/dies/jigs/fixtures helps the workers or owner–managers to continuously improve the production process and reduce the run-time of the part or component. This knowledge becomes essential to survive and compete in the market, as it helps reduce costs, and improve quality and productivity. About 36 per cent of the firms were capable of making such improvements, and this was much higher in the Chennai and Pune regions (Table 5.3). The firms in Chennai and Pune were able to make improvements in the process largely because of the initiatives of the parent firms to improve productivity, and transfer skills and technology to the sub-contracting firms.

Another important capability is understanding and undertaking product and process drawings of the component. This capability varies across firms, and it can range from not doing any drawings to drawing on CAD/CAM. Firms which did not make any process drawings for the components were largely in the NCR (37 per cent), and Ahmedabad and Rajkot region (20 per cent). The owner–managers and workers in these regions did not have the capability to undertake the drawings, and they often felt it was not essential (Table 5.3). In both these regions, the firms were largely dependent on the replacement markets, both domestic and export, and were manufacturing parts or components either through reverse engineering or copying. Process and component drawings become essential for original equipment manufacturing; for the replacement markets, products can be manufactured without these drawings, by just checking the measurements.

About 22 per cent of the firms did not develop process drawings for the production process. They undertook manufacturing with the help of the drawing provided by the customer. This was largely because these firms did not have the capability and could not afford to hire technical personnel to undertake the process drawings. In such informal enterprises and small firms, the owner–manager along with his foreman or skilled workers decide on the different processes that need to be in place for producing the component and the machines to be used. They then assign the different process operations to the workers, and give instructions on the operations by studying the component drawing. When the component is a difficult one they develop rough drawings and give a copy of the particular process drawing to the workers. The practice of developing rough drawings was prevalent only in 10 per cent of the firms, largely in the Chennai–Coimbatore and Pune regions (Table 5.3). The reason for not undertaking process drawings cannot be completely attributed to the lack of such capabilities within the firm. It is often likely that the processing of the components is quite simple and does not require any drawings. The workers or owner–manager can study the component drawings and decide the different processes.

The experience of an entrepreneur from Pune neatly captures the differences among the regions. He had visited a small firm in Rajkot to check the machine he wanted to buy and was surprised at the quality of autocomponents that were produced there. The component manufacturer was well known in the area, and was a supplier to a number of well-known customers. The entrepreneur therefore assumed that the quality of his products would be good. But, to his surprise, he found that the manufacturer did not have any understanding of the drawing, was not aware of the different sizes, the accuracy and limits that needed to be maintained, and the measuring instruments to use. He was told by the Rajkot supplier that he could reproduce any sample given to him and that his customers did not bother much about the quality of the job. The entrepreneur from Pune concluded that there was absolutely no quality consciousness among auto-component makers in Rajkot. According to him, they manufacture components in huge lots, and while a particular component that is made in Pune for Rs 200–250 is available in Rajkot for Rs 20, the quality is very inferior.

Given a component drawing for a manufacturing part or component, about 25 per cent of the firms used CAD/CAM to make their drawings. The proportions of such firms were higher in the NCR and in Chennai–Coimbatore. About 20 per cent of the firms made the drawings manually as they could not afford computers. The drawings were also simple and not complicated. Developing manual drawings was seen to be much higher in the NCR, and in Ahmedabad and Rajkot (Table 5.3).

About 9 per cent of the firms developed component and process drawings from rough drawings provided to them by the customer (parent firm). These were largely supplier sub-contractors. These firms actually developed the component drawing for the parent firm as they had better technical knowledge of the component. For instance, in the Pune region a reputed parent firm gives the sub-contracting firm the component drawing with certain specifications, but several details such as measurement and other aspects of the component are not mentioned. The engineers of the sub-contracting firm work out the full details and give it to the parent firm for its final approval and stamp. Once approved, the process drawings of the component are developed in-house and then the production process starts. Design development and structure is also at times undertaken by the sub-contracting firm, if it has better expertise. We came across another case where, for producing a new component, the parent company discussed with the sub-contractor what kinds of jigs and fixtures to use, what tools were needed, what the processes should be and whether there was the possibility of reducing the number of processes. The parent company also asked the sub-contractor to develop the component drawing and in-process drawings. A higher proportion of such firms were found in the Pune and Chennai–Coimbatore regions, which were largely catering to the OEM market. This linkage between the sub-contracting firms and small firms provided the latter with an opportunity to develop component or process drawings.

Entrepreneurial Capabilities

A form of entrepreneurial capability, or his capacity to exploit the market and also to innovate, is captured by the education level of the owner–manager (Table 5.1). The capability of the owner measured in terms of education showed that about 16 per cent of the owner–managers had technical education, which includes an engineering degree (B.E). This proportion was much higher in Chennai–Coimbatore (21 per cent) and the NCR (20 per cent). About 22 per cent of the owner–managers had technical degrees or diplomas in mechanical engineering from Industrial Training Institutes (ITI); this proportion was higher in the Pune region (27 per cent). And about 34 per cent of them were graduates or postgraduates, these proportions being higher in the NCR, Rajkot and Ahmedabad. In about 30 per cent of the firms, and this was high in the Pune region, the owner–managers had education below the higher secondary level.

It is interesting to note that a large proportion of owner–mangers across the regions were educated below the higher secondary level or were graduates, without any technical degree. They were able to set up their enterprises due to the specific skills attained through experience and the contacts established at work. Of the owner–managers across different firm sizes in the different regions, 70 per cent had work experience in an auto-components or machine-tool firm before they set up their own units, and most of them had established their contacts from their previous companies, which enabled them to get regular work orders.

Sub-Contracting Relationships: Vertical and Horizontal

There are differing views on sub-contracting. Some view it as being exploitative since it allows large firms to externalize the burden of labour and product market uncertainties, and to shift the burden to small firms, often using them as 'shock absorbers', in the current competitive markets. Others argue that the sub-contracting relationship is efficient as the numerous processes are segregated and handled by different companies, linked through the flow of work, to achieve appropriate scales for each process. Within this argument is the notion that the strategies of large firms are willingly complied with by their sub-contractors, including cost and risk-sharing. We would like to move beyond both the above arguments to see if sub-contracting arrangements help small and informal firms to develop their capabilities with regard to technology and skills. Thus, in this section we analyse whether there is scope for learning and skill development in the vertically integrated production process. We also explore the extent to which the diffusion of technology and skills takes place across firms that are vertically integrated. We further examine the horizontal flow of work among these firms, and the nature of such networks.

Vertically Integrated Production Process

In the vertically integrated production process, the sub-contracted firm is dependent upon the parent firm to supply raw material or design or equipment to undertake the production process, though the form of sub-contracting may differ. Small firms and informal enterprises undertake part or component manufacturing and machining processes down the supply chain. About 80 per cent of the firms in the sample were sub-contracting in work, which consisted of both job work and manufacture of parts or components with material. The nature of the sub-contracting activity that we observed in the autocomponents sector across the different regions can be classified into four categories: capacity sub-contracting, specialization sub-contracting, supplier sub-contracting and component sub-contracting.

Capacity sub-contracting basically 'involves the farming out of excess work that could normally be done in-house except for a current excess of orders relative to installed operative capacity'. Within this category could also be included 'job work', wherein the machining process is undertaken as per the specification once the material is provided. *Specialization sub-contracting* is a form of a contract wherein the sub-contractor has something to offer (skills, machines etc.) that the parent firm does not possess. *Supplier sub-contracting* refers to an 'independent supplier with full control over the development, design and fabrication of its product'. The supplier, however, is willing to enter into a sub-contracting arrangement to supply a dedicated or proprietary part to the parent firm. *Component sub-contracting* involves carrying out all the manufacturing processes and then selling the final product under its own name. While the first three are part of the supply-driven chain, the last is part of the buyer-driven chain and it caters, to a large extent, to the replacement segment in both the domestic and export markets.

About 41 per cent of the firms undertook capacity sub-contracting, which largely included 'job work'. This was mostly in the Chennai–Coimbatore and Pune regions and a majority were informal enterprises. Specialization sub-contracting largely involved developing parts or components, and was undertaken by 46 per cent of the firms. A higher proportion of firms undertaking such activity were in the NCR and Pune. The specialization sub-contracting firms were provided the process design of the component and they had to develop the drawings and manufacture the prod-

TABLE 5.4   *Sub-Contracting and Technical Assistance Attained through Linkages*

	NCR	Chennai	Pune	Ahmedabad–Rajkot	All Firms
Forms of Sub-Contracting					
Capacity	30.0	57.1	48.5	0.0	40.6
Specialization	63.3	39.3	48.5	0.0	45.5
Supplier	6.7	0.0	15.2	0.0	6.9
Component/Part Supplier	46.7	17.9	0.0	100.0	28.7
Undertaking Sub-Contracting Work for					
Tier 1 Supplier	33.3	42.9	21.2	0.0	28.7
Tier 2 Supplier	20.0	50.0	12.1	0.0	23.8
Tier 3 Supplier	43.3	14.3	66.7	0.0	38.6
Written Contracts	80.0	75.0	81.8	0.0	71.3
Verbal Contracts	13.3	21.4	30.3	100.0	29.7
Source of Getting Orders					
Through friends or personal relations	16.7	50.0	63.6	40.0	43.6
Through previous work contacts	36.7	7.1	30.3	0.0	22.8
Established contacts	46.7	42.9	6.1	60.0	33.7
Technical Assistance Provided by the Sub-Contracting Firm					
Process Drawing	63.3	85.7	78.8	–	76.2
Component Drawing	23.3	21.4	24.2	0.0	20.8
Machines	6.7	14.3	12.1	–	10.9
In-Process	93.3	89.3	78.8	–	84.2
Vendor Development Process	26.7	64.3	33.3	0.0	36.6

Source: Same as Table 5.1.

uct, part or component. Most of these firms had both skill and technical expertise which they had developed over time, that allowed them to manufacture at a comparatively low cost. Supplier sub-contracting was restricted to a very small proportion of firms (7 per cent), and was largely undertaken in the Pune region (Table 5.4). These firms had complete control over the development, design and fabrication of the product, and entered into a sub-contracting arrangement after negotiations. The firms undertaking supplier sub-contracting were supplying gearshift assembly, accelerators, clutch assembly, brakes, moulded plastic components, brake rods, rod hangers, etc. Component sub-contracting was undertaken by 29 per cent of the firms, largely in the NCR, Ahmedabad and Rajkot, and they catered to both domestic and export replacement markets.

All these firms undertook specialization, supplier and component sub-contracting work for Tier 1 (29 per cent), Tier 2 (24 per cent) and Tier 3 (39 per cent) suppliers. In the Pune region, we saw about 67 per cent of the firms undertaking sub-contracting work for Tier 3 suppliers. In the Chennai region a larger proportion of the sub-contracting work was undertaken for Tier 1 and Tier 2 suppliers. One of the features of sub-contracting relates to the legality of the relationship, whether or not there exist proper written contracts (purchase orders). About 71 per cent of the enterprises had written contracts and 29 per cent had verbal contracts. A larger proportion of informal enterprises received verbal contracts, probably because they undertook 'job work' or capacity sub-contracting (Table 5.3).

To receive orders in the vertically integrated production process, it is most important to establish customer contacts. In 23 per cent of the firms, sub-contracting relationships were established through contacts from previous employers. This helped the owner–managers get a regular flow of work once they set up their own enterprise. This phenomenon was much higher in the Pune and NCR regions. Relationships established through personal contacts helped the parent firm by reducing uncertainty and search costs to determine competency, and there was also the factor of contractual trust. In the case of 44 per cent of the firms, personal contacts or friends had helped with orders and 34 per cent of the firms had established new contacts (Table 5.3). However, all the firms had to go through the vendor selection process[8]

[8] The vendor selection process largely involved identification of firms by quality inspectors or engineers or owner–managers of the firms, and checking the machine capability of the firms and skill capability of the workers. If the quality inspector or engineer found that the firm had the potential and capability, then it would be asked to give quotations, pricing and raw material costs, and asked to provide batch samples. If the samples were found to have consistent quality and were cost-efficient, the firm would be given orders to manufacture. This entire process would take about fifteen days to six months depending upon the criticality of the process, part or component.

before they were selected to manufacture parts or components or to undertake the machining process. Establishing customer contacts gave the subcontracting firm the stability to undertake the job. However, it was very difficult for most of them to get new orders as there was fierce competition among the firms to reduce the price below the threshold limits. All the firm owners reported that they continuously try to expand their customer base, towards which they spend a couple of hours every day.

Technical Assistance

Sub-contracting relationships are also considered a vehicle of technology transfer wherein small firms and informal enterprises receive technical assistance, guidance and knowledge from their parent companies or customers. This could be in the form of providing the necessary tools, jigs and fixtures, drawings for components, inspection equipment, selection of machinery, training of workers, etc. Empirical studies show that such transfers do exist in certain industries and regions (Nagaraj 1989; Gupta and Goldar 1995; Holmstrom 1998; Chaudhury 1999). However, the extent to which sub-contractors receive technical assistance from parent firms differs from case to case, depending upon their association or relationship. The most important reason for such transfers is improving the technological capability and quality of the small firms, and maintaining the tolerance limits of the components.

We had observed in Chapter Two that for the manufacturing sector as a whole, the proportion of sub-contracting firms receiving technical assistance in the form of design specification was about 93 per cent. At the micro level, we found that all firms undertaking capacity and specialization sub-contracting received such assistance. A major form of technical assistance that the sub-contracting firms received was related to technical drawings. While the capacity sub-contracting firms received process drawings (76.2 per cent) wherein the processes, technical parameters, dimensions and measuring instruments were specified, the specialization sub-contracting firms received component drawings (20.6 per cent) and developed their own process drawings (Table 5.3). The supplier sub-contracting firms too developed their own drawings, which had to be approved by the parent firm. All the firms reported that they approached the parent firm if they needed assistance in the drawings. A smaller proportion of firms (11 per cent) received technical assistance in machines, either in selecting or in making modifications in the machine to undertake the process, or in being supplied with one of the parent firm's machines. In the Chennai–Coimbatore region, for instance, a sub-contracting firm wanted to perform the turning operation in a CNC so that the quality could be maintained, but this was proving to be very expensive. The parent firm came up with a cost-effective idea of doing that particular process in a copy turning lathe. A comparatively higher proportion of such instances were reported in the Chennai–Coimbatore and Pune regions, as many of these enterprises were informal and highly dependent on such assistance. The sub-contracting relationships between the firms in these regions were also much closer than in the other areas.

A large proportion of the smaller firms (84 per cent) also received technical assistance for the manufacturing process, where by the engineers of the parent firm would visit the enterprise and check the process. If there were any alterations necessary, they would suggest improvements or changes in the procedures, make adjustments in the machine, suggest improvements in jigs/fixtures/dies, and also check the instruments. If there was a problem with the castings or fixtures, the enterprises would consult the parent firm and resolve the problem. Sometimes the parent firms would check the operation sequence and help them reduce the operation time.

There were also some exceptional cases (7 per cent) where the firm's engineer along with the sub-contractor tried to develop a component to a desired quality. For instance, in the Chennai–Coimbatore region, a team from the parent firm visited the sub-contracting firm and helped it to develop a process for a particular component till they achieved satisfaction. If the problem was with the forging of the raw material, which led to a machining problem, then the parent firm would try to resolve the problem together with the forging supplier. This was a form of knowledge exchange where there was an attempt to search for mechanisms to operate at higher levels of certainty in order to retain higher joint efficiency. The information flow that is transferred across firms through such joint activity is of tacit knowledge. Similarly, for the development of the product, either samples or drawings were provided to the sub-contractors, and engineers from the parent firm visited these units on a regular basis to help them develop the product (Table 5.4).

The raw material to manufacture parts or components purchased by the sub-contractor was as per the specifications provided in the purchase order. In the case of critical and low-volume components, the parent firm provided tools, dies, jigs or fixtures to the sub-contracting firms. In other cases, the sub-contractor developed the tools and dies in-house, at his own cost, or contracted it out (45 per cent). This also showed the capability of the sub-contractor, as mentioned earlier. In Chapter Two we had observed that in the unorganized manufacturing sector, about 7.3 per cent of the firms were supplied with equipment. If there was any technical assistance needed in the product development, they approached the customer sometimes, but most often they had their own network of informal and small firms whom they approached for assistance. This strategy helped them improve their credibility with their customers. Engineers or supervisors from the parent firm made regular visits to the sub-contracting firm, and such visits, a form of supervision, were much higher for the informal enterprizes.

Technical assistance was also provided by the parent firms through the vendor development process, wherein the parent firm conducted regular meetings with the sub-contractors on issues such as ISO 9000, production schedules, delivery schedules and delivery rates. Also, a lot of emphasis was laid on quality, reducing prices, reducing rejection, improving in-process development, house-keeping, and so on. Some of the parent firms organized meetings with the top vendors every month, in which the improvements made by these vendors were shared with all the others. This form of vendor development was prevalent for 37 per cent of the firms across all regions, and it was very high in the Chennai region (64.3 per cent).

Diffusion of Skills

For firms to grow, continuously get orders and expand markets, it is essential that they follow certain practices. These practices also allow for the diffusion of skill. An important aspect in the diffusion of skills relates to the maintenance of machines. It is argued that operators or workers need to be assigned the primary responsibility for basic maintenance since they are in the best position to detect signs of malfunction (Seth and Aggarwal 2004). The maintenance of machines on a regular basis, the maintenance of history cards for the machines, overhauling of machinery, cleaning, painting and training of workers are practices that every worker operating a machine should follow. This will help in reducing breakdowns of the machine, and improve its efficiency and productivity. The parent firm was often seen to give advice and training towards the maintenance of machines and to reduce the run-time costs incurred by the small firms and informal enterprises. Firms usually tend to postpone or ignore these tasks when they need to meet peak production targets, performing them only during the slack periods. We found that almost all the firms followed the practice of daily maintenance of machines, while only 56 per cent did preventive maintenance and only 32 per cent maintained history cards. The informal enterprises did not practise any preventive maintenance or have history cards for the machines. Lack of time and manpower was argued to be the main reason for not undertaking preventive maintenance among the informal enterprises (Table 5.5).

The parent firm also provided assistance to improve the work methods. This included in-process control, process charts with specifications, use of measuring instruments by workers, rejection analysis, work place man-

TABLE 5.5   *Diffusion of Skills in the Firms within the Workshop or on the Shop Floor*

	NCR	Chennai	Pune	Ahmedabad–Rajkot	All Firms
Maintenance of Machines					
Preventive	50.0	71.4	51.5	50.0	56.4
History Card	30.0	42.9	30.3	10.0	31.7
In-Process Control					
Manual	73.3	82.1	87.9	100.0	83.2
Automatic	13.3	17.9	12.1	0.0	12.9
Work charts	46.7	57.1	33.3	10.0	41.6
Production planning	76.7	64.3	45.5	70.0	62.4
Rejection analysis	23.3	46.4	24.2	0.0	27.7
QMS	13.3	71.4	0.0	10.0	24.8
Tool Room	50.0	35.7	42.4	40.0	42.6
Testing Lab	36.7	17.9	15.2	60.0	26.7
5 S	40.0	46.4	45.5	60.0	45.5
Certification					
ISO	43.3	35.7	33.3	50.0	38.6
TS16949	13.3	3.6	3.0	20.0	7.9

Source: Same as Table 5.1.

agement and ISO certification. Most of the firms reported in-process control in the production process to reduce errors and for consistent quality. The process control in most firms was manual (83 per cent); only in a small proportion of firms (13 per cent) was it automatic. The manual in-process control comprised checking the piece after every process by the worker/operator with the help of measuring instruments. If there was any error, the production process was stalled and it was corrected. In firms where the workers were not able to identify the defects, the foreman or line supervisor did the task. The in-process control varied from process to process, depending upon the criticality of the process. If the process was critical, every piece was checked; otherwise, every fifth, tenth or twentieth piece was checked. To improve the process and reduce the margin of error so that the effectiveness of the process was improved, process sheets or play cards were put up on top of every machine for the worker to check if necessary. The play cards had the process drawing, tools to be used, dimension specifications, instruments to be used for checking and production quantity (Table 5.5). This practice was being followed largely in the Chennai–Coimbatore region and NCR.

      Rejection analysis for corrective and preventive measures, either on a shift or daily basis from inputs to end-products, and maintaining rejection records at each stage was practised by 28 per cent of the firms. A larger proportion of firms in the Chennai region followed this practice as they already had quality management systems in place. Most of the firms also received quality feedback reports from their customers. The feedback report mentioned the reason for part or piece rejection, what the problem was, how they could correct it and what preventive measures needed to be taken. The practice of having a tool room and testing lab within the firm had been adopted by 43 per cent and 27 per cent of the firms. Both these are very important for firms to grow, and to be able to meet the quality parameters set by the parent or sub-contracting firm (Table 5.5).

The core of the new systems of production organization is management of the work place. To become a sub-contractor or supplier, it has become mandatory for firms to follow certification procedures like ISO 9000: 2000 and TS-16949, which maintain and improve quality. About 40 per cent of the firms had ISO certification and a few more were in process of getting it. To get this certification, apart from a number of other parameters, work place management and cleanliness measured by the Japanese 5S (Sort, Systematize, Sweep, Sanitize, Self-discipline) are very essential. About 8 per cent of the firms had TS-16949 certification, largely in the NCR, and Ahmedabad and Rajkot region. These were medium and large firms.

The practice of maintaining the work place was adhered to by 46 per cent of the firms. Though the proportion of firms adopting quality management systems was high in the Chennai region, only a few of them had ISO and TS-16949 certification. This is largely because the firms in Chennai are very stringent about the rules, and tried to put their systems in place before going in for certification. In other regions, especially the NCR, on the other hand, some of the firms that were given certification were actually not following any of the practices and neither did they have their systems in place (Table 5.5). There is increasing pressure by the parent firms on the small firms to get certification, without which they could lose their contracts. The pressure from large firms was basically because they wanted to become TS-16949 companies. For a firm to have TS-16949, it is mandatory that all its sub-contractors have ISO certification.

Apart from the diffusion of technology and skills, a crucial question related to sub-contracting is whether the informal enterprises and small firms are able to grow. It is a crucial issue because the sub-contracting relation is not one of transaction equality and there exists an institutionalized asymmetry. This could be observed in the price negotiations, when there were periodic price cuts due to rising prices of raw materials, untimely delivery or quality issues. There was often the risk that the parent firm could be dissatisfied with the sub-contractor resulting in loss of the contract. This forced the sub-contractors to expand their customer base, which helped them in spreading the risk and also led to growth of the enterprise. Most firms (87 per cent) had multiple vendor sources for the sub-contracting work they undertook. Though diversification of order sources made the sub-contractor less vulnerable, it still did not allow them to negotiate better conditions. Almost all the firms showed an increase in sales turnover, which to a large extent also depended on market behaviour. Most of the firms were able to expand, by expanding their customer base (87 per cent), or shifting to part or component production (33 per cent), or supplying to firms outside the automobile industry (25 per cent). These strategies helped them not only to grow, but also to reduce their risks in the present competitive environment.

Horizontal Flow of Work

There is very little mention in the sub-contracting literature of horizontal relations between small firms and informal enterprises. The literature tends to assume sub-contracting to be vertical, while the relations among small firms are seen to be competitive. Some documentation has been done for Ota ward in Japan where there exists extensive trading links among small firms, often encouraged by specialization, which has been termed '*confrere trading*' (Whittaker 1997). This means that in the vertically integrated production process there is scope for horizontal flow of work, wherein the sub-contracting firm further sub-contracts out some part of the production process to firms in the neighbourhood. This kind of sub-contracting might also take place due to the specialization of some of the firms in certain processes. Such networks of sub-contractors were considered to have a potential for forming 'skill concentration networks' in certain regions. Here, we digress a bit from the original concept which referred to such networks as being part of not the 'volume type' of production but the 'skill concentration type', low-volume production. In the regions that we surveyed, we found that there is a possibility of existence of 'skill concentration networks' even while dealing with 'volume type' production. As long as there is scope for product and process development, and innovations, there is scope for such networks to exist in the present competitive environment.

In our sample we found that there exists horizontal flow of work across small and informal enterprises. The firms that sub-contracted in work from the different tiers in the automobile industry further sub-contracted out that work to other informal, small or medium enterprises. The form of sub-contracting that was observed was either capacity or specialization sub-contracting. We found that 79 per cent of the firms, both small and informal, accepted orders for which they could undertake only a limited number

TABLE 5.6   *Horizontal Flow of Work across Sub-Contracting Firms* (percentages)

Size of Employment	NCR	Chennai	Pune	All Firms
Proportion of Firms Sub-Contracting Out	83	79	73	79
Capacity Sub-Contracting	58	71	55	64
Specialization Sub-Contracting	80	76	68	73
Subcontracting Out to				
Informal Enterprises	–	14	73	28
Small Firms	92	86	27	71
Medium Firms	8.0	4.5	4,2	6
Sub-Contractors Approved by the Customer	4.0	4.5	27	12
Verbal Contract	100	100	100	100
Number of Firms Sub-Contracting Out	25	22	25	72

Source: Same as Table 5.1.

of processes in-house, and sub-contracted out the rest of the processes to other informal or small enterprises (Table 5.6). The firms in the Ahmedabad region were not sub-contracting out, but the other regions reported high proportions of such sub-contracting. Capacity sub-contracting, wherein a firm sub-contracted out similar production processes to other small or informal enterprises, was reported by about 64 per cent of the firms, and this was much higher in the Chennai region. This form of sub-contracting out was largely undertaken by firms that have a regular flow of work with the parent firms, to further their business in that particular process. We found that when firms sub-contracted out the same process to others in the area, they paid a lower price and were able to make a profit. However, they had to regularly monitor the quality of the production process in these firms.

Specialization sub-contracting was observed among 73 per cent of the firms, wherein a firm which received regular orders undertook the machining task and sub-contracted out other tasks such as plating, powder-coating, hardening, wire-cutting, EDM, welding, sheet metal, and grinding and turning operations, to other small and informal firms in the same locality (Table 5.6). This kind of sub-contracting paves the way for 'skill concentration networks' to form, as informal and small enterprizes work together in similar neighbourhoods, and accumulate skills and technology.

There are certain processes that cannot be segregated, and it is more efficient or profitable for the informal and small enterprises to coordinate these processes among themselves. The parent firms are often not aware of production processes being undertaken by a network of informal firms. However, in the case of specific operations like plating, welding, hardening or powder-coating, the parent firms approve certain other sub-contractors (12 per cent) to do the work, when the sub-contracting firm does not have the expertise. The practice of approving sub-contractors for different processes was quite high in the Pune region, with Tier 1 and Tier 2 sub-contractors approving informal enterprises for undertaking specialized tasks. Apart from certain specialized production processes, the other activity that takes place in these informal networks is development of tools, jigs and fixtures. About 40 per cent of the firms sub-contracted out their tooling operations. The proportion of work that was sub-contracted out by these firms ranged from 5 to 30 per cent of their sales turnover, being similar across firms and regions.

The relationship between small firms and informal enterprises with horizontal flow of work was often informal, most of the contracts being verbal, and the sub-contracting relations were normally based on personal connections. Technical competence was a necessary but often not a sufficient condition to contract out work. Work was sub-contracted out to 78 per cent of the informal enterprises, 71 per cent of the small firms and 6 per cent of the medium enterprises, and on average to two to three firms. In the NCR and Chennai, the firms sub-contracted out largely to small firms, while in Pune a larger proportion of firms sub-contracted out to informal enterprises. The impediments to such links could be quality and delivery problems, but the firms seemed to overcome these through constant supervision of the tasks that were farmed out. Informal cooperation between small firms ranges from lending tools and workers, to consultation on technical and personnel matters. There was competition tempered by mutual encouragement and assistance, resulting in technical and managerial improvements. Due to perpetually low wages and little surplus left for capitalist accumulation, cooperation seemed to be the best strategy when there was abundance of work.

The presence of a large number of specialists to undertake the production process and tooling jobs along with 'jobbing shops' facilitated the horizontal flow of work, and developed the potential and scope for 'skill concentration networks'. In these network clusters where capital or technology was scarce or primitive, we found that there was potential for innovation. Many of the small and medium enterprise owners and engineers reported that they visited the informal enterprises to see what innovative mechanisms or ideas they were experimenting with, or the kind of modular manufacturing they had come up with. They then often borrowed some of these innovative ideas and developed tools, dies or fixtures within their own enterprises. We found that the Pune and Chennai–Coimbatore regions had more scope for development of such networks which allowed innovations to take place. We present below some examples which throw light on the possibility for such 'skill concentration networks' to develop in informal enterprise clusters.

Innovation in Informal Enterprizes

One such instance was reported to us by a firm owner who had got an innovative idea from an informal enterprise to develop the die and tool for a gear-shaft lever assembly component. This particular component had to be bent on both sides, which meant that they had to make special-purpose machinery to undertake the particular operation. The time taken to undertake the process/operation on both sides was about 5 minutes each, which proved to be very time-consuming and expensive. The owner–manager was looking for an alternative mechanism. During one of his visits to the informal enterprise cluster, he observed a bending operation being undertaken on a drilling machine. This being an efficient way of undertaking the operation, he borrowed the idea for his assembly component and developed a fixture that was uni-directional with 24-point bending. The fixture allowed him to undertake the operation in one and half seconds for each side. In one sense, this was a process innovation. It enabled him to save huge costs and make the component more efficiently without having to develop special-purpose machinery.

In another instance, an informal firm making press components on mechanical press machines was approached by a reputed large firm to manufacture brake rods in a cost-effective way. The brake rods were being manufactured on turning lathes or CNC machines as the specifications varied at various ends of the rod. The owner of the informal enterprise had extensive experience in maintaining hydraulic and mechanical press machines in large firms before he set up his own firm. Using his experience, he developed a special-purpose machine. He attached a hydraulic cylinder to a simple mechanical press and then developed the die in such a way that in a single operation, with the help of hydraulic pressure, the material could be gathered on the rod as per the specification. The ingenuity lay in developing the special-purpose machine and the die. Following this innovation he was able to develop a number of products related to rods, for which he has become a single-source supplier. Though some of these details and the functioning of the machine were shared with us, normally none of his customers are allowed to enter his firm for fear that the technique and process would be copied by them.

Similarly, in another firm we found that a turning lathe machine was being used for a grinding operation. We found that, to undertake certain processes, informal enterprises often added a copy attachment to a simple lathe machine, which allowed smooth production process with quality being maintained at a comparatively low cost. In the Chennai–Coimbatore and Pune regions, we were informed that a group of four to five firm owners and tool specialists would often get together to solve production problems or to improve the processes in different components. They did production trials and were able to improve the quality or process of the component over a period of time. These examples show us that immense potential and skills are available in the informal enterprises for skill concentration networks to form. If the skills are tapped properly, they could lead to improvements in the production process, and help these small and informal firms to grow.

Factors Determining the Growth of Firms

In this section we make an attempt to determine the factors that aid the growth of firms. There could be a number of endogenous and exogenous factors that influence the growth of the firm, but for this analysis we restrict ourselves to certain crucial variables that are technology and worker-related. We assume that exogenous factors like markets have a strong influence on the growth of the firm, as markets for this particular sector are growing not only domestically but also internationally, and firms have the opportunity to enter either replacement markets or original equipment manufacturing, depending upon their capabilities and contacts.

We empirically analyse the growth of a firm's function using the simple production function equation,

$$Y_{gi} = a_i \cdot b_1 \, Age + b_2 \, TI + b_3 \, PS + b_4 \, CAP + b_5 \, LINK + b_6 \, SK$$

wherein

Y_{gi} refers to the growth of sales turnover in the ith firm over the period 2000 to 2004.

Age refers to when the ith firm started, in number of years.

TI refers to the technology index, which has been constructed taking into consideration three criteria: the type of machines that the firm possesses (manual, semi-automatic, automatic, programme logit control (PLC) and computerized numerical control (CNC)); whether the machine is newly bought or second-hand; and whether the machine is imported or locally made. Taking these criteria into consideration, values are assigned for every machine that the firm or enterprise owns, and added up for each enterprise, to construct the technology index. For the first criterion, the values take 1 to 10 for different machines, as described earlier. A computerized numeric control (CNC) or vertical milling machine (VMC) is assigned a value of '10'; the special purpose press, injection-moulding machines and pneumatic logit control (PLC) moulding machines are assigned a value of '8'; automatic mixing kneaders and hobbing machines, rubber and plastic wire-cutting machines, the hydraulic power press, and hardening, plating and power-coating machines are assigned a value of '7'; the Herbert 2 Capstan lathe and G D Weiller lathes are assigned a value of '6'; the manual power press, spot welder and press-mounting machines are assigned a value of '5'; spring coiling machines and computer-aided controlled coiling machines are assigned a value of '4'; semi-automatic grinding, moulding and mig welding machines are assigned a value of '3'; the manual small hand press and multiple function simple lathes are assigned a value of '2'; and manual single function lathes, mixing mills, mixing and grinding machines, and small grinders are assigned a value of '1'.

The second criterion is whether the machine is newly purchased or second-hand. If the machine is newly purchased, we have assigned a value '5'; and if it is second-hand, we have assigned a value '3'. The third criterion is whether the machine is imported or locally made. We have tried to distinguish between machines made locally in Chennai, Coimbatore, Bangalore and Pune, and those made in Ludhiana and Rajkot. The distinction is made because the owner–managers of firms often informed us that the quality and accuracy achieved in a component using Chennai, Coimbatore, Bangalore and Pune-made machines were much higher than in those made with Ludhiana and Rajkot machines. We assigned values 1 to 8 for this criterion. If the machine is imported, we have assigned a value of '8'; if it is made in Chennai, Coimbatore, Bangalore or Pune, we have assigned a value of '5'; if it is manufactured in other regions we have assigned a value of '3'; and if it is made in Rajkot or Ludhiana, we have assigned a value of '1'. The higher the index, one would expect higher growth of the firm, and so the expected sign of the variable would be positive.

PS refers to process skills possessed by the workers in a firm. To construct this index, we took into consideration four criteria. For each criterion we assigned values, which were then summed up for each firm. The criteria are in-process control, that is, whether there are checks after every process; the criticality of the component, which is captured by taking into consideration how often the component is checked when in production; the final inspection procedures before dispatch; and whether the workers use measuring instruments for checking the component. For in-process control, the values assigned are '2' for automatic, '1' for manual, and '0' for no control. For criticality of the component we have assigned values from 1 to 5. If every component is checked, we assign a value of '5'; if every fifth component is checked, we assign a value of '4'; if every tenth component is checked, we assign a value of '3'; if every twentieth or twenty-fifth component is checked, we assign a value of '2'; and if every fiftieth component is checked, we assign a value of '1'. For the final inspection procedures, we have assigned values from 1 to 3. If every piece is checked before dispatch, we assign it a value of '3'; if every fifth or tenth piece is checked, we assign a value of '2'; if the components are randomly checked, we assign a value of '1'; and if there is no checking it is '0'. The last criterion of whether or not the workers use measuring instruments while checking the components takes a value of '0' if they do not use instruments, and '1' if they use instruments. This variable would have a positive sign: the higher the index, the better would be the firm's performance. We expect that if the process skills are transferred to the workers, the quality of the part or component would improve, which would lead to fewer rejections and more orders for the firm.

CAP refers to the capabilities of the firms where, intuitively, the workers' capabilities are also captured. We constructed an index of this variable by taking into consideration three criteria: the drawing capabilities of the firm, whether the firm fabricates machines, and in-process innovations. We have assigned values for each of the criteria and these values are then summed up to construct the index. The first criterion takes values 1 to 5. If the firm undertakes component and process drawing, it takes the value '5'; if the firm undertakes process drawing using computer-aided design (CAD), we assign it a value of '4'; if the firm undertakes process drawing manually, it takes the value '3'; if the firm undertakes only rough drawings, we assign a value of '2'; and if the firm does not undertake any process drawings either because it does not have the capability or because the process is simple, we assign a value of '1'. The second criterion takes a value of '1' if the firm fabricates machines and '0' if does not. The third criterion of in-process innovation could be either in machines or tools to improve quality and productivity, and to reduce costs, by developing the dies, jigs and fixtures within the firm. If the firm has undertaken any in-process innovation, we assign a value of '1'; and if there has been no innovation, we assign a value of '0'. This variable would also have a positive sign, and the capabilities of the firm would help the firm move from undertaking just 'job work' to developing parts or components, as the workers acquire more skills.

LINK refers to whether the sub-contracting firm receives any form of support from the parent firm to help it improve its technology and skill base. To construct this variable we have taken three criteria into consideration. These are technical assistance in the selection of machines; technical assistance in the process, which includes the kind of dies and jigs that need to be used; and whether the firm is part of the vendor development programme of the parent firm. We assigned values for each of these criteria and then summed them up to construct the index. A firm could be receiving technical assistance from the parent firm in various forms. If the parent firm helps in the selection of machines, we assign it a value of '3'; if the parent firm helps in the modification of machines so that the firm can undertake a particular process, we assign a value of '2'; if the parent firm supplies the firm with one of its machines, we assign a value of '1'; and for the remaining, a value of '0'. With regard to the second criterion of technical guidance in-process, we assign a value of '1' if the firm receives technical assistance from the parent firm, and '0' otherwise. For firms which receive technical guidance in-process from the parent firm, we further segregate them and they take values 1 to 5. If the engineers of the parent firm visit the firm regularly (that is, every two to three days) to check the process, we assign it a value of '5'; if they visit the firm once a week, we assign a value of '4'; if they visit the firm once in fifteen days, we assign a value of '3'; if they visit the firm once a month or once in two or three months, we assign a value of '2'; and if they visit once a year, we assign a value of '1'. For the third criterion, we assign a value of '1' if the firm is part of the vendor development programme of the parent firm and '0' otherwise. Linkage is supposed to have a positive effect as the firm gets more orders, and acquires better technology and skills over a period of time.

SK refers to the proportion of skilled workers to production workers. We have used the definition of a skilled worker as defined by the owner of the enterprise and not on the basis of education. Theoretically, one would expect that the higher the growth of the firm, the higher would be the proportion of skilled workers to undertake complicated tasks and for using better technology. However, this need not be the case with small firms where growth could also take place with better utilization of semi-skilled workers. So the coefficient could take either a positive or a negative sign.

Table 5.7 presents the estimated results of the firm's growth. The age of the firm had a significant negative sign, implying that firms which have come up in the last few years were able to grow faster than the established firms, which could be either due to the linkage effect or to specific skills that the firms possess. We found that TI was negative, though not significantly so, which could mean that the firms that grew faster did not have better or branded technologies, and that they grew using conventional machinery. What this perhaps implies is that the firms were able to utilize to the optimum even the conventional technology they had. PS had a positive sign, as expected, but, was not significant, implying that the process skills of a firm had a positive impact on its growth. CAP also had a positive sign but not significant. This could mean that improving the capabilities of the workers would help the growth of the firm. The variable that had a positive

TABLE 5.7   *Factors Determining the Growth of Small Firms*

Variables	Coefficient	T-Statistic
Age	−0.9677**	−2.9681
TI (Technology Index)	−0.005	−0.3846
PS (Process Skills)	1.9420	1.4320
CAP (Capabilities)	0.4578	0.25349
LINK (Linkages)	2.4924**	2.5810
SK (Skilled Workers Proportion)	−0.06046	−0.06706
R Square 0.44		
Adjusted R 0.19		
Observations 101		
F 2.3303		
Significance F 0.04289		

Note: ** Significant at 0.1 per cent level of significance.

sign and was significant was LINK, which very clearly shows that in the automobile sector, which is vertically integrated, small and tiny firms have a huge potential to grow if they are linked with large firms. Through this linkage they get not only regular orders, but also technical assistance in various aspects. The last variable, SK, had a negative sign, though not significant, which means that the small firms that grew faster did not necessarily have a higher proportion of skilled workers, and they were able to increase their turnover by using the services of semi-skilled and unskilled workers.

What this analysis very clearly shows is that given the opportunity, small firms have a huge potential to grow as certain products and markets are expanding. Because of their entrepreneurial capabilities, small firms have the ability to train even workers with low skills. Proper or assured market linkages between large and small firms are a crucial factor in the growth of the autocomponents sector.

Conclusions

This study examines the possible advantages of sub-contracting linkages for small firms or informal enterprises through the diffusion of technology and skills in the context of the autocomponents industry. It was seen that technological capabilities increased with the size of the firm. The Chennai–Coimbatore and Pune regions had better machines both in terms of their brand and technological levels. A significant proportion of the firms also had the required knowledge to develop their own dies, jigs and fixtures for parts or components they manufactured. In the NCR, and Ahmedabad and Rajkot region, some of the small firms further had the capability to fabricate machines or to make special-purpose machinery to undertake specific production processes.

The growing market for autocomponents provided more scope for innovations in improving the production process or developing techniques of production. As the capabilities of the firms improved, the opportunity to seize better returns from the growing market for autocomponents also improved. Firms that had better entrepreneurial and technological capabilities had better access to component development and also scope for innovation.

We found vertical integration of the production process in the autocomponents sector with three major forms of sub-contracting arrangements: capacity (job work), specialization and supplier sub-contracting. The most widely used form was capacity sub-contracting. Diffusion of technical knowledge, formation of skills and managerial practices were prevalent to a large extent in firms undertaking capacity and specialization sub-contracting. There was a tremendous effort on the part of the parent firms to help these firms improve their processes through regular interaction. The parent firms also provided them support to develop their capabilities in parts and components, often by giving them opportunities to manufacture samples. Firms that had better technical and skill capabilities were able to benefit the most from these relationships.

We found that there was potential for a number of skilled personnel from the formal sector, most of whom had very good command over technology and skill, to set up informal enterprises and small firms. No doubt, most of the work sub-contracted out, especially through 'capacity' sub-contracting, was to exploit the low labour and capital costs in the informal enterprises. But this strategy also helped the informal enterprises to earn an income that was above the market wage in the formal labour market, and these workshops then became training centres for workers entering the labour market and unskilled workers.

The horizontal flow of work across these firms drew out the vast skill and innovation potential that exists even within the informal enterprises, which could be utilized efficiently in the production process. An important aspect is the potential and scope for the development of 'skill concentrated networks' in these informal enterprise clusters if there is continuous support, largely in the form of assured markets. Most of the informal enterprises showed a keen interest in innovation due to diversified products and market demand. There is absolutely no doubt that the present competitive environment and flexible production processes have given small firms and informal enterprises an opportunity to innovate and grow. The case of autocomponent clusters shows that small and informal enterprises have a lot to gain from the growing competitive markets if they are willing to acquire both technical knowledge and skill capabilities.

CHAPTER SIX

The Process of Skill Formation in the Autocomponents Industry

How did the changes in production organization or the restructuring of the automobile industry into a tiered system, affect labour processes? What was the impact on workers in the already segmented labour market, of these changes and the inflow of new technologies into the system? In the previous chapter we saw how the skill embodied in the worker helps to improve the technological capability of firms. In Chapter Three, we presented two measures of the skills of workers using macro definitions of education levels and occupational categories. In this chapter we discuss the skill content of workers in the autocomponents sector and define the skills of workers – skilled, semi-skilled and unskilled – at the micro level of the firm. This definition is based on the various technologies used in informal enterprises and small firms. Using the earlier definition of skills based on education, we work out a matrix of education levels of workers with the new definitions of micro skills. We note that workers with even low levels of education have the potential to acquire skills, based on a micro definition, to become skilled workers. We also address the issue of how skill formation takes place in this sector, what it means across different technologies and processes, and how much time it takes to gain experience in the use of a particular machine or process. Lastly, we explore whether upgrading technology or bringing in new technology to the firm leads to deskilling or displacement of workers, or whether the old workers are absorbed with upgradation of their skills.

Flexibility in the Labour Market

The autocomponents sector underwent a major change in the 1990s to keep pace with the operation and quality standards demanded by global auto manufacturers entering India (Okada 2004). The primary or formal labour market in the sector till then was associated with relatively good employment conditions in terms of wages, stability and promotion opportunities, and protected by labour laws and collective agreements. However, the changes in production organization resulted in downsizing of firms, retrenchment of workers and a shift towards contractual employment. The changes in production organization also presented the challenge of upgrading the skill base of component suppliers to meet the demands of the globally competitive market.

The reduction in permanent workers and rise of contractual employment was largely because firms were reducing their core work force and transferring activities to smaller production settings that typically offered lower wages, fewer benefits, less employment stability and less opportunity for union representation (Brown *et al.* 1990). In the autocomponent units that we surveyed, we found that the proportion of contractual and daily wage workers had risen tremendously in the last decade, accounting for 48 per cent of the workers in 2004 as compared to 38 per cent in 1995, across various regions in the country.

The growth of contractual and daily wage labourers was especially high in the National Capital Region (NCR) and Pune (Table 6.1), and this rise was seen across firms of all sizes. The growing use of contractual workers led to an increase in the size of the peripheral work force, raising issues of social protection and representation for these workers. In about 8 per cent of the firms, the entire shop floor was contracted out to labour contractors to undertake the production process. The contractors were paid by production lots and it was their responsibility to complete the production in the specified time. They paid the workers on a piece-rate basis. The major reason for larger firms to adopt such a strategy was to reduce costs and improve productivity.

While the majority of the firms provided the workers with some bonus, other benefits such as Employees State Insurance (ESI), Provident Fund (PF) and productivity-based incentives were limited. Of the firms surveyed, while 86 per cent gave bonus in the form of one month's salary at the time of festivals, only 11 per cent provided ESI, 8 per cent provided PF and 26 per cent gave productivity-based incentives. The firms in the NCR were

TABLE 6.1   *Growth of Workers in Autocomponent Firms, 1995–2005*

	Permanent	Contract	Daily wage	Total
NCR	6.51	17.06	10.93	8.11
Chennai–Coimbatore	1.03	3.78	3.81	1.86
Pune	3.08	13.20	8.02	5.31
Ahmedabad–Rajkot	12.95	12.29	0.40	7.35
All Regions	5.10	8.30	4.63	4.71

Source: Same as Table 5.1.

TABLE 6.2   *Benefits Provided by the Firms to the Workers* (percentages)

	NCR	Chennai	Pune	Ahmedabad–Rajkot	All Firms
ESI	23.3	10.7	3.0	0.0	10.9
Provident Fund	16.7	7.1	0.0	10.0	7.9
Gratuity	6.7	3.6	0.0	0.0	3.0
Overtime	3.3	3.6	0.0	10.0	3.0
Production-based Incentives	43.3	14.3	3.0	80.0	25.7
Bonus	70.0	96.4	97.0	70.0	86.1
Union	6.7	10.7	3.0	0.0	5.9
On-the Job Training	93.3	100.0	93.9	100.0	96.0
Regular Training	23.3	21.4	18.2	30.0	21.8
Rotation of Workers	83.3	85.7	78.8	50.0	79.2

Source: Same as Table 5.1.

most likely to provide these benefits (Table 6.2). All large firms provided ESI and PF to their permanent work force in compliance with the labour laws under the Factories Act, but not to the contractual or daily wage labourers. The exception was some large firms in the Ahmedabad–Rajkot region, which provided production incentives to a much larger extent. These benefits were not given to their workers by the small and informal enterprises. Only 3 per cent of the firms paid overtime wages to their workers, though in many of them, the workers worked beyond the stipulated 8 hours, for up to 10–12 hours, in all the regions surveyed.

New organizational patterns are also associated with a diminished role of trade unions. Only 6 per cent of the firms reported having unions, this proportion being much higher in Chennai and the NCR (Table 6.2). Poor unionization of workers has a significant indirect effect on wage inequality, causing the wages of unskilled workers to fall since they have no bargaining power. In the NCR it was observed that though unionization was low, a number of workers in these firms attended union meetings. If there was a problem, the workers approached the union to resolve it. About 20 per cent of the firms in this region reported such instances. However it was not clear to what extent the unions helped address or resolve the problems. The owners of the firms very clearly resented workers who attended union meetings and tried to alienate them from other workers so as to prevent unionization within the firm.

Though the workers did not receive many of the benefits that were due to them, what they gained in the process of working in such firms was on-the-job training, regular training to upgrade their skills and multi-skilling as a result of rotation of work. On-the-job training was reported by 96 per cent of the firms in the sample, across regions. Emphasis on regular training for workers so that their skills could be upgraded over a period of time was prevalent in 22 per cent of the firms (Table 6.2). An important asset that workers accumulated through working in the informal and small enterprises was skill acquisition.

Skill Content of Workers

The skills and knowledge of workers are the most important assets of an organization. However, workers' skill has long been underestimated in the analytical framework of mainstream economics, where it has been seen as playing only a supporting role to physical capital. Koike (1990: 4) argues that apart from labour, almost all the other factors that affect competitiveness, such as machinery or technology, can be bought or imported. The only exception is workers' skill, which is embodied in non-transferable human beings.

Lall (1992: 170) defines human capital as 'not just the skills generated by formal education and training, but also created by on-the-job training and experience of technological activity, and the legacy of inherited skills, attitudes and abilities that aid industrial development' (as quoted in Sargeant and Mathews 1997: 1671). This definition of skill indicates that there are both technical and attitudinal dimensions to it. According to Cappelli (1993), 'a skilled worker has traditionally been defined as a person who can perform a complex task while working without direct help and supervision'. Along with skill, knowledge of the product, experience and an understanding of the customer's needs are essential.

The skill that the worker possesses is crucial for the growth of the firm as well as for introducing new technology within it. Most empirical studies define skills on the basis of the level of education that the worker possesses. According to the commonly used definition, a skilled worker is one with a minimum of higher secondary level education and above. However, during our field survey we found that defining skills on the basis of education alone is probably not sufficient, as the skill content of a worker is the knowledge he possesses and the process he is able to perform. In the case of a production worker, skill may have nothing to do with formal education. To be able to capture the skill content of the worker, we asked the owner–managers of all the firms that we interviewed to define the skilled, semi-skilled and unskilled workers in the various production processes, and to classify the workers into these categories based on their skill content.

Definitions of Skills: A Micro View

A skilled worker is one having knowledge of the machines and understanding of the component drawings, and the ability to set tools or dies, visualize the different processes for a given component, and produce the component as per the given specifications and within the tolerance limits specified.

This definition of skilled workers using different production technologies and undertaking different processes in the autocomponents industry is arrived at as discussed below. In our understanding, these skills can be acquired only through experience on the shop floor in the autocomponents sector and are, to a large extent, independent of higher formal education.

We define workers as 'skilled', 'semi-skilled' and 'unskilled' depending on their involvement in production processes using conventional and computer numeric control (CNC) machines, and in the tool room. This is based on the information provided by the owner–managers of the firms we surveyed. There are some variations in the definitions across the various regions studied, which are highlighted.

Production Using Conventional Machines

The conventional machines that the firms operated, such as the Herbert 2D Capstan lathe, G D Weiller and the conventional single-operation lathe machine, were different depending on the number of functions they could perform. The G D Weiller machines were found largely in the Chennai–Coimbatore region. These machines had a number of functions similar to those of CNC machines, the major difference being that they had to be operated manually. These were sophisticated lathe machines with the possibility of multiple operations within a conventional lathe. The Herbert 2D Capstan lathe machines, largely used in Pune, were not as sophisticated as the G D Weiller, but also had multiple functions. Due to the differences in the technologies used, the definition of the skilled worker varied across regions and firms.

Skilled worker

An entrepreneur in the Chennai region provided a comprehensive description of a skilled worker: a worker who is capable of doing a 'job' as per the drawing specification without any support, has knowledge of the machine, tool and component, the drawing, has knowledge of tolerance levels, can read the symbols (grinding, turning, finishing), and knows how to use the measuring instruments.

For most owners of informal and small enterprises, a 'skilled worker' in the production line is one who can operate manual or semi-automatic machines, and can undertake the different processes to produce a component, given a drawing, according to the specified quality. This means that the worker must have knowledge about the drawing, about what machines to use and what operations to perform in what sequence, and the ability to set a die, fix the tools/jigs/fixtures in the machine, measure the critical dimensions and complete the job within the stipulated time. In the case of a problem in the machine, a skilled worker is expected to have the knowledge to identify it and solve it. The worker is also expected to continuously work towards reducing the run-time of the job, thus improving productivity. A worker who is good at the production of non-standard components during the trials is defined as 'skilled'. According to most owners a skilled worker is supposed to have the ability to guide semi-skilled and unskilled workers.

The content of skills varied for different operations. For example, in plating operations, the skilled worker would be expected to have basic chemical and technical knowledge about electroplating. Similarly, on a hobbing machine, the hobber or setter was expected to know the component, the setting of gears, the module of hob, pitch thread depth and gear depth to be used, and to have good knowledge of the machine. In a milling machine, the worker should be able to run the machine without assistance, put the clamp, and identify and solve any problem that arises.

Semi-skilled worker

A 'semi-skilled worker' was one who had to be trained in every job, and the machine had to be set up for him before he could undertake the mechanical process. He possessed the skill to measure the components with different measuring gauges such as snap gauge, plug gauge, etc.

In the Chennai–Coimbatore region, the semi-skilled worker was expected to have knowledge of the machine, understand the critical dimensions of the components to maintain quality and process them as per the drawing, and to undertake minor adjustments. The worker was expected to understand at least a single drawing and to set machines for simple jobs.

Most owners agreed that a semi-skilled worker could undertake production of a routine kind and of a standard component, not non-standard components. They could not understand drawings of or produce a new component. A semi-skilled worker in the mechanical press line was supposed to have knowledge of setting a die, after which the worker could undertake only that particular press operation. In electroplating, a semi-skilled worker was expected to have basic knowledge about plating passivation.

Unskilled worker

An 'unskilled worker' was defined as a helper who could perform rough operations once the machine was set and the tools sharpened. This was the most consistent definition that we found for machining processes, though there were some variations across firm sizes.

Production through Computer Numeric Control
Skilled worker

A 'skilled worker' operating a computer numeric control (CNC) machine is one who has knowledge of programming, hardness of the component, cutting tools, and can understand the drawing, decide what tools are needed for the operation, take care of production and minimize problems of the machine.

Semi-skilled worker

A 'semi-skilled' worker is an operator with at least a diploma in mechanical engineering (DME), a requirement in some of the firms. The operator is expected to know the basic principles of operating CNC machines. He should know how to take zero return or references, adjust and readjust the components, and change and adjust tools if there is a problem in the component. He should also have knowledge of how to load and unload the components, and the production of the component as per the dimensions displayed in the drawings.

Unskilled worker

An 'unskilled' worker is a trainee or fresh candidate, and has knowledge of how to load or unload the components and to make the offset required for different tools. He requires regular monitoring and advice to undertake his tasks.

Tools and Dies

We came across a number of small and informal enterprises making tools, dies, jigs and fixtures in the Pune region, and decided to include them in our sample to understand their role in the autocomponents industry. The skills and knowledge required by the workers about the components in these enterprises were much higher compared to those involved in the production process. This was because the worker in the tool room was expected to have complete knowledge about the component in order to make the necessary tools, dies, jigs or fixtures required for the particular process of production. We define the skill levels required for workers in tool-room workshops, below.

Skilled worker

A 'skilled worker' manufacturing tools, dies, jigs or fixtures was one who had knowledge of the component, the production process and the tools. He was able to understand a component drawing, visualize the different processes and design the tools in such a way that the component could be manufactured with a minimum number of operations. The most important skill of the tool-room worker was accuracy in machining and the ability to comprehend the entire task. As a tool-maker he also required the ability to outsource work, oversee quality standards and get work done within the stipulated time.

Semi-skilled worker

Semi-skilled workers were largely assistants to the skilled workers. They maintained tools and dies, and were involved in die-fitting and bolting, apart from being continuously trained by the skilled workers in making tools and dies.

The Skilled Work Force in Autocomponent Firms

In this section we work out a matrix of education levels of workers using the definitions of skills presented above (Table 6.3). According to the information provided by the owner–managers, among the production workers in the enterprise, about 8 per cent are employed as supervisors, 38 per cent as skilled workers, 22 per cent as semi-skilled workers and 32 per cent as unskilled workers, across all the regions. The supervisor was a skilled worker who planned the different processes for the component when the drawing was given to him; assigned the production tasks to the workers; had knowledge about the different machines and knew which operation needed to be done where; undertook all major repairs of the machines; ensured a smooth production process and quality requirements; and inspected the components in the production process. A comparatively large proportion of unskilled workers are employed in informal and small enterprises as the labour costs are low, and most owners prefer to train unskilled workers with low wages rather than hire skilled workers.

Comparing the skills of workers by the macro and micro definitions, a larger proportion of workers were found to be skilled (46 per cent, including supervisors) by the micro definition, as compared to the traditional/macro definition based on educational qualifications (34 per cent) for all regions. Across the regions, we found that enterprises in the NCR employed a higher proportion of unskilled workers by the micro definition, thus reducing costs. This strategy probably worked well for them as they largely catered to the replacement market. Even in the Pune region, which largely supplied to OEM (original equipment manufacturing), enterprises employed a comparatively high proportion of unskilled workers to reduce costs, and trained them eventually. In contrast, the Chennai–Coimbatore region had a higher proportion of skilled workers, thus emphasizing quality. Different recruiting strategies were adopted by the firms across the

TABLE 6.3 *Education Levels of Production Workers by Skill Definition*

	Education Level	Supervisor	Skilled Workers	Semi-Skilled Workers	Unskilled Workers	All Production Workers
NCR	Illiterate	1.0	0.8	9.0	7.0	5.4
	Primary	0.0	6.1	30.7	23.6	18.9
	Middle	11.5	3.6	9.6	12.5	9.2
	Secondary	12.5	47.2	27.6	27.9	32.2
	Higher Secondary	9.4	7.4	19.7	29.0	19.3
	Graduate	1.0	0.0	0.0	0.0	0.1
	ITI	64.6	34.9	3.4	0.0	14.9
	Total	6.8	27.8	25.1	40.3	100
Chennai–Coimbatore	Illiterate	0.0	1.1	0.0	9.4	1.9
	Primary	0.0	0.5	1.5	1.0	0.7
	Middle	0.0	5.9	5.4	12.5	6.1
	Secondary	20.0	43.0	71.5	74.0	49.9
	Higher Secondary	22.9	14.6	13.1	3.1	13.6
	Graduate	4.3	0.2	0.0	0.0	0.5
	ITI	52.9	34.6	8.5	0.0	27.1
	Total	9.5	59.6	17.7	13.1	100
Pune	Illiterate	0.0	0.0	1.0	0.0	0.2
	Primary	2.3	0.6	0.0	28.8	10.2
	Middle	9.3	18.9	26.5	24.4	21.5
	Secondary	23.3	45.1	63.3	35.3	43.6
	Higher Secondary	14.0	18.3	8.2	11.5	13.4
	Graduate	4.7	0.6	1.0	0.0	0.9
	ITI	46.5	16.5	0.0	0.0	10.2
	Total	9.3	35.6	21.3	33.8	100
Ahmedabad–Rajkot	Illiterate	4.2	3.0	0.0	32.2	5.9
	Primary	0.0	43.2	35.1	50.8	40.6
	Middle	0.0	0.0	12.8	16.9	4.3
	Secondary	0.0	0.0	48.9	0.0	9.0
	Higher Secondary	20.8	0.0	0.0	0.0	0.9
	Graduate	0.0	0.0	3.2	0.0	0.6
	ITI	75.0	53.7	0.0	0.0	38.6
	Total	4.7	65.3	18.4	11.6	100
All Regions	Illiterate	0.5	0.8	5.7	6.0	3.5
	Primary	0.5	2.7	19.0	21.9	12.2
	Middle	7.2	7.2	11.5	14.7	10.5
	Secondary	17.2	45.0	43.4	34.7	39.2
	Higher Secondary	14.8	12.4	16.3	22.7	16.7
	Graduate	2.9	0.2	0.2	0.0	0.3
	ITI	56.9	31.7	3.9	0.0	17.5
	Total	8.0	38.1	22.4	31.5	100

Source: Same as Table 5.1.

regions, based on the type of workers required. This issue is addressed in the next section.

Though the macro definition of skills based on education does not include secondary education as contributing to the skilled work force, we found that about 45 per cent of skilled workers in all the regions had completed secondary education (Table 6.3). Besides only about 10 per cent of the skilled work force in all the regions had low levels of formal education. Their skills, by the micro definition, were largely attained through on-the-job training and experience. This matrix clearly captures workers who, even with low levels of education, have the potential to acquire skills and become skilled workers by the micro definition provided by the owner managers. It is clear that the skill content is embodied in the worker, and is acquired through on-the-job training and experience.

Process of Skill Formation

There is no doubt that skill formation is very crucial for human capital formation and for the development of a quality work force. The process of skill formation in the small and informal enterprises was largely enterprise-specific, dependent on the nature of work, the kind of machines used and the kind of workers recruited. Skill formation in most of these consisted of on-the-job training over a long period of time. This was because the content of the skill was such that it was best transferred to new workers through an extended apprentice system (Koike and Inoki 1990).

Recruitment process

Though most informal and small enterprises would prefer to hire workers who are qualified, they were often unable to do so as the reservation wages of such workers were quite high, or because it was difficult to get skilled workers for particular jobs. To minimize their production costs, of which a substantial proportion was the wage cost, the firms preferred to hire labour with low levels of education and train them on-the-job. The informal enterprises and small firms operated more or less like training workshops where workers were trained at a very low price, for the apparent benefit of both the employer and the worker.

Across regions, every firm had its own strategy for employing workers. In the NCR and Pune, the preference was to hire unskilled young workers from outside the region as they were available at low wages and were more regular at work. Educational qualification was a priority while hiring skilled workers only in the large enterprises. Most of the informal enterprises did not give much emphasis to higher education. Instead, they hired a skilled worker for his experience, his way of operating the machine, knowledge of instruments and capability to set dies.

In the NCR, firms preferred hiring workers from villages in Uttar Pradesh and Bihar who belonging to a particular caste, who had absolutely no training or experience in undertaking manufacturing activity. Recruitment of the workers took place based on information on health, land ownership in the village, ancestral occupation, family background, number of dependants at home and the nature of food intake. These criteria were important in order to decide whether the workers were healthy enough to undertake strenuous jobs and their commitment to the employer if hired.

In the Pune region, there was a clear preference for hiring unskilled workers from villages in Karnataka, Orissa, Bihar, Uttar Pradesh and also from Rajasthan. A network was developed and workers returning home during festivals would come back with others to work in these informal workshops. Neither education nor experience was a criterion for employment, only fitness was considered. Most of the workers who came from villages had low levels of education and were hired as unskilled workers at low wages and trained on-the-job. The other reason for firms preferring hiring labour from the villages was that they were regular in their work; the local labourers would not work for more than 18 days in a month, which affected smooth functioning of the production schedule.

It was only in the Chennai–Coimbatore region that the level of education and experience was given importance while recruiting workers. This was mainly because of the higher levels of technology used in this region, especially in the larger firms, as indicated by the technology index in Chapter Five. Some of the enterprises had strict competency or recruitment policies whereby workers were required to have studied at least till the 10th standard of higher secondary education whether they had passed or failed the examination, even to be hired as helpers or unskilled workers. To undertake skilled work using both conventional and CNC machines, the firms preferred to hire workers with formal education up to at least the 10th standard.

Most of the enterprises made enquiries about the family background of the worker, the company he was previously in, his understanding of the machine, his character, his capacity to adjust with the administration and cooperate with the supervisor and other workers, and asked for references as well. Informal enterprises that preferred to hire workers with low levels of education and no experience looked for sincerity and commitment on the part of the worker. Hiring experienced workers was avoided since they could be difficult to mould and argumentative, which would affect the production process. Besides, the experienced worker was not cost-effective for the informal enterprises and they preferred to train unskilled workers.

To test whether the worker had knowledge about the operation for which he was being employed, he was hired on a trial basis for up to a couple of days, during which time he was asked to perform the particular operation as per the specifications in the drawing. This helped the employer gauge whether the worker had the skill and experience needed for the job. The employer could also evaluate the number of components the worker was able to manufacture without any defects, and check the quality and accuracy of the component. The worker would then be hired on the basis of these factors.

Most often, unskilled and semi-skilled workers were recruited through announcements on notice boards, or through other firms or personal contacts. Skilled workers were mostly employed through known contacts. Some of the larger enterprises also hired workers through placement and consultancy agencies.

On-the-job training

The process of skill formation largely depended upon the kind of workers that were recruited. If the workers recruited were unskilled, on-the-job training for them would begin with basic training. The workers in small and informal enterprises were trained either by the owner–manager, supervisor or experienced skilled workers. The newly recruited unskilled workers were initially asked to do a number of small chores before being assigned to a machine and taught how to operate a particular setting. Further training was then provided at the machine: accuracy, how to produce the component, use the measuring instruments, and the specifications required to be checked on a component. This took about a week to a fortnight. Later, depending upon the capability of the worker, he was taught other operations. In some of the enterprises the workers were rotated across the different machines and made to observe the different operations.

The new recruit initially worked under the close supervision of an experienced worker from about six months to a year. During this time he was given training about different aspects of the machine: its handling and daily maintenance, inspection and supervision of parts, identification of faults in it and checking the bearings. He was taught how to use measuring instruments, how to set the component and perform operations, and how to sharpen the tools or set a die. It took almost a year for an unskilled worker to get trained and to start operating the machine independently. To a very large extent, this depended upon the skill level of the worker; some workers picked up the skills in a few weeks to six months, while others took longer. Some even remained helpers, never graduating to skilled work.

During the training period, most of the operations these workers performed were routine, repetitive and monotonous jobs, and their skills were measured by the speed and exactness with which they performed the task. They were paid low wages during training; the wages increased with improvement in skill. Newly hired workers were paid only 60 per cent of the wage of that particular grade of worker. Depending upon their performance, the wage was increased slowly. It took about two to three years for them to get the market wage rate. On-the-job training in these firms was carried out on a continuous basis, depending upon the workers' capacity to acquire more skills and knowledge about other operations.

Small firms which had ISO 9001 or TS 16949 developed a skill matrix and gave continuous training to their workers. The skill matrix defined the education level of each worker and the skills he possessed. Training was provided on the basis of the matrix and the worker's performance. The training programmes also involved orientation programmes and training programmes for employees on product knowledge, the use of raw material, the entire process of a product, quality aspects, testing equipment details, the use of testing equipment, types of quality – stage-wise, testing labs, quality parameters, knowledge about the shop floor – manpower allocation/handling, shift schedule, machine knowledge, coordination with quality/purchase, vernier document testing, quality system (QS), quality system awareness and its requirement, the importance of certification, design/customer registration, the internet, new product development and various stages of product development, customer requirements – quality, material, and case studies of customer complaints. These training programmes varied across departments and across the range of skilled workers.

The skill matrix also helped firms to observe whether the workers were acquiring skills over a period of time, and whether there was upward mobility of the workers. Regular training in one of these firms was for two to three weeks in a year, during which time the workers in a particular department or section, say, the press shop or machine shop, were trained. Or, one of the senior or experienced workers in the tool room would give training for a week on quality standards and processes. Engineers were sent abroad for training in CAD/CAM. In one of the firms, an engineer was sent to the Tata Company to develop a product with their engineers.

Time taken to gain experience

The time taken to become an experienced worker depended upon the kind of operation, the criticality of the component, and the skill, knowledge and capability the worker possessed, for which knowledge of the machine, process and component was essential. The various operations on

TABLE 6.4   *Time Taken to Become an Experienced Worker and to Gain Skills*

Machines	Number of Years of Experience
Centreless lathe – grinding	4
Cylindrical grinding	8–10
Turning, facing and threading	4–5
Conventional turret machine	1.5–2
G D Weiller machine	6–8
Herbert 2 Capstan machine	6–8
Drilling and tapping	0.6
Turned components	4–5
Milling machine	2–3
Vertical milling machine	2
Tool-setting	1
Moulding shop	3
Mechanical press	2
Press operator	2
Tool maker	5
Special-purpose machinery	3–4
CNC setter	2–3
Programmer	5
Operator	1
Skilled worker	3–4

Source: Same as Table 5.1.

different machines and the average number of years taken to gain experience are presented in Table 6.4. There were only slight variations across the various regions.

On a centreless lathe, turning, grinding or milling machine, it takes about four to five years for a fresh recruit to become an experienced and skilled worker. By this time, the worker would have gained complete knowledge of the machine, understood the drawings and processes that need to be undertaken, the sequence of the process, and how to handle the machine if there is a problem. It takes a worker about eight to ten years to become experienced and skilled in the use of a cylindrical grinding machine. It takes that long because different dimensions need to be achieved in the component at the same time and in one operation. On a mechanical press, it takes about six to eight months just to operate the machine if the die is already set for the worker. It takes about two years to understand the drawings and to do the die settings on the machine, and four to five years to have complete understanding of the component. On drilling and tapping machines it takes about six months to become an experienced worker, while on a conventional turret machine it takes about one-and-a-half to two years to gain experience.

Broadly speaking, it takes about three to four years to become an experienced worker in a particular process, and there are about 50 to 60 processes in the autocomponents industry. It takes about fifteen to twenty years to learn all these processes, many of which are inter-related. If any worker does one process wrongly, the next worker should be able to identify the mistake and correct it. For a fresh recruit to be able to undertake rough unskilled jobs it takes about six months to a year; it takes about two to three years to become a semi-skilled worker; and to become a skilled worker on mechanical and semi-automatic machines, about four to six years. There was a slight variation across the various regions in the number of years taken to become a semi-skilled or skilled worker.

As we noted while defining the skill sets, the skills the workers possess are different for the production line, and for making tools, dies, jigs and fixtures. Further, the skills needed to operate a manual or semi-automatic machine in the production line could be different from operating CNC and automated machines.

On a CNC, it takes about two to three years to become a setter, and five years to become a programmer. To become a CNC operator it takes from six months to a year. It takes three to six months for an operator on an electronic drawing machine (EDM) to gain experience, and about a year for him to become a programmer. Similarly, on a vertical milling machine (VMC), it takes about two years to become an experienced worker.

Multi-skilling

An important skill that is becoming essential for a worker is the ability to carry out multiple tasks. This enables firms to reduce costs and helps in taking care of absenteeism, by allowing for continuity and smoothness in the production process. There is a mixed opinion in the literature with regard to the assigning of tasks to workers: whether they should be taught multiple skills in order to improve their employability, or whether they should be assigned specific tasks in which they can become skilled over a period of time.

We found that about 79 per cent of the firms rotated workers across departments and processes, and this was much higher in the Chennai–Coimbatore and NCR regions as compared to the Ahmedabad–Rajkot region. Firms that did not rotate their workers argued that improved efficiency, productivity and maintenance of quality might be lost with rotation. The reason given for rotating workers was to take care of absenteeism so that production continued smoothly and the production schedule was not disturbed. According to the owner–managers, although the primary motivation was absenteeism, the workers eventually became multi-skilled, which helped them in their careers.

Most of the production workers in the sample enterprises did not remain in one job throughout their life, but moved from an easier to a more demanding one that helped them to improve their skill content. They gained experience in a number of jobs and moved frequently within a cluster of workshops that were closely related in terms of technology. This strategy helped them gain multiple skills and experience, and allowed them to move from unskilled, semi-skilled and skilled worker status to being a foreman or supervisor. There was the prospect of further upward mobility for these workers too, as they could set up their own workshops or enterprises, depending upon their entrepreneurial capability. The most impressive aspect of these firms was their skill formation process which allowed a completely untrained worker to acquire skills over a period of time in various processes and, depending on his capacity and capability, achieve upward mobility within the enterprise.

Impact of Technology Upgradation on Labour

Firms need to upgrade their technology and the quality of their production process to be globally competitive. This is also considered a mechanism whereby the demand for and returns to skilled labour can increase. There is substantial evidence in the literature to suggest that increased use of integrated manufacturing (IM) could have very positive consequences for skill development in the developing countries (Cappelli and Rogovsky 1994; Lall 1992). However, doubts have been raised as to whether such upgradation of technology actually leads to skill development. These concerns were first raised in the 1970s when Braverman (1974) argued that the introduction of advanced technology results in 'deskilling' rather than 'upskilling'. His argument was that numerically controlled machinery and other forms of advanced automation often serve to replace skilled workers, having examined a number of negative consequences for direct labour of these new technologies. On the other hand, there exists a significant body of research that indicates a link between the use of computer-controlled production machinery and skill development. Wilson (1992), for instance, found that maquilas using a substantial degree of computer-controlled machinery were more likely to implement practices resulting in multi-skilling of workers and their participation in problem diagnosis, machine maintenance and quality control, than firms that did not use these technologies.

Any improvement in technology leads to displacement of labour by capital and, at times, this could be accompanied by deskilling of the labour force in the production process. There is enough empirical evidence to support such a hypothesis. There is no doubt that technological change and the introduction of modern techniques leads to the deskilling of workers in outdated production processes, but this is very specific to certain processes and technologies. We explore this from our limited evidence in the autocomponents sector.

Technological change or upgradation is largely due to the customer's requirements and to survive in competitive market. Improvements in technology help maintain quality, consistency and repeatability of the product. That apart, another reason for upgrading machines or technology is to be able to supply semi-finished or finished products to the customers, and to reduce outsourcing. Upgradation of technology also helps to reduce errors, and improve quality and productivity.

In the machining process, the conventional manual lathe, semi-automatic, automatic, NC (numeric control) and CNC (computer numeric control) machines are used to undertake turning, grinding and finishing operations. In each of these machines there is gradual technological progress, and enterprises would acquire the higher or better technology depending upon the task or operation it needs to perform. Similarly, the skill levels required for a conventional manual lathe machine are very different from that required for CNC. Informal enterprises and small firms in our sample would normally use conventional manual lathes to undertake different production processes, moving towards machines of better technology over time.

When an enterprise upgrades its technology from conventional lathes to CNC turning lathes or the vertical machining centre (VMC), there is a probability that the workers will be deskilled. In most cases, semi-skilled workers are trained to load and unload components, and to operate the CNC machine. Skilled workers will no longer be required to undertake these processes on conventional machines, and this might lead to their deskilling. They will be, instead, hired to set the die or tools on the CNC or VMC. However, the semi-skilled and unskilled workers do not acquire the skills and knowledge to make the components using the conventional machines.

In most of the firms that had acquired CNC or VMC machines, there was no displacement of the work force, though deskilling did occur to some extent. Most of these firms were expanding, so they set up a tool room wherein the skilled work force was employed. Some of the operations like cylindrical grinding which cannot be done on CNC required conventional lathe machines, and so the skilled workers were employed to undertake such operations. The skill levels required for the conventional lathe machines are very high.

However, most enterprises preferred to train their old workers who operated conventional machines to operate the CNC machines. They hired a programmer who often had a DME to do the programming for the CNC. Some enterprises were not willing to invest time and money on training old workers, and hired new workers with high qualifications to operate the CNC machines. In such enterprises, both the conventional and the CNC machines were operated simultaneously, with only the critical dimensions being undertaken in CNC. In most firms in this industry there was neither deskilling nor displacement of workers.

The need to upgrade technology in some firms was based on customer demand, which wanted firms to reduce errors and improve productivity. In others, the reasons were to improve the production process, prevent rejection, improve quality and productivity. In many cases technological change was impelled by the need to expand, to exploit the growing market. In some of the enterprises we observed more operations being brought within the firm, like tapping or drilling machines, which allowed in-house operations as opposed to sub-contracting out.

In one of the enterprises, a new automated technology was purchased that combined three operations, wire-cutting, crimping and soldering, into one process and one machine. By bringing in this new technology the firm was able to replace six workers with one worker. The surplus workers were moved into assembly and the enterprise decided to expand by undertaking additional operations for the component within the firm. There seems to be a lot of opportunity for work with the growth in this sector, and firms are expanding and bringing in new and better technologies. In the short run, this is not leading to displacement of labour as there is opportunity for the firms to expand. However, the same may not be true in the long run, when the demand for the components reduces.

Even though firms are upgrading their technology by bringing in CNC machines, in most firms these machines coexist with the conventional machines. By upgrading their technology, firms are also trying to deliver semi-finished or finished products to their customers. The conventional machines and CNC machines continue to coexist for two reasons. One, forging in India is not as accurate as in developed countries like Japan. Because of this, the components need to be machined in conventional lathe machines which are more cost-effective, labour being cheap. The component is fed into the CNC for final 0.001 mm accuracy. If the component was directly fed into the CNC machine after forging, as is done in Japan and other developed countries, the lifespan of the CNC machine would be reduced from twelve years to a year. Two, there are certain tasks or finishing of products that cannot be done in a CNC machine. The case of the cylindrical machine was mentioned earlier. Similarly, internal boring, which is a turning operation, cannot be done in a CNC machine. So it is done on a semi-automatic turning lathe machine.

Conclusions

This chapter focused on the changes in the labour market in the autocomponents sector alongside changes in the production organization in the automobile sector. The changes in production organization have provided an opportunity for a number of small and informal enterprises to enter the market and undertake production processes at the lower end. As most of these enterprises are unorganized, they engage labour on a contractual or casual basis. Thus we found a rising trend of contractual and casual employment over the last decade in the autocomponents sector in the regions that we surveyed. Most of these workers hired on a contractual or casual basis were not entitled to social security benefits like ESI, Provident Fund or pension. However, they were entitled to receive a yearly bonus of one month's salary at the time of festivals. The other benefit these workers received was in the form of on-the-job training and rotation of work, which helped them attain skills even while subsidizing the production costs for the entrepreneur.

An important aspect of this chapter is the alternative micro definition of the skill of workers. In developing economies like India, the traditional definition of skill by educational levels does not fully capture the skill embodied in a worker. We found, in our survey, that the education level of a worker ranged from illiteracy to an ITI degree, and there was a larger concentration of workers with secondary education who, in the traditional definition, would not be classified as skilled. The definition of a skilled worker in relation to different production technologies and processes is one 'who has knowledge of the machines, an understanding of the component drawings, the ability to set tools or dies and to visualize the different processes for a given component, and the ability to produce the component as per the given specifications and within the tolerance limits specified'. These skills can be acquired only through experience on the shop floor. For the production worker on the shop floor in the autocomponents sector, higher education did not seem to be a necessary criterion to undertake a number of non-specialized tasks. Even workers with low levels of education had the potential to acquire skills and become skilled workers.

There is no doubt that education, especially in ITIs, helps in acquiring theoretical knowledge, but most workers cannot enrol since they do not meet the minimum levels of education required for admission into these institutions. In the absence of such education, informal and small enterprises become good, subsidized learning schools. Small and informal enterprises provide an opportunity for skill formation to their workers and we provide a detailed account of this. We also found that there was clear upward mobility for them from being unskilled to semi-skilled to skilled workers, and also a movement across firms. Some of them eventually set up their own informal enterprises. This was perhaps due to the expanding markets for this industry, and the situation may not be true for all industries.

Finally, we explored whether the upgradation of technology or introduction of new technology led to displacement or deskilling of workers. We found that there was no displacement of workers since there was scope for the firms to expand and absorb these workers into other activities, but there was a definite deskilling. Skills required for the operation of the conventional lathe machines were regarded as superior compared to those needed in handling a CNC or VMC. Semi-skilled workers were being trained to operate CNCs, but these workers did not necessarily acquire the skills and knowledge necessary to make components in conventional lathe machines.

CHAPTER SEVEN

Labour Market Changes in Japan's Manufacturing Sector

The economic growth of Japan heralded in the 1980s, preceded by its progress from a war-ravaged economy to 'miracle' growth in the 1960s, is a matter of wide discussion in the discourse on developing economies. This tremendous growth was due to a number of factors, which included improvement in productivity in every sector of the economy and the shift of labour from low-productivity to high-productivity sectors (Iyotani 1995). Japan followed a path of export-oriented growth which reaped great benefits and it became a trend-setter for many of the Southeast Asian economies in the region which emulated its growth process. The most impressive aspect of Japan's economy was that the returns of economic growth were transferred to the labour market in terms of improved wages and employment opportunities. This led to an improvement of the quality of the labour force, and a sense of equity and social justice among participants in labour (van der Hoeven 2001).

This growth, however, was not sustainable, and Japan experienced high unemployment rates and a decline in lifetime employment in the early 1990s. There was an increase in flexible and part-time employment (Rani 2006), a hollowing-out of manufacturing industries, and a shift of firms to Southeast Asian or other countries. Small and medium-sized firms found it difficult to survive in Japan due to the credit constraint in the economy. In this context, the present chapter discusses two specific issues. First, the shifting of Japanese firms or the establishment of subsidiaries in China, South Asia and Southeast Asia because of rising labour costs and recession in the Japanese economy. As Japanese firms invested abroad, in new locations like India, we explore whether there was a transfer of technology and skills to workers in India as practised within enterprises in the home country. Second, what strategies did the small and medium-sized firms that continued production in Japan adopt to survive? We also explore the question of skills, which is becoming an important concern in the Japanese economy.

The chapter begins with a brief analysis of economic growth and the labour market situation in Japan. The characteristics and conditions of small and medium-sized firms in the manufacturing sector, and the problems faced by these firms in the recessionary economy are discussed. The Japanese initiative in technology and skill transfers to enterprises set up in India is analysed next, through case studies of firms. The strategies adopted by small and medium-sized firms to survive in the Japanese market during the recessionary period are explored. Finally, the problems related to transfer of skills in the present scenario and the process of skill formation in Japan are discussed.

Economic Growth and the Labour Market

During the period of high economic growth, Japan's competitive success involved not only effective management of production, investment and macroeconomic policies, but also effective extraction of surplus value from workers by (state and private) capital, and its effective conversion into means of expanded production and monetary accumulation (Burkett and Hart-Landsberg 2000). The success of Japanese growth hinged on the conversion of machine industries from production mainly for the domestic market to a strong export orientation, and this was achieved by keeping unit labour costs low largely through expanded use of temporary and sub-contracted labour. Although the repeated restructuring of its industrial base maintained the dynamism of the Japanese economy until the mid-1980s, the eventual result was a hollowing-out of domestic industry, and substitution of foreign investment and financial speculation for productive domestic investment. This eroded the domestic industrial base required to sustain Japan's earlier rapid growth rate.

The economic environment changed dramatically with the appreciation of the yen in 1985, at the Plaza Agreement.[1] The Plaza Accord caused a brief recession and high unemployment (2.6 per cent). The export industries were severely hit and imports began to rise with the newly industrializing economies (NIEs) becoming serious competitors to Japan in both domestic and overseas markets (Nakamura 1992). There was also increasing pressure from the US on Japan to open up its market in hi-tech (integrated circuits) and agricultural (rice) products. These factors slowed down the economy for a short period, but production resumed its upward trend in

---

[1] In September 1985, the finance ministers of the world's major industrialized countries, including the United States and Japan, met at the Plaza Hotel in New York city and introduced the 'Plaza Accord'. The objective of the Plaza Accord was to lower the trade deficit that the United States had with the rest of the world. Under its terms, it was agreed that the value of the dollar would be lowered in relation to the yen.

1987. To maintain competitiveness worldwide, large parts of the motor vehicles, electrical machinery, precision instruments and machinery industries were 'hollowed-out' and relocated abroad, mainly in Southeast Asian countries and China to take advantage of their cheap labour. The other force that impelled Japan's recovery was the famous 'bubble economy', an investment and construction boom driven by an escalating upward spiral of stock, share, land and housing prices. Monetary policy was accommodative, as interest rates were kept low for the bigger Keiretsu corporations (Nakamura 1995).

Japan's continuous export dependence, and its regional and global production strategy which was used to maintain its export competitiveness had adverse consequences, however, for the Japanese working class in particular. Some of these industries were heavily dependent on female labour and with the relocation of production overseas, female employment began to decline.

The impact of shifting manufacturing firms overseas began to be felt in labour market by the beginning of the 1990s. Unemployment began to rise – although lower than in other countries, it was still high by Japanese standards – and became a sensitive political issue (Nakamura 1992). As in other developed countries, there was an increase of temporary or part-time workers with specific knowledge and skills. Some of these workers found employment through placement services, which was prohibited by the law.

The Japanese economy grew at a meagre 1.6 per cent in the early 1990s and managed a weak recovery in 1994–95, but the yen appreciated sharply, forcing companies to invest overseas. The shift in the manufacturing industry was not restricted to large companies alone but also involved small and medium manufacturers, leading to a 'hollowing-out' of industry. This undermined domestic investment, although information technology did create considerable impetus for new investment. The already weak economic conditions were aggravated by the financial crisis – especially nonperforming loans including bad debts. The economy suffered another severe blow when the Asian financial crisis erupted in 1997, with a fall in stock prices. The stock market crash sharply increased the bad debt burden of large banks and other financial institutions (Koshiro 2000).

In the early phase of the recession, permanent employment in firms was not affected. Employment adjustment was carried out by reducing the number of hours much more sharply than during earlier recessions. The work force declined by 0.01 per cent during the 1990s. Unemployment was at an unprecedented high, almost reaching 5.8 per cent by 2002. The slowdown in the growth rate of the economy and the ageing of the labour force generated problems that were difficult to address by piecemeal adjustments involving only parts of the employment system (Ariga, Brunello and Ohkusa 2000).

The gap between successful and floundering firms widened from the beginning of the 1990s. Japanese companies were forced to address the flaws in traditional management practices. There was enormous pressure to change business practices and restructure corporations, to make organizations leaner, more cost-efficient and flexible, leading to retrenchment of workers in all the major corporations. Thus the Japanese employment scenario underwent tremendous changes in the 1990s.

In an effort to retain/recover competitive advantage in the market place during this deep and long recession, firms tried to reduce labour costs. Companies also started to take bolder steps to reduce the number of full-time employees as labour costs rose, and resorted to hiring part-time workers. The three most common measures taken by the companies were: (1) reduction of workers with full employment benefits (with lifetime employment, seniority-based salaries and full retirement packages); (2) replacement of workers with full benefits with other, more flexible workers (new workers recruited in mid-career, part-time workers, contracted workers, temporary workers supplied by staff placement agencies); (3) switching from a seniority-based salary structure to a merit system that reflected each individual's capability to carry out tasks and make contributions to the company. These changes resulted in an increase in the part-time or flexible work force (24 per cent in 2001, with male part-timers comprising 12 per cent and female part-timers 39 per cent of total workers).

The Manufacturing Sector in Japan

The change in employment practices was a major effort at restructuring on the part of firms in Japan, hitherto known for their worker-friendly and lifetime employment systems.

Small and Medium-Size Enterprises

The manufacturing sector in Japan accounted for 19.7 per cent of the GDP and 19.3 per cent of the total number of persons employed in 2002. The Small and Medium Enterprises Basic Law defined small and medium enterprises (SME) in the manufacturing sector as enterprises with capital of less than 300 million yen. Medium enterprises were those with a regular work force of less than 300 employees, and small enterprises those with less than 20 employees. The law guaranteed special financing and tax concessions to SMEs. Within the manufacturing sector, SMEs accounted for 74.1 per cent of total workers in 2001, and within that, small enterprises

FIGURE 7.1   *Growth Rates of Number of Employee and Value Added*

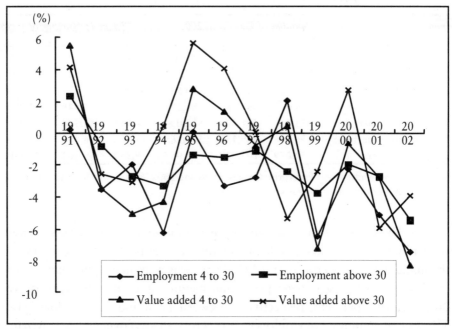

Source: Census of Manufactures (various issues), Ministry of Economy, Trade and Industry, Government of Japan.

accounted for 33.5 per cent (Census of Manufactures 2001). In the machinery industry, which included general machinery, electrical machinery, transportation equipment and precision machinery, SMEs and small-scale enterprises accounted for 58.3 per cent and 21.6 per cent, respectively, of total workers employed in 2001. We are interested in this group of industries since it contains the automobile and autocomponents sectors.

The growth rates of value added of the manufacturing sector, and within it the small-scale sector, fluctuated over the period 1991–2002 across different employment sizes (Figure 7.1). There seemed to be some recovery in value added in the years 1995, 1996 and 2000, before it slid again. The value added growth of medium and large enterprises that employed 30 and more workers exceeded the level of 1991 between 1995 and 1996. If we look at trends in the machine industry, the picture is different. While general machinery and precision machinery peaked in 1991, electrical machinery had a boom between 1996 and 2000, and transportation equipment after 2002. Small-scale enterprises of the three machinery industries, excepting electrical machinery, had a decline in gross value added during this period.

TABLE 7.1   *Number of Workers Engaged in the Manufacturing Sector, 1996–2001, Japan*

Industry Group	Number of Persons in 2001			Change in Number of Persons, 1996 to 2001		
	Less than 30	30 to 299	300 and more	Less than 30	30 to 299	300 and more
Manufacturing sector	3,731,424	4,514,866	2,879,855	–740,207	–589,473	–466,209
General machinery	419,070	460,168	288,292	–47,428	–45,848	–43,099
Electrical machinery	275,045	681,624	872,004	–54,931	–58,306	–102,921
Transportation machinery	156,796	319,152	550,268	–14,492	–16,806	–74,234
Precision machinery	70,079	107,829	72,087	–9,340	–9,802	–26,910

Source: Establishment and Enterprise Census, 1996 and 2001, Ministry of Internal Affairs and Communication, Government of Japan.

There was a general decline in the total number of employees, represented by regular workers,[2] sole proprietors[3] and unpaid family workers, in the manufacturing sector after 1991. There was a decline in the number of employees in small-scale enterprises and medium and large enterprises, by 26.3 and 19.7 per cent, respectively, between 1996 and 2001 (Table 7.1). The decline in number of employees was across all employment sizes. Across industry groups it was observed in all establishments with more than four persons, except for food products. The number of employees in general machinery, electrical machinery, transportation equipment and precision machinery declined by 23.2, 33.1, 13.2 and 39.2 per cent, respectively, between 1996 and 2001. The value added recovered in the latter half of the 1990s in electrical machinery and transportation equipment, and there was no increase in employment after 1996 (Table 7.1).

The Establishment and Enterprise Census provides more detailed data on size-wise numbers of workers who were working at the establishment the day of the census. They include workers who are dispatched to other establishments run by different companies. They do not include workers who are dispatched from other establishments and not receiving wages or allowances. In the case of sole proprietors, they include family members who are not getting wages or allowances. There was a decline in the number

---

[2] Regular workers are persons who (a) are employed on an indefinite or longer-than-a-month labour contract, (b) are employed for eighteen days or longer during previous and current months out of casual hire on a daily or less-than-monthly basis, (c) are dispatched by temporary employment agencies and are loaned workers from a parent company, (d) work full-time and receive monthly remuneration as directors, executives, etc., and (e) are the family of a solo proprietor and work for him, earning monthly salaries or wages.

[3] Sole proprietors and unpaid family workers are defined as sole proprietors engaged in business and their families who work full-time for them without remuneration.

of workers engaged in SMEs and this had an impact on the manufacturing sector as a whole. The decline in the number of workers engaged in large establishments mainly contributed to the reduction of employment in electrical machinery, transportation equipment and precision machinery. In 2001, the percentage shares of workers engaged in large enterprises in the manufacturing sector, general machinery, electrical machinery, transportation equipment and precision machinery, were 25.9, 24.7, 47.7, 53.6 and 28.8, respectively. In electrical machinery and transportation equipment, large enterprises absorbed more employment than small and medium enterprises.

The decline in employment, to a very large extent, was due to the closure of establishments and retrenchment of employees. Since 1991, many of the large companies have resorted to retrenchment for rationalization of employment under the continuous recession. Some big companies closed

TABLE 7.2 *Number of Workers Engaged in Manufacturing Sector across Different Firm Sizes in Existing, Newly Organized and Abolished Industries, 1996–1999, Japan*

	Existing	Newly Organized	Abolished
Manufacturing			
Less than 30	–301,137	257,070	–597,985
30 to 299	–289,911	220,702	–341,307
300 and more	–403,630	70,394	–83,913
General machinery			
Less than 30	–17,972	29,132	–54,229
30 to 299	–21,598	18,523	–29,550
300 and more	–26,332	5,830	–6,540
Electrical machinery			
Less than 30	–14,197	28,302	–56,058
30 to 299	–24,745	42,246	–55,756
300 and more	–104,074	18,699	–23,592
Transportation equipment			
Less than 30	–8,415	11,940	–21,173
30 to 299	–25,442	14,455	–22,803
300 and more	–68,408	8,671	–9,339
Precision machinery			
Less than 30	–3,531	5,889	–9,882
30 to 299	–5,360	5,950	–6,099
300 and more	–17,155	2,818	–3,295

Note: The dates of the Census were 1 October 1996 and 1 July 1999.
Source: Establishment and Enterprise Census, 1999, Ministry of Internal Affairs and Communication, Government of Japan.

down their establishments to concentrate on profitable areas, while others shifted abroad. While closure of establishments contributed to reduction of employment in SMEs, it led to retrenchment in large enterprises (Table 7.2). This was a common phenomenon in the manufacturing sector as a whole, and especially in the machinery industries.

The 2002 Employment Status Survey showed that 5 million workers had left their jobs in the manufacturing sector between 1997 and 2002, and only 48.5 per cent of them were still gainfully employed. The major reason for leaving jobs was retrenchment and voluntary retirement (14.3 per cent); bankruptcy and closure of establishments was also a significant cause (10.3 per cent). These figures show the huge impact of retrenchment and closure of establishments in the manufacturing sector on the labour market.

The Condition of Japanese Small and Medium Enterprises

There was a decline in the number of SMEs in the manufacturing sector by 3 per cent from 1991 to 2001. High start-up and closure rates were a characteristic of SMEs (Table 7.3).[4] They accounted for more than

---

[4] Method of calculation of start-up rates and closure rates based on the number of establishments, according to the Establishments and Enterprise Census of Japan:

(a) Periods between 1994 and 1996 and between 1999 and 2001.

1. Annual average number of set-ups of establishments. The Census groups the number of establishments according to the period of establishment. In the 2001 Census, the number of new establishments since 2000 was 407,452. As the survey period from 1 January 2000 to the date of the survey on 1 October 2001 is 21 months, the number of new establishments is divided by 21 and multiplied by 12.

2. Annual average increase in the number of establishments. The annual average increase in the number of establishments is calculated by dividing the increase in the number of establishments from the date of the previous survey on 1 July 1999 to 1 October 2001 by the period between the surveys (27 months) and multiplying by 12.

3. Annual average number of closures of establishments. The annual average number of closures of establishments is calculated by subtracting the annual average increase in the number of establishments from the annual average number of set-ups of establishments.

4. Set-up rate. The set-up rate is calculated by dividing the annual average number of set-ups of establishments by the number of establishments at the time of the previous survey, and multiplying the result by 100.

5. Closure rate. The closure rate is calculated by dividing the annual average number of closures of establishments by the number of establishments at the time of the previous survey, and multiplying the result by 100.

(b) Periods between 1991 and 1994 and between 1996 and 1999.

1. Annual average number of set-ups of establishments, annual average number of closures of establishments. The Census groups the number of establishments into new establishments, closed establishments and continuing establishments according to their status of change. The number of new establishments and the number of closed establishments are each divided by the period from the date of the previous survey and

TABLE 7.3   *Trend of Start-up and Closure Rates in the Japanese Manufacturing Sector* (percentages)

Industry Group		1991–94	1994–96	1996–99	1999–2001
All	Start-up	4.6	3.7	4.1	3.8
	Closure	4.6	3.8	5.9	4.3
Manufacturing	Start-up	3.0	1.5	1.9	1.6
	Closure	4.5	4.2	5.3	4.3
General machinery	Start-up	3.4	1.6	2.2	1.7
	Closure	4.3	3.1	4.5	3.3
Electrical machinery	Start-up	5.4	2.2	2.8	2.6
	Closure	5.4	5.3	5.9	5.0
Transportation equipment	Start-up	3.5	1.4	2.1	1.9
	Closure	3.2	2.8	4.6	2.5
Precision machinery	Start-up	3.3	1.7	2.5	2.0
	Closure	5.0	5.4	4.7	4.2

Source: Establishment and Enterprise Census, 1996, Ministry of Internal Affairs and Communication, Government of Japan.

99.4 per cent of the total number of establishments in 1991 and 2001, with the number of large establishments being negligible. After 1991, the start-up rate declined in the manufacturing sector and in the four machinery industries. This was argued to be because of the large impact on one's livelihood of potential failure in business, the strong preference for white-collar employment, the averseness to economic risk as a national characteristic, and the shortage of knowledge, skills and business know-how required to set up an enterprise (White Paper on Small and Medium Enterprises 2003). The most important reason was the deterioration of the business environment, which not only restrained start-ups but also caused closures of existing establishments. Some of these issues are discussed below.

Firstly, subsidiaries of parent companies shifted abroad and this had a major impact on the economy. The appreciation of the yen in 1985 due to the Plaza Agreement led many companies to shift labour-intensive processes from Japan to other Asian countries, mainly China, in order to take advantage of the cheap labour there. The increase in foreign direct investment (FDI) from Japan to China between 1993 and 1995, which was more than 600 billion yen, accounted for 20 per cent of total FDI in this period.

_____

multiplied by 12 to calculate the annual average number of entries of establishments and annual average number of closures of establishments.

2. Set-up and closure rates. The annual average number of set-ups of establishments and annual average number of closures of establishments are each divided by the number of establishments at the time of the previous survey and the result is multiplied by 100.

TABLE 7.4   *Number of Overseas Affiliates by Year of Establishment or Capital Participation*

		1988 and earlier	1989–91	1992–94	1995–97	1998–2000
World	Manufacturing	2,965	1,123	1,198	1,600	571
	Four machinery industries	1,576	554	568	829	364
Asia	Manufacturing	1,514	603	903	1,163	303
	Four machinery industries	752	285	397	563	187
China	Manufacturing	212	132	572	509	115
	Four machinery industries	104	55	234	219	64

Source: Survey on Overseas Business Activities 2001, Ministry of Economy, Trade and Industry, Government of Japan.

The Survey on Overseas Business Activities has data on the number of overseas affiliates by year of establishment or capital participation (Table 7.4). The number of Japanese manufacturing affiliates established or capital participation in Asia, China and the world increased in the period 1992–97. The increase in overseas investment and shrinkage of the domestic market raised the overseas production ratio (sales of overseas affiliates vis-à-vis sales of domestic companies) from 7.4 per cent in 1993 to 17.1 per cent in 2002 in the manufacturing sector.

The FDI involved not only setting up new units but also the shifting of units from Japan. The impact of this shift on domestic production and employment was three-fold: a reverse imports effect, an export-inducing effect and an export substitution effect. There was an increase of reverse imports from overseas affiliates and exports of interim products to overseas affiliates. Exports bound for Japan from overseas affiliates, i.e. re-imports, increased from 1,678 billion yen in 1992 to 6,352 billion yen in 2002. The ratio of re-imports within Japan's total imports rose from 6.5 per cent to 16.5 per cent during the same period. Re-imports from Asia, which was the most important overseas base, accounted for 81.8 per cent of total re-imports in 2002. There was an increase in the exports of intermediary goods to overseas affiliates in the manufacturing sector from 4,100 billion yen in 1992 to 15,091 billion yen in 2002. The ratio of exports of interim products within total exports of Japan grew from 9.8 per cent to 30.1 per cent during the same period.

The development of foreign trade with overseas affiliates caused bipolarization of the SMEs. Some of the units lost their business due to their clients shifting abroad, and were forced to close down. However, other units got an opportunity to supply their products to the overseas affiliates. The annual growth rates of value added per unit in establishments with 30 and more employees were 2.0, 5.2, 2.0 and 2.6 per cent in manufacturing, electrical machinery, transportation equipment and precision instruments, respectively. And, the annual growth rates of value added per unit in establishments with 4 to 29 employees were 1.2 per cent, 5.2 per cent and 1.1 per cent, respectively, in the manufacturing sector, electrical machinery and precision instruments. This showed that the existing and operating establishments were maintaining their profitability even in small units.

Secondly, big companies reduced their sources of procurement to reduce costs, and this meant that more stringent procedures were used to select their suppliers. Even the selected SMEs were forced by the big companies to reduce their sales prices to be competitive in the global market, and the entry of new firms became difficult.

Thirdly, banks restrained loans to sick and small companies due to the accumulation of non-performing assets. Small establishments depended on bank loans to a larger extent than large establishments. In 2002, loans from financial institutions accounted for 53.4 per cent, 50.3 per cent, 37.7 per cent and 23.9 per cent of total funds in establishments with less than 20 employees, 21 to 100 employees all 101 to 300 employees and more than 300 employees, respectively. Loans are the most important source of funding for SMEs, without which it is very difficult for these firms to operate.

Fourthly, there was the problem of finding a successor in proprietory firms because the younger generation was hesitant to join the manufacturing sector either as workers or owners. Most of the SMEs were family proprietorships, and the younger generation was hesitant to join the family

FIGURE 7.2   *Number of New Employees from Universities 1990–2002*

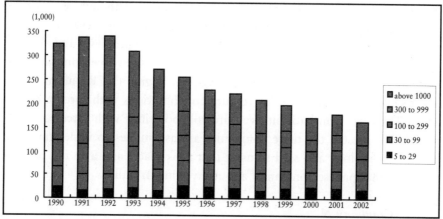

Source: White Paper of Manufacturing Base, 2004, Ministry of Economy, Trade and Industry; Ministry of Health, Labour and Welfare; and Ministry of Education, Culture, Sports, Science and Technology, Government of Japan.

business because of the uncertainty and high risks involved. As a result, age-ing of sole proprietors has become a serious concern. The White Paper clearly points out that 43.3 per cent of sole proprietors are above 60 years of age.

Despite the rise in unemployment rates, many establishments have illegally employed foreign workers without working visas, due to the non-availability of a local labour force with adequate skills or for lower wages. Under the present recession, many large units have also refrained from em-ploying new labour. Some of them have closed down their domestic units and shifted abroad. This too has led to a sharp decline in the entry of uni-versity degree-holders into large establishments (Figure 7.2). In SMEs, the entry of new employees has fluctuated. The Japanese manufacturing sector as a whole thus has a serious problem in the form of succession of skills, which may affect technological development.

Japanese Initiatives in Technology and Skill Transfer to India

Since the 1980s, many Japanese companies have invested and set up factories in India. The machinery was imported from Japan to these facto-ries, but a number of local workers and engineers were employed and trained. Initially, core components were imported from Japan with the remaining components being manufactured locally. Later, however, due to regulations, they had to procure all parts and components locally from Indian comp-anies or joint venture companies within India. To meet this requirement, the Japanese companies started helping the local companies to improve the quality of their products.

Technology and management methods were transferred from Japa-nese companies to Indian companies through localization of components and human resources. Inside the factories, engineers and workers were trained directly by Japanese engineers and skilled personnel. Although some of the sub-contracting Indian companies were advised by the Japanese companies, these enterprises also needed to improve the technological level and skills of the workers through their own initiative. We visited five companies in Gurgaon and NOIDA in the National Capital Region (NCR), all of which had technical or financial joint-venture collaborations with foreign comp-anies. Three of them had joint-venture collaborations with Japanese com-panies. We present the three companies as case studies to understand the kind of technology and skill transfer that took place, and also the percep-tions of the Japanese companies about investing in India.

Company N

This company was set up in India in 1997 to manufacture power press and dies. It imported second-hand machinery from Japan, including the machining centre, vertical machining centre and a 400-ton capacity power press. Japanese technology is heterogeneous and the technological level of this company was of medium range, and so the machines imported from Japan were not of the best technology. Thus there existed a technology gap, as there were better, hi-tech machines available in Japan. However, the quality of the product could be improved substantially despite the low level of machinery. All it required was skilled workers who could identify the faults.

Company N worked with a group of companies from Japan to develop the skill of its workers through on-the-job training. A Japanese engineer from the group was brought to India to train the workers, and workers from the Indian company were sent to the Japanese headquarters and other companies in the group for six months to acquire skills on-the-job. The recruitment policy of the firm was to hire diploma holders to operate CAD/CAM, and ITI or 12th/10th standard workers for the shop floor. Since one Japanese engineer could not handle all the workers, the company did not have job rotation among workers.

For a worker to absorb skills in die-making in CAD/CAM, it takes twelve to fifteen years. When a new worker joins the drawing department, the normal practice was to first appoint him in the workshop, where he would spend a minimum of five years trying to understand and recognize what kind of dies are best for production. This helped the worker to develop a precise drawing for particular dies. However, this practice was not always possible or practical in small or medium-sized firms.

Company N was a medium-sized one and did not send its new workers to the workshop initially, but hired them directly for the drawing department. The best dies and moulds were those in which no modification were required, and meant that the worker understood the drawings and was able to produce a good die. If the mould required modification and the finishing was not good, it meant that the worker did not understand the die drawing. Modifying the die and mould was a time-consuming and expensive task. In die-making, a CNC cannot reach many of the internal parts and curves of the die, and these operations need to be done manually. The worker can find out if the product is good or defective by the feel of it. This implied that the company relied on the experience and skill of the workers for quality products, and made the effort to train them.

The company had introduced some of the management systems used in Japan on its shop floor, such as Kaizan (continuous improvement of the product or process), Kanban (suggestions for improvements) and 5S. It maintained an accurate inventory of the dies and the dispatch goods were properly displayed. Production and process data-sheets were in place. To overcome communication gaps between the Japanese group leader and the workers, since most of the workers could not read or understand English, there was an interpreter to translate. The firm has not been able to introduce a quality circle and are working towards it.

One problem that the company is facing currently is that the workers are not committed to the company, and the job turnover ratio is quite high. So, having made large investments in training and skill development, the company is running at a loss. It takes about three years to acquire the minimal skills, and once the workers acquire them they start looking for new jobs where they might get better wages. The company had recruited twenty workers in the CAD–CAM department when it was set up, and now only seven remain.

Another issue was with regard to the confidence levels of the workers. While the Japanese worker would solve any problem encountered in the process himself, the Indian worker, in a similar situation, would wait for help from either a fellow worker or his superior. His superior's confirmation was considered to be most important by the Indian worker. This lack of independence could be partly because of the way training was imparted to Indian workers, and partly because of the lack of good-quality basic and technical education in India.

Company M

This was a joint venture between a Japanese and an Indian company, started in 1996. It manufactured plastic automobile parts such as front-bumper assembly with grills, sub-assembly dashboard/instrument panel, assembly parts for doors, mirrors and handles, wheel-caps, rear-bumper assembly, and so on. The main production machinery included injection moulding machinery of various capacities, vibration welding, and two paint booths. These machines were imported from Toshiba in Japan and any problem with the machines was addressed by calling in service engineers from Toshiba itself. The company had an annual service contract with Toshiba by which service engineers from Toshiba visited it once a year.

Dies and moulds are most important in the manufacture of plastic automobile parts. Die-making companies in India are heterogeneous, with the top die manufacturers exporting to Japan and Europe. Company M provides the concept and technical know-how of dies and moulds to die-makers, and checks the drawings. Technical know-how is provided to both Indian die-makers and to sub-contracted die-makers of Honda. Honda also requested the company to share its know-how with other local sub-contractors in order to raise their technical level, without which it is difficult for Honda to survive in the market. Honda emphasizes local development of the Indian automobile or components industry because it finds it difficult to source its products from abroad all the time. The moulding business is not cost-effective, and if the Japanese collaborator has to manufacture moulds, it is an expensive process and the import duty too is quite high. Apart from Honda, Toyota and Maruti are also trying to develop local technical know-how in dies and moulds.

Company M sends its engineers, mostly diploma-holders and engineering graduates, to Japan for training, under the Overseas Training Scholarship of the SME, to small and medium companies, for three months. The company also took the initiative of sending one of the engineers to its headquarter company in Japan, for training. The company invites Japanese engineers to India, to provide technical assistance to its workers. One of the problems it faced was that once a worker or engineer was trained, he left the company and all the investments made by Company M were lost.

Company M also pointed out the differences in the work culture and management style between India and Japan. It faced a union problem for about six months because the workers wanted wage hikes, promotions and were against the new system of two shifts. This led to work sabotage, black bands and absenteeism. However, production was not stopped as the company hired casual labourers and tightened security. After an enquiry nine workers were terminated and the issue was subsequently resolved. The Japanese and Indian counterparts perceived the union problem differently. The Japanese management realized that there was a problem with promotions, and that there was little contact between the workers and the management. This had led to defects that needed correction or reworking, and they thought that this should not occur in the future. The Indian management had a completely different point of view. They thought the battle had been won as the production supply continued despite the strike and they had succeeded in dismissing nine workers.

According to the Japanese management, the problem in India is that a worker can become a supervisor after about twenty years of experience, while a supervisor cannot become a manager, however much experience he gains. This is not the case in Japan, where an experienced supervisor becomes a manager, over time. According to them, it is unfortunate that Indians think low of skills at the workshop level, and try to get a degree instead of learning a skill.

The Indian system is rather inflexible and hierarchical, and there are limits to the upward mobility of workers. More importance is given to acquiring a degree than a skill. In fact, skill acquisition at the shop floor is seen as having less value and these workers are seen to be lower in the hierarchy than workers with degrees who are supervisors or managers.

Company M has not started quality circles, but they have regular meetings of workers at which they are given awards for their contribution in either identifying or solving a problem. There is interaction between the manager, supervisor and engineers with the workers on the shop floor, except when they are developing parts for a new car model. All other management systems in place are just as in a Japanese firm and the infrastructure inside resembles that of a Japanese firm.

Company S

This company has had a number of technical tie-ups with companies in Japan for different components since 1983. It also has joint ventures with companies in Germany, Korea and other countries. The collaboration with the Japanese company now is for technical and financial assistance.

The company has received technical help from the collaborating company in Japan, and has sent Indian workers and engineers to the company in Japan for training. There is co-development of prototypes or new products with the Japanese company. The company manufactures components and exports them to Japan. It has thirty quality circles and regular meetings are held with the workers. All management systems are in place.

The company provided the workers with regular training, organizing different types of daily training modules on a day-to-day basis. Specific training for handling, processing and management of specific products was conducted. Further, visual image training was provided on the shop floor. The workers were required to memorize all the drawings for a job so that it could be done quickly and efficiently. During the making of samples, the skilled workers were provided with support from the supervisor and engineer, which helped them develop their skills.

The case-study analysis of the three companies clearly shows the emphasis placed on workers' skills by Japanese companies in India and the efforts they make in developing them. They hire workers with some education and give on-the-job training on the shop floor. They also send workers to Japan to get technical knowledge and improve their skills. Though it is not always possible for these companies to follow the training methods practised in their home country, they do try to incorporate better skill-training modules and methods, and provide regular and specific training to the workers.

Strategies Adopted by Small and Medium Enterprises in Japan

We undertook a survey of twenty small and medium-sized enterprises in May–June 2004, in the Ota-ku ward of Tokyo and the Joyo ward of Southern Kyoto Prefecture, to understand the strategies adopted by small firms in Japan in the current recessionary period and the process of skill formation in these firms. In this section we look at what lessons can be learnt from these, for small and medium-sized enterprises in developing countries like India. We must, however, mention at the outset that all the twenty firms we surveyed were perhaps the most successful of the firms and were willing to share their experiences. A number of other firms refused to give us interviews and we assume that they were struggling to survive. This is, therefore, a biased sample, and could lead to bias in our analysis. Despite this caveat, perhaps there are lessons to be learnt from the Japanese experience.

The employment size of the firms ranged from 5 to 140 workers, and these were firms working for automobile, electrical equipment, semi-conductor, machine tool and transportation equipment companies. Most of them had computer aided design (CAD) and computerized numeric control (CNC) machines. Three firms had overseas affiliates, and one was in the process of setting up an overseas affiliate.

During the high growth period, most of these SMEs were sub-contractors for large firms and undertook specified work. The current recessionary trend has also led to a weakening of the Keiretsu[5] system, leading to more competition among sub-contractors. The relations between the parent and the sub-contracting firm used to be asymmetric, and there was dependence on the parent firm for tools and machinery. There has been a change in this trend since the hollowing-out of firms over the last decade, towards a more symmetric relationship between the parent and sub-contracting firm. This could be because the SMEs that had decided not to move out were the most successful ones, which had upgraded their technology and were capable of finding their own niche market without depending on the parent firms. In the 1980s, when the large firms started moving to the Southeast Asian countries, many of the small firms could not follow suit due to capital shortage. Having stopped getting orders from the parent firms, they improved their technical know-how and skill expertise and shifted to manufacturing precision products as samples and prototypes, and thus gained independent technological strength.

The development of technical skills and expertise by small and med-

---

[5] The general structure of a Keiretsu is an association of companies formed around a bank. They cooperate with each other and own shares of each other's stock. These conglomerates are called Keiretsu. There are two types of Keiretsu: horizontal and vertical. The horizontal relationship is across industries, where they usually have one enterprise in each business sector to enjoy economies of scale and avoid competition within the group. The vertical ones are smaller than the horizontal groupings. One large company is a member of the horizontal Keiretsu but has its own independent vertical group, integrating a pyramid of suppliers and component manufacturers (sub-contractors) in one structure. The advantage of this structure is that many sub-contractors work as 'buffers' for the core firm during economic downturns.

ium enterprises has become an advantage for large firms and multinational enterprises. The large firms often seek their cooperation for research and development, and to meet certain high technical demands. Some of the small firms also compete with the large firms in certain niche products. The two major strategies adopted by the small and medium-sized firms in the face of recession were to concentrate on research and development and the manufacturing of core precision parts, and to diversify their products.

Research and Development

Many of the small firms that did not move out along with the parent firm went into venture business oriented towards research and development. They tried to develop diversified products for different producers. This helped them to innovate, and accumulate skills and technical expertise. Of the twenty companies in our sample, three were engaged in research and development-oriented venture businesses, and a few others in process and product development. These small venture companies were looking for niche markets and had the capability to develop various products.

As the small firms gained specialized skills and technical expertise, the large firms became dependent on them for certain products. One such case was reported by the owner of a small firm: a large firm had approached him for automating and improving an assembly line because it did not have the required technical know-how. The perception of owners of small firms was that while the large firms which were largely engaged in the production line had good technical expertise about manufacturing processes and products, they had limited knowledge about improvising hardware and looked to outside sources for this. This opened up opportunities for small firms to create their own niche markets.

In Company P, the most important development was the indexing equipment used as an automatic jig changer for an automated welding line, which was developed for Honda Giken. In the automobile industry where volumes were becoming low, there were wide-ranging products and the product life-cycle was changing fast, and it was not cost-effective for companies to have separate welding lines for each car. So this innovation by a small firm actually helped large firms to cut down costs because the automatic jig changer allowed four-wheelers of different sizes to be manufactured in the same assembly line. The company shared a joint patent with Honda Giken, and also got patents from Japan, Germany, UK and USA. Similarly, Company Q developed prototypes for large firms as per drawings and specifications, for different products. The large firms often did not inform them what these parts were going to be used for due to competition and to maintain secrecy.

Some of the companies were also engaged in process innovations for large firms, with the owners of some of them being equipped with skills to undertake three-dimensional and complicated processing activities. The SMEs constantly came up with new innovations and efficient systems of production to survive in the market. For example, Company R manufactured parts of a semi-conductor-producing machine, where the error had to be within 5 microns. To minimize the error to 5 microns, they needed to know how to fix the part for grinding. If the part was made of iron a magnet could be used to fix it, while for aluminium or steel they had to vacuum and maintain the temperature inside the machine to prevent the shape of the part getting distorted. In grinding, oil and water were used to reduce friction, and it was essential to maintain the temperature of the oil and water. The owner of the company succeeded in manufacturing a vacuum machine and temperature-maintaining machine to overcome this problem, through his experience and know-how. However, despite the innovation, he was not able to patent the process because he had not collaborated with the parent company in developing it.

In the semi-conductor industry, Company S developed a process technique in the grinding machine to break the veneer beneath the silicon without damaging the silicon. For this process innovation, it obtained a joint patent with the parent company. Earlier, big semi-conductor companies used to curve the silicon with laser, which was a very inefficient process. The innovative technique was more precise, cost-effective and efficient.

Some of the small firms were also accumulating technical know-how and improving capabilities to develop sophisticated precision products. Company T was well known for its sophisticated precision products, and charged very high rates for processing or developing them. Larger companies generally approached it only after they had failed to develop the product elsewhere. Sometimes the company got indirect orders from small firms who were unable to manufacture the product, and who learnt the know-how in the process. Often the original customer was unaware or did not have the know-how to undertake the process. Thus the strategy has been of concentrating on high value added activity, i.e. development and low-volume production of important parts at cheap capital costs.

Diversification of Products

During the high-growth period of the 1980s, large companies and their sub-contractors aimed at the major markets and undertook mass production. However, in the 1990s, with flexible and lean production systems, the production volumes declined and the product variety or range increased. This meant that the small firms had to adjust to survive in the emerging market and also change their management practices. Initially, very few of them could change their management systems or move from mass production to producing small volumes of a wide range of products. Later, however, a number of small and medium firms diversified their products to survive in the market. For example, Company T already had a wide range of products, and introduced new products according to customer demand and depending on the market.

Some of these firms also adopted a strategy of manufacturing the core parts of machinery (especially semi-conductor-making machines, as there was an increasing demand for these) or machine tools or precision products. Some others made and pressed dies, for which Japan had good technical expertise and skill. These firms also invested abroad in press and die manufacturing to expand their base and reap profits. They were able to obtain profits in press manufacturing but were struggling with dye manufacturing since the transfer of skills in this process took longer. These firms also made efforts to expand their market and obtain orders from other countries.

Mix of Simple and Sophisticated Machines

After the bubble burst, many of the parent companies asked the small and medium enterprises to reduce costs without any compromise on the quality, which was the most important aspect of competing or surviving in the market. To reduce costs, many of the SME adopted a production strategy of using both simple conventional and sophisticated machines to manufacture products. For example, to manufacture a product with precision, Company U used only one hi-tech machine and the others were simple machines. According to this company, investment in the latest or sophisticated machines was not always profitable as the turnover was often not enough to compensate for the investment, and with the margin of processing declining, even survival became an issue.

Networks

The shifting or hollowing-out of large firms from Japan to the Southeast Asian countries and China from the beginning of the 1990s had a huge impact on small and medium-sized firms. Most firms in Ota-ku could not make the shift to foreign countries because it was very difficult to raise the capital, and therefore had decided to stay back. The Ota-ku Municipality tried to develop collaboration among the small companies, to share information about sales, production and defects with one another. The Ota Industrial Association provided them with services, such as measuring and inspection equipment, whenever needed. However, this transition towards sharing and collaboration among companies takes time. As the market is competitive, most owners are secretive about their contacts and processes, and thus it is not easy for a network of small-sized firms to develop.

Problems

Some of the serious problems faced by most small and medium-sized companies were related to the issue of succession. The next generation was not keen on ownership of these firms as the risks were too high and the competition was fierce, preferring to work instead for some other company. This was observed in at least five out of the twenty companies surveyed. Another issue related to the practice, now being followed in Japan, of customers (the large companies) taking die drawings from small firms and giving them to Chinese companies to manufacture. This is done to reduce the costs of the large firms, but it renders the small companies uncompetitive.

Skill Formation and Technological Development

In the 1990s, recession and unemployment rates in the Japanese economy rose rapidly. There was also a shortage of skilled workers. Even big companies that had their own training systems faced a shortage of skilled workers. The following decade saw a shortage of engineers and workers in Japan.

Asai (2002) defines technology as a system of knowledge on the basis of science. It can be formulated by numerical values, letters and figures, and can be transmitted to others easily. On the other hand, skill is a practice formed or learnt through experience, is embedded in an individual and is more difficult to transmit to others.

A manufacturing process goes through six stages: development, design, industrial engineering, production management, maintenance, operation. Both technology and skills are required at all six stages (Ogawa 1996). First, firms develop new products on the basis of their accumulated research, marketing and the strategy of companies. Designing depends not only on technology but also on management. Second, designing new products requires broader knowledge. Engineers who have a high educational background play an important role in the process of development and design. As the life-cycle of products is becoming short, new products become obsolete very quickly. It is then the responsibility of the designer to supply high-quality products at low costs, quickly, to meet the changing demand.

Third, industrial engineering, consisting of operators, machinery, tools, materials, works in process, inventories of products and transfer systems, helps to improve the efficiency of the production process. Process design, which decides the method of production, is important at this stage. Fourth, production management aims to control quality, supply products before deadlines and maintain production costs below targets. Fifth, maintenance is important for operations to run smoothly; while problems with equipment should be solved immediately, the repair of equipment is becoming more difficult as technology develops. Six, all operations need a good combination of technology and skill. If a company wants to supply its products to a niche market, the volume of production would be low and so it would use labour-intensive technology or adopt outsourcing, both of which reduce costs. Conventional machines require the skills of workers for precise processing. If a company introduces sophisticated machinery, the workers must have basic technological knowledge of the machines.

Technology can substitute for skill. Information technology (IT) has changed skill formation dramatically. Since the spread of computer-aided design (CAD), computer-aided manufacturing (CAM), computer-aided engineering (CAE) and computer numerical control (CNC) machines in developing countries, firms there have been able to catch up with firms in the developed countries. CAD made it possible to draw using personal computers. CAM and CNC machines rendered sophisticated processes easy. CAE made it possible to analyse products without tests and trial production. IT made it possible to fill the gap in skills between developing and developed countries. As a result, Korea, China and Thailand started to export dies and moulds to Japan, although they continue to import sophisticated dies and moulds from Japan. Improvement of technology also facilitates the development of more sophisticated products. To produce more sophisticated products, higher levels of skill are necessary. However, technology cannot cover all aspects of skill. Skill needs to be developed with technology. The Government Report of Japan points out what kind of skills are necessary in small and medium enterprises in the following industries (The Small and Medium Enterprise Agency 2000).

Casting and Moulding

This process, which depended on manual work, has been automated as a result of mechanization and the introduction of IT during the 1980s. Programming skills to operate the new machinery and to process designs that were appropriate for new technology became a necessity. During the 1990s, the development of simulation software helped pattern production, which needed sophisticated skills. This included insight into the whole process, including indication of pattern production, ability to judge the kind of additive to be mixed, and materials to be added to the pattern when melted. Depending on the melted material components, maintaining the temperature became a necessary skill.

Forging

During the 1970s, the forging tool changed from the hammer to the press. This led to the replacement of technology by human skills. Development of machinery made it easy to process materials like aluminum, which were earlier difficult to process. However, skills remained necessary and essential to process the complicated shapes at the final stage of the process, and broader knowledge of technology became essential for the worker.

Cutting and Grinding

Before the 1970s, basic skill was defined as the ability to process products by conventional machines on the basis of drawings. After the spread of numeric control (NC) machines, the skill required was the ability to develop the programme to operate the NC machine for a particular operation. In the 1980s, with the entry of CNC, CAD and CAM machines, there was further diffusion of technology, and the level of precision became much higher. This, in turn, required higher skills.

The Government Report argues that as technology develops, necessary skills also change. At the present technological levels, this would mean that a skilled worker should have broader knowledge and be familiar with IT. The old skills accumulated from conventional machines are still useful in small and medium enterprises for some companies continue to use only conventional machines. It needs to be noted that skill cannot be mechanized, and that both skill and experience are essential to develop new technology and to solve problems.

Skill Formation in Small and Medium Firms

As in India, the small and medium-sized firms in Japan operate both conventional simple lathe machines and computer numeric control (CNC) machines, to undertake production, processing or development of prototype products. Most companies use a mix of conventional and CNC machines. If the volumes are low, firms prefer to use conventional machines since the costs can be reduced. All the firms emphasized that skill acquisition and training are essential for their workers, but every firm had its own policy and approach.

Skill Certification

Some of the firms that we visited had a policy of skill certification for their workers. This meant that when the workers joined the company, they had to fulfil a condition of continuing with their studies and getting skill certificates. It took about three years to obtain a secondary certificate and nearly ten years to obtain a main certificate. The certificate helped the worker to get a wage rise and boosted his self-confidence. In many of the companies, workers had skill certificates which they had attained through on-the-job training and studying books. However, there were some that did not believe in encouraging their workers to obtain skill certificates; instead, they had their own internal tests which the workers had to pass in order to receive better wages.

Training Manual

Firms had different strategies or policies for training their workers. Some of them had developed a manual, so that there was continuous training of their workers and upgradation of their skills. To train workers, the companies followed three principles of production control, called QCD (quality control, cost-effectiveness and meeting deadlines). In some companies with both manual and CNC lathe machines, it was necessary to ensure that the workers were initially trained in the manual machines and then moved on to the CNC. This helped them acquire skills in both, which was very helpful especially in the die development, a critical process. In die development, 70 per cent of the processing was done on CNC machines and 30 per cent on manual lathe machines.

In another company, there was a clear manpower planning programme with four standards called ILUO, where I stood for 'beginner', L for 'worker can manage', U for 'independent', and O for 'capable of teaching somebody'. The management insisted that the workers move across the ILUO grades over a specified period of time. The manpower upgrading programme encouraged competition among the workers. All the employees needed to have knowledge of computers. The university graduates among them took about six months to get trained. The training was conducted with the help of manuals and experienced workers. All workers were encouraged to obtain authorization-of-skill certificates, both primary and secondary. The contract workers employed were also provided training and given manuals. According to the company, it is very essential to impart training especially to workers who are hired for semi-conductor assembling.

On-the-Job Training

Company U provided only on-the-job training to its employees. When new recruits were taken, they were initially given training in different sections of the company for short periods of time. In each department, the workers underwent training under a senior, experienced worker who supervised and taught them. The transfer of skills was largely possible because of the age composition of the workers, which ranged between 20 to 50 years. As the workers of the drawing department were trained in the workshop department, it gave them sound knowledge of the machines, and helped them use this skill and experience to make drawings.

Another company had a policy wherein all workers who joined newly had to go though training in scraping (Kisage). 'Kisage' is a scraping tool, used in all machine-tool factories, with which the metal product is scraped in the finishing stage. The training is largely on-the-job and the skill attained is valued very highly in the industry.

In some of the companies, initial training was given on CNC lathe machines and the workers were then moved to manual lathe machines. These were companies that had a combination of manual and CNC lathes. However, not all firms were able to train their workers in both CNC and conventional lathes.

In Company V, new employees were trained for three months before the company decided whether to hire them or not. After about a year, the firm asked the employee whether he would continue to stay there or leave the job. If the worker was good with programming, he was appointed in the CNC and machining centre. If he was good at processing and enjoyed his job, he was appointed to grinding operations on a CNC grinding machine. Grinding was considered a very important process that required special skills for the worker was required to judge the finishing and have a feel for the product.

Firms also gave a lot of emphasis to the rotation of workers across various jobs so that they were multi-skilled. Workers in the drawing department had to get experience in the workshop so as to be able to make good drawings with fewer defects. There was an effort in a number of companies to document the know-how of workers and bring it out as manuals. They were also trying to document the skills of workers and how to transfer such skills.

According to one firm owner, the most important aspect of manufacturing is failure, which actually leads to more learning. A number of owner–managers mentioned that many workers had developed their skills on-the-job and learnt by making mistakes. One of the companies had a policy of allocating the development of a product both the programme and the process, to a single worker. If there was any problem or clarifications that were needed, the worker dealt with the customer directly. Similarly, if there were any defects in the drawing, he consulted with the customer to improve the drawing. This strategy helped the worker to attain skills and also experience in dealing with customers. A long career in conventional machinery was very important, and a combination of low technology (manual machines) and high technology (CNC lathes) was needed to manufacture high-class precision products.

Training Centre

The Ota Industrial Association has a training centre to which many of the companies sent their new workers for training. The basic skill and knowledge to undertake simple processing on conventional machines can be acquired in one year here, and if the workers trained for four to five years, they became skilled workers. In the case of finishing a die or a drawing, a worker took five to ten years to gain experience and become a skilled worker. In the case of CNC lathes and machines, it took only about five years. The skill required for CNC lathes was that of programming and pressing the button, in which the workers can be relatively easily trained.

With regard to programming and operating CNC lathe machines, a single person can ideally perform both operations, but this would lead to loss of time and be inefficient. So, from the productivity and efficiency point of view, it is better if these operations are specialized. There were no strict rules, and workers were free to make their choice about what they wanted to do: programming or undertaking an operation. This did not mean that there was no need for skill, only that the way skill was defined was different.

For example, if the material undergoes a change, the production process also changes and the maintenance of temperature becomes important, especially for maintaining the curves during grinding. The programming then needs changing and so too the operational method. Conventional manual machines can be handled only by skilled workers, but CNC machines can be handled by anybody. Knowledge of the operation and programming is most important, and this can be gained through experience. In conventional machines, overall knowledge about the machine, tools, dies, components, processing and finishing is very important, which is probably not the same with CNC.

Problems of Transferring Skills

Acquisition and transfer of skills in the small and medium-sized firms to a large extent depended upon the financial position of the firm, the proportion of senior and junior workers operating conventional machines, and the policy adopted by the firm. To operate conventional machines, certain specific skills were essential which could be transferred only if the company had both senior and junior employees. The evidence was, however, mixed. In most of the companies, senior employees operated conventional machines and junior employees operated CNC machines. The skills required for conventional machines were not transferred from senior to junior employees due to the restriction of time in many companies, while in some there was such a transfer of skills. The training programme within the firm facilitated smooth transfer of skills to young workers.

The small companies faced a problem with the transfer of skills to the younger generation on manual lathe machines, while this was not a problem on CNC machines. For the manual lathe machines, both time and labour are required, which the small firms could not afford. The CNC was developed in Japan to undertake processes that both skilled workers and unskilled workers can perform. Part of the skill of using a manual lathe has been absorbed by the new CNC technology. Earlier, a skilled worker did each operation manually, which meant different kinds of skills were needed. But with CNC, all the operations are done on one machine without any knowledge of the skills required for a manual lathe. Therefore, increasingly, these skills are no longer taught to the workers.

Transfer of skills also means stoppage of the production process and a loss for the company, and many of these companies could not afford it. In the case of Company W, they required both CNC and conventional machines as CNC could not produce the complete range of products. Conventional manual machines operated by skilled workers are essential for certain products, and also help in attaining precision. In this company, the skill to manufacture with manual machines lay largely with the older workers, and this skill was not transferred to the young workers. To train workers on a manual machine, the trainer and trainee would be engaged on a machine which could not then be used for manufacture. Since many of the companies can no longer afford this, they are in a dilemma about how to train the younger workers.

To gain skills is very tough; both the teaching and the learning take time. For example, in one of the companies that we visited, a worker who had a skill certificate participated in a Skill Olympic contest in which he was asked to manufacture a product, but he failed. The reason for the failure was that the worker had concentrated on programming skills, at the expense of skills that had to be learnt from other operations. This shows that for a skill to improve, it is essential to have knowledge and experience of all other tasks.

Lessons Learnt

Our analysis of the Japanese labour market shows its increasing flexibility as large firms moved out to Southeast Asian countries and China. The hollowing-out of large firms from the economy also led to weakening of the Keiretsu, which were a large support for the small firms. The small firms that could raise the required capital moved out along with the large firms, while the remaining firms either closed down or adopted different strategies of survival.

One of the strategies adopted by the firms that remained in Japan was to upgrade the technology and skill levels of their workers. This helped them enter certain niche activities where they both developed products for the large firms and innovated. This was possible largely because of the skills attained by the workers over the years, allowing the firms to manufacture sophisticated machinery parts or components, or even change the jigs, fixtures or dies in an assembly line. Firms that did not have such skills tried to attain them, to survive in the market.

The second lesson learnt in Japan was the skill formation process itself, where a lot of emphasis was given to working on the shop floor to gain knowledge about the component or the process before the workers moved into their defined tasks of drawing or designing. The importance attached to working on the shop floor, irrespective of qualifications, is an aspect that could benefit firms in India. The Indian companies lacked this practice, as engineers or highly qualified personnel did not think highly of skills at the workshop level. This practice of gaining knowledge on the shop floor would help the workers to gain skills in different departments, help in improving the quality and provide opportunities for innovation.

In spite of the good skill-training practices in Japan, some of the Japanese small firms are liable to face problems in the future, as has been presented in the case studies. First, the younger generation does not want to take on the responsibility of succession as the market risks are too high. Second, there is the problem related to the transfer of skills from the older generation to the younger generation. Japan was known for the skill formation process in which skills were transferred from old to young workers, as the age-gap was small. Skill transfers also took place across firms through interactions and development of products. With the hollowing-out of large firms, skill transfers across firms declined drastically; and, within small firms, skill transfers are becoming difficult because of the age-gap between old and young workers. That apart, the firms do not have the time or machines to spare with which a worker can learn these skills. The third problem is related to the quality of the work force in the small firms. Earlier, under the Keiretsu, the cream of high-school graduates would join the large firms, learn the skills and gain experience. But now, most of them are moving towards higher education and university degrees, and only the average students join the small manufacturing firms. The absorptive capacity of these workers is low. It takes a lot of effort and time to train such students, and it is also difficult for the small firms to spare experienced workers to train them.

The third lesson to be learnt is that of the technology and skill transfer of Japanese firms investing in India. The technology that was brought in from Japan was probably not the best, but even with such technology, the firms were able to penetrate the market. There was an attempt towards technical collaboration, which was much more beneficial to the firms in India. As far as skills were concerned, the firms were unable to follow the systems used in Japan due to the size of the firm and lack of technical personnel. The Japanese collaborative firms in India tried to put management systems in place, but it took time because of the existing systems and culture in the local economy.

There was also a lack of commitment of the workers to the firm, as observed in two of the cases of joint-venture collaborations in India, which worked negatively towards the functioning of the firm and the maintenance of quality. It reduced trust and enthusiasm on the part of the employer towards the worker. Due to this, it became difficult for firms to accumulate knowledge within the firm, which would help in research, development and innovations.

CHAPTER EIGHT

The Challenge of Skills and Technology

Labour and small enterprises in India are facing a challenge to remain afloat or competitive in the current context of globalization. In this book we present the story of two axes along which they are struggling to face the challenge: improving education or skills, and technology. We argue that rising skill premiums in Indian industry are due to the widespread entry of skill-biased technological change. The choice before labour is to improve skills or be fired. For small enterprises, the challenge is to upgrade technology or become uncompetitive. Therefore, better skills and technology appear to be the only life-line for labour and small enterprises in the current economic environment. This final chapter, while summarizing the main findings of the book, also attempts to focus on the options facing the policy-maker if he wishes to foster inclusive growth in the years to come. The policy options we deal with are only those that directly flow from our analysis in the book.

Higher Education in a Globalizing Society

Debate on the role of education in a developing society has thrown up two perspectives. One is a broad, liberal vision of education that Krishna Kumar (2008) argues for, which helps in the creation of a democratic and transformative space for all people in our national development. This liberal education is expected to increase curiosity and the imagination, and is associated with the humanities, arts and literature. It is supposed to produce good citizens learning to ask searching questions, and reject shoddy historical arguments. Such an education is also expected to create more original and creative thinking in both the arts and sciences. In fact, it is exactly what a developed country at the cutting edge of research and technology expects of its educational system.

The second is a more materialistic view of higher education intended to produce skilled workers fit to undertake the jobs being created in the economy. Such skilled workers perform repetitive and imitative jobs efficiently, and are useful in an economy that is growing rapidly with mass production and service industries. Increasingly, the emphasis in education today is towards vocationalization and skill development in an effort to fill the 'skill gap' perceived by industry.

Higher education has been a neglected field in both research and policy. In the economics literature, growth and distribution of physical capital was central to the debate on economic development, while human capital received attention since the early twentieth century. An influential strand in this literature showed that the returns to education were negatively related to levels of education, that social and individual returns to elementary education were the highest (Schultz 1988; Psacharopoulos 1994). This had the direct policy effect of tilting the limited resources in countries towards investment in elementary education, to the neglect of higher education.

Recently, however, several studies have noted increasing returns to levels of education or a collapse of the returns on primary school in African and Asian countries (Moll 1996; Kingdon and Unni 2001). More recent analysis at the Asian Development Bank also notes increasing returns to levels of education in four countries in Asia – India, Indonesia, the Philippines and Thailand – during the early 1990s and mid-2000 (ADB 2007). An even more interesting result of this study was that the levels above higher secondary and post-secondary education showed increasing returns this decade. Across industry groups, the returns to educated workers in the tertiary sector were the highest and also rose the fastest. The advantage of investing in higher education is now more apparent to both the individual and policy-maker.

Another reason to foster higher education of the broader variety is that the technological spill-overs from research in the developed countries are on the decline. For example, while crop research in the developed countries has shifted from improvement in yields to the appearance of crops and environmental effects, developing countries like India still require research on improving yields in semi-arid conditions (Kapur and Crowley 2007). Similarly, medicine-related research in the developed countries no longer focus on infectious and other diseases that are still rampant in developing countries.

With all the changes in the current economic scenario, higher education is finally back on the agenda of researchers and policy-makers in developed and developing countries. However, the debate on whether a more liberal education or a materialistic short-term one is most relevant today continues. It is increasingly argued that there is a skill gap or a mismatch between the demand and supply of skilled workers, which might soon act as a constraint to growth in the Asian region, particularly India.

Technology and Skills in a Globalizing Society

Solow's model of growth theory brought out the importance of technical change by acknowledging the heterogeneity of labour in terms of observable and non-observable characteristics such as skills, dexterity, adaptability and motivation. The measurement issue with regard to the skills of workers was acknowledged. Endogenous growth theory took this further and technology was considered an endogenous variable (see Chapter One). Capital accumulation consisting of both physical and human capital occurred mainly through 'learning by doing'. Technology therefore clearly included accumulation of skills. In the globalizing world of today, heterogeneity of labour inputs plays a decisive role. Besides the theoretical progress in the growth literature, the real world is also taking note of the development of the 'knowledge economy'.

Pandit and Siddharthan (2008) refer to two types of technology and technology transfer. Technology transfer between and within firms, often through foreign equity, mainly involves tacit technology that is not codified and may still be evolving, and it may transfer other forms of tacit technology such as brand name, goodwill and managerial practices. Such technology is more compatible with the growth of an indigenous skilled work force at the firm level. A second type of technology is what is termed arms-length technology, and its transfer could occur through import of technology. Such technology is likely to be codified and standardized, and transferred between firms through designs and drawings.

Pandit and Siddharthan conducted a cross-section study of large enterprises in thirty-three manufacturing industries in India using proxies for these two types of technology and skilled labour. They found that industries using the first type were more likely to have a positive employment growth. Enterprises undertaking modernization through intra-firm technology imports and product differentiation by using a more skilled work force experienced higher growth of employment.

In our study of the autocomponents industry, we focus on the first type of technology at the firm level. The point we would like to make is that development of skills at the micro level is linked to the technology used. If skill is a measure of productivity, then the productivity of workers is implicitly linked to the technology they use and therefore the two, skills and technology, are closely linked.

Definitions and Measurement of Skills and Technology

One of the problems encountered in an empirical study of skills and technology is the issue of measurement. Measurement of the levels of skills of workers and technology used by firms, in turn, hinges on the definitions used. When we attempted to examine the issues of changing skills of the work force and technology in the economy at various levels of disaggregation, we noted that there was no one definition that could be employed at both the macro and micro levels. A key contribution of this book is a definition of skill and technology at the two levels. At the risk of repetition, we discuss below the definitions we evolved and used in this study.

Measurement of Skills

Autor *et al.* (2001) categorize the literature on the demand for skill into two. The first strand analyses shifts in the demand for skills from trends in occupation, education and gender composition of employment. These characteristics constitute macro definitions of skills and are useful to study long-term trends in the skill content of the work force. The second strand empirically tests the complementarities between technological change and workers' learning and problem-solving capabilities at the individual and organizational level. Such a definition is what we have evolved at the micro level with information from the owner–managers of enterprises.

Macro definitions of skill

At the aggregate macro level, the literature in labour economics uses two methods to identify skill. One uses the international occupational classification which gives the broad categories of non-production workers and production workers. The non-production workers including professional, managerial and administrative, clerical and sales workers, are better skilled. Among them, managerial and professional workers can be considered to have the highest levels of skill. The production workers consist of workers engaged in manual and non-manual production, and service activities including construction. These workers can also be further divided into unskilled and skilled workers depending on their position as supervisors, and depending on whether they conduct activities manually or with the use of machines.

The second method of identifying the skill level of a worker is based on the level of education. This method assumes that the completed level of education is used by the employer as a screening device to identify skills. Those with education above high school diplomas and college degrees may be treated as skilled workers. Persons with schooling above middle school could constitute semi-skilled workers, and illiterate and primary school-level workers as unskilled.

Each of these methods of identifying the skill of a worker has its own problems. The occupational classification is a broad method of classifying workers by what they do. It does not indicate whether the worker was actually trained to do the job, and assumes that the workers engaged in an activity were either formally trained or acquired training through experience. This method cannot differentiate between persons who are good at a particular job or bad at it, or the actual skills acquired by such workers.

Definition by level of education is problematic because of the large proportion of illiterate workers in India. It would be inaccurate to assume that all illiterate workers are unskilled. These workers have various forms of skills acquired through informal training and experience, such as traditional handloom workers. The case of the autocomponents industry discussed in the book clearly brings out that there is no one-to-one association between formal schooling and the skills defined by employers.

Micro definitions of skill

Autor *et al.* (2001) define five levels of skills using the *Handbook of Analysing Jobs*, Department of Labor, US. These are:

1. Routine manual tasks: ability to move fingers and manipulate small objects with fingers rapidly and accurately.
2. Non-routine manual tasks: ability to move hand and foot coordinately with each other in accordance with visual stimuli.
3. Routine cognitive tasks: adaptability to situations requiring the precise attainment of set limits, tolerance or standards.
4. Non-routine cognitive/interactive tasks: adaptability to accepting responsibility for the direction, control or planning of an activity.
5. Non-routine cognitive/analytical tasks: general educational level and mathematics.

In our discussions with the owner–managers of small enterprises in the autocomponents industry on defining skilled, semi-skilled and unskilled production workers, many dimensions of these broad indicators were observed. The entrepreneurs and managers drew a clear link between the skills of workers and the technology used. We present below the definitions of skills of production workers using conventional production technologies for undertaking different processes.

Skilled worker. A 'skilled' worker was capable of doing a 'job' as per specifications without any support, had knowledge of the machine/processes, could study the drawing/formulae, had knowledge of the tolerance levels/limits, could read the symbols, knew how to use the measuring instruments, and was able to produce the product as per the given specifications and within the tolerance limits specified. This is similar to 'routine cognitive tasks' or skill level 3.

Semi-skilled worker. A semi-skilled worker was one who had to be trained in every job and the machine/instrument had to be set for him before he could undertake the process. He possessed the skill to measure the components/compounds with different measuring instruments. This is broadly 'non-routine manual tasks' or skill level 2.

Unskilled worker. An 'unskilled worker' was defined as a helper who could undertake rough operations once the machine/instrument was set and the tools/chemicals were ready. This is broadly 'routine manual tasks' or skill level 1.

The higher levels of skill, 4 and 5, defined by Autor *et al.* (2001) as 'non-routine cognitive/interactive tasks' and 'non-routine cognitive/analytical tasks' relate mainly non-production workers at the level of managers (skill level 4) and professionals (skill 5).

Measurement of Technology

As in the case of defining the skills of workers, the usefulness of a macro definition and measure of level of technology is to analyse long-term trends, and that of a micro definition to study its complementarity with the skills of workers at an individual or organizational level.

Macro definition of technology

One measure is the growth of total factor productivity (TFPG), which is the difference between the growth rate in value added and a weighted sum of growth rates of capital and labour, and is estimated for the manufacturing sector using the growth accounting technique. TFP growth is a residual productivity growth and includes the effects of technological change, better utilization of capacities, skills and organization. Therefore it measures technological change in a broader sense than just the physical technology.

A second measure of technical change used in this book is based on the relative wage bills for skilled and unskilled workers. The assumption is that wages are directly related to the productivity of the worker, which is also dependent on the use of technology. That is, when skilled workers are paid more, or there is an increase of skilled workers in the industry, this is due to an increase in the productivity of skilled workers which occurs due to a change in technology.

Other measures of technology used in the literature, particularly when analysing large enterprise or aggregate industry-level data, are technology purchase, percentage of expenditure on R&D, participation in foreign equity and discounted value of capital.

Micro definition of technology

A standard measure of the level of technology in a firm is the value of investments in plant and machinery. The micro definition of technology that we developed from discussions with the owner–managers of enterprises was, like the micro definition of skill, a combination of technology and the skill capacity of the entrepreneur/worker.

Two measures were developed at the micro level: a technology index as a measure of the level of technology used in the enterprise, and the technological capacity of the workers in the firm as a measure of the technical capability of the firm.

The technology index was computed taking into consideration three criteria: the type of machine – manual, semi-automatic, automatic, programme logit control (PLC), numeric control (NC), computer numeric control (CNC); whether the machine is new or second-hand; and whether the machine is made locally or imported. For each firm or enterprise, the values of these three variables were summed up to arrive at a technology index. A higher technology index meant better technological capability of the firm both for innovation and expansion.

The *technical capability of the firm* was the skill embodied in a worker or owner–manager that helped to improve the technical capability of the firm.

Why are Skills at a Premium in the Globalized Economy?

It is more or less universally agreed that most countries, including India, have seen a rise in their skilled work force, however defined. In the first chapter, we put forth six hypotheses prevalent in the literature to explain why the countries of the world have seen a rise in skilled work force and a premium on their wages. The first hypothesis, put forth by trade economists, is that trade liberalization through factor endowments is the main source of the increasing gap between wages of skilled and unskilled workers. The second hypothesis rejects the trade-related hypothesis and argues that skill-biased technological change is the main reason for rising skill premiums. The third hypothesis combines the trade and skill–technology hypotheses to argue that innovations that replace skilled for unskilled workers occur only in some countries where, for example, trade liberalization induces their adoption. Hence trade patterns and technology adoption jointly determine skill premiums. The fourth hypothesis points to global outsourcing and domestic production-sharing, leading to inflow of technology to small firms in developing countries. This leads to continuous upgrading of skills and rising skill premiums. The fifth hypothesis is a micro understanding of the impact of quality upgrading of firms to remain competitive within globalized production processes. This leads to adoption of improved technologies as well as upgrading of skills of workers, and results in rising wage premiums. The sixth hypothesis is a micro understanding of why individual investments in education and skills in response to the rising returns to skilled workers further enhance skill premiums. This book has made the effort to empirically test some of these hypotheses. We do not accept the purely trade-related argument, the first hypothesis, and hence do not attempt to test it empirically. The sixth hypothesis of individual investments in education and skills is not the theme of this book and therefore is not tested either.

We tested the skill-biased technological change hypothesis (second hypothesis) using a simple framework (Chapter Three). Skills were measured by level of education and technology was measured by the relative wage bills. The services sector had greater technical change, and rise in skilled workers and skill premiums. This fact was corroborated by an interesting result in a study by Papola (2005), that the relative productivity in services vis-à-vis industry was exceptionally high and rising in India, as compared to other Asian countries. Technical change and rising skill premiums were more likely to occur in activities that engaged mainly male compared to female workers, regular salaried compared to casual workers, and workers in urban compared to rural areas. Intuitively, each of these segments of the work force (male, regular salaried and urban workers) appear to have had the benefits of higher skill training and use of technology, and consequently enjoyed rising wage premiums.

We extended the analysis to test for the combined trade and technology-related hypothesis (third hypothesis, in Chapter Four). We classified manufacturing industries into trade categories that were export-promoting, import-substituting, and those that shifted from export-promoting to import-substituting categories or vice-versa, over the decade of the 1990s and early 2000s. The impact of trade liberalization on inflow of technology, rise in skilled workers and skill premiums was noted to be most prominent in the export-oriented industries. This could imply that these industries were better poised to take advantage of the trade liberalization measures. Within the export-oriented industries, it was mainly the male workers who gained from the process of trade liberalization and rising wage premiums. The only export-oriented industry group where women seemed to have benefited was the wearing apparels or garment industry. The skill premiums of women were enhanced mainly among the production workers.

A recent study using the latest National Sample Survey data on Employment and Unemployment argued that there was no evidence of skill-biased technological change and that skill premiums rose mainly due to differential growth patterns across industries (Abraham 2007). The evidence presented was the growing wage differentials within educational categories such as secondary school or above, and not between the educational categories. We reject this thesis on the ground of what we described earlier as the limitations of the measurement of skills by levels of education. The micro definition of skill also points to this limitation by arguing that in developing economies, even with low levels of education certain highly specialized technical skills can be attained.

The widening inequality within the top educational category of 'above graduation' actually indicates a wide variation in skills within the group. Persons educated above graduation have differences in levels of qualification and in the quality of education: for example, business management graduates from Indian Institutes of Management (IIMs) versus other schools of management, or engineers from Indian Institutes of Technology (IITs) versus other engineering or technical schools. Graduates from renowned schools are at a premium not merely because of their skills, but also because their wages and productivity are higher from being employed in enterprises using higher technology. Arguably, these widening wage disparities within the higher educational categories are evidence of increasing wage premiums for skilled workers. The widening wage inequalities within the services sector may also be evidence of differences in the skill content or skill intensity within these industries, and not just due to faster growth of the industry. In our view, these recent macro data provide further evidence of skill-biased technological change. These changes may or may not be caused by the trade liberalization process in the economy.

The fourth hypothesis about global and local production linkages was framed in the literature we reviewed (Chapter One) as a macro hypothesis. Though we did not formally test it, we discussed the impact of sub-contracting linkages between large firms, both foreign and Indian, and small firms in the autocomponents industry on fostering technical change and increasing skill levels of workers at the micro level of the firm (Chapter Five). We documented various cases of such linkages with large or parent firms helping small firms to improve technology, as defined at the micro level through a technology index and the technical capability of the firm. We observed that in the Chennai and Pune regions, much of the improvements in production processes occurred through the help of parent firms which encouraged transfer of skills and technology to the sub-contracting firms. The inflow of new technology into the small firms also led to the transfer of skills to the workers employed by them. A simple model of the determinants of growth of small firms was tested, where we found that sub-contracting linkage, measured by whether the firm received any support from the parent firm to improve technology or its skill base, was the most significant positive variable.

The experience of joint-venture firms with Japanese collaboration showed that the Japanese parent firms transferred technology to the Indian firms, though not necessarily the best technology. The Japanese parent firms hired workers in the Indian firms with minimum qualifications and made a lot of effort to train them on-the-job. A number of workers and engineers were also sent to Japan for training in the parent firm. These joint-venture firms, however, felt that there were limits to the upward mobility of skilled workers in India due to the rather inflexible and hierarchical structures which prevented a supervisor on the shop floor from becoming a manager. However, the cases of Indian small firms and Japanese joint-venture firms showed that the production linkages between large and small firms, which helped to improve technology and skills at the firm level, was definitely an important way in which small firms could grow in the current competitive environment.

The fifth hypothesis was a micro understanding of the role of the firm in quality upgrading through improved technologies leading to increased skill intensity and rising wage premiums for skilled workers. This process was partly documented in Chapter Five as part of the linkages with large firms. We further discussed the process of upgrading of technology in the firms, which sometimes did lead to deskilling of workers but mainly resulted in improved skill intensity (Chapter Six). The quality upgrading of firms often occurred due to an increase in demand in an expanding market. The firms obtained new machines that were of better technology and capable of undertaking a number of tasks in order to meet the new demand. Either the old workers were trained to operate these new machines, or new/ better skilled workers were hired. Quality upgrading of firms also occurred through improving existing machines or new technology, and this helped to improve the production process, prevented rejections, improved the quality of the product and improved the productivity of the workers.

Overall, the macro and micro empirical data presented here argue in favour of both the trade and skill–technology explanations for the rising skill base of the work force and consequent rise in skill premiums. However, we do present macro and micro evidence of the increasing contractual and casual nature of employment as a result of which most of the workers do not receive social security benefits like ESI, Provident Fund or medical benefits. In fact, with the increasing competitive nature of the manufacturing sector, the only benefit that the workers seem to be gaining is in the form of on-the-job training and rotation of work. This helps them to attain new skills and perhaps subsidizes the production costs of the entrepreneurs. The inflow of new technologies in the trade-liberalized regime, therefore, helps the workers to improve their skills and employability, while the firms gain through improved productivity. There is no doubt that the skilled workers or workers who are trainable gain in this context of growth of a competitive market, in terms of a rise in wage premiums. However, with a large proportion of workers having little formal education or skill training, and a large proportion of children and youth out of school, the issue of how to improve the security of these current and future workers remains a major policy question.

Lessons from Japan

The Japanese model of export-led growth set a trend in the early 1960s and was followed by most of the Southeast Asian countries. This model was laudable in that the benefit of the growth was transferred to the workers through improved wages and employment opportunities. The other interesting feature was the inter-linkages between large and small firms through sub-contracting arrangements in the manufacturing sector, which involved both transfer of technology and upgrading of the skills of workers in the small firms. The Japanese labour market of that period was known for lifelong employment and there was continuous upgrading of skills. The model, however, began to collapse in the mid-1980s as other economies grew and became capable of producing at lower costs using similar systems (Chapter Seven).

The original Japanese model followed the Keiretsu system, where long-term sub-contracting relationships were developed between large and small firms in a production chain. Transfer of technology and skills was established through these chains. However, with the recession in the economy during the early 1990s, many companies moved base to Southeast Asian countries and, more recently, to China, where labour was cheaper. One of the strategies adopted by the firms that remained in Japan was to enter into certain niche markets with the help of better technology and workers' skills. This was possible because of the experience and skills attained by the workers over the years.

A lesson to be learned from Japan is the process of skill formation on the shop floor. The old Keiretsu system of skill-training on the shop floor allowed young school graduates to attain skills on-the-job and to accumulate various skills in the process. In India, too, as we noted in the case study of the autocomponents industry, on-the-job training is one of the main ways in which the skills of workers are enhanced in small and informal enterprises. However, there are limits to the possibility of upgrading the skill of workers in larger firms, which was clearly brought out by the case of

Japanese joint-venture firms. These relate to the low educational level of workers at the entry level, which sometimes does not equip them to read the drawings and instructions. However, despite this limitation the workers were trained on-the-job in the joint-venture firms, and also sent abroad for improving their skills and gaining technical knowledge. The firms tried to incorporate better skill-training modules and methods to improve the skills of the workers. An important lesson to be learnt from the Japanese experience is the movement of workers from production to non-production cadre. The hierarchical nature of labour markets in India prevents skilled workers on the shop floor to graduate to the next level of a manager. This has an impact on the working culture within the organization, and also reduces the motivation of workers towards new learning techniques.

The strategy adopted by Japanese firms to continue production in Japan in certain niche markets highlights the importance given to research and development even by small firms. It was investment both in technological and skill accumulation that allowed them to diversify into different products, using a mix of simple and sophisticated machines. In the present competitive environment where the production base keeps shifting across regions in search of low labour costs, such specialized investments allow firms to exist rather than close down.

Another important lesson from the point of view of the worker and ensuring quality within the enterprise could be the skill certification process practised by Japanese small enterprises. This could be in addition to the vocational training method that already exists in India. The Japanese manpower planning programme with four standards, ILUO, which is followed as a skill training matrix in large firms in India, could also be introduced in small firms.

The Japanese experience of networking and providing support to small enterprises in terms of sharing equipment or information from industrial associations could also be adopted. Networks do exist in India in the form of local industry associations, Chambers of Commerce, etc., but they need to be made functional and more integrated with the changing scenario.

Lessons for Policy-Making
Definitions and Statistics for Skills and Technology

In the new competitive era, skills and technology are the engines of growth in the economy. In such a situation, it is important to have an assessment of the skill and technology levels that exist in individuals/firms, industries and the country at large. It is with this view that we discuss the need for definitions and data collection on these issues.

Skills

At the policy level, in many countries, there has been a debate on the definition of skills. This is particularly important in countries that attempt to provide vocational or skill training to its youth in schools or those who have passed out of schools. In the early 1950s and 60s skill was easily defined, based on the activities undertaken in the manufacturing sector, in terms of the manual dexterity and technical know-how of a shop floor worker, or the academic skills of a scientist or engineer. In recent years, with the increasing share of the services and retail sectors, 'skill' has acquired a broader meaning to include 'softer' skills such as personal and social skills to communicate with people and work in a team.

There is no established definition for skill or technology in the statistical systems of our country. The recent NSS Surveys of Employment and Unemployment (55th and 61st Rounds) define workers with thirty to thirty-five specific skills, such as driver, electrician, computer programmer, etc., as skilled workers. These specific skills do not cover many of the specialized production activities undertaken even within the manufacturing sector. The percentage of skilled workers so arrived at is a truncated one, and a small percentage of workers are found to have such skills. Persons with skill were also measured by the formal and informal institutions through which training is acquired, which again led to a very low proportion of workers reporting themselves to be skilled.

In developing countries like India, nearly half the work force has education levels below primary schooling. Further, as we observed in the autocomponents industry, the most common method of skill training is on-the-job. Under such conditions, it is important to have some assessment of the skill content of the work force. A large majority of the workers possess some traditional skills imbibed through household occupations or training from family members, neighbours and friends.

In order to assess the level and nature of skills possessed by the population, and devise a more inclusive skill-training programme, it is important to produce a more accurate data-base on skill. The starting point for such an exercise is to devise a definition of skill, which has to take into account the micro context of skill formation. In this book we have suggested a micro definition of skill for data collection purposes. This micro definition is sector and product-based. As mentioned earlier, the skill spread would increase if one takes into consideration a whole range of sectors and activities. This provides a starting point to get into a discussion on what constitutes skills when a large proportion of workers have low levels of education but have skills acquired on-the-job. An expert group needs to be constituted, consisting of people from various industries, to arrive at a workable definition of skill. The NSS could then commission some methodological studies to test this definition.

Technology

A similar dilemma exists with respect to technology. Technology was earlier defined to include only value of plant and machinery. Total factor productivity is a black box that includes everything but capital and labour: labour skills, learning-by-doing, capacity utilization and scale economies (Bhavani 2002).

The growing literature on innovations, learning-by-using and learning-by-doing has resulted in a wider definition of technology. Technology includes the physical processes of transformation of input to output, the organizational methods that structure this process, and the information flows required to carry out this process (Bhavani 2002). However, a strict definition is still elusive. 'Technology' can refer to material objects of use to humanity, such as machines, but can also encompass broader themes, such as methods of organization and techniques.

The micro definition of technology used in this book allows one to develop a technology index taking into consideration various parameters like the machine used, innovations made and the capability of workers to fabricate machines, which is much more comprehensive and a better indicator of technology than just computing the price value of the machine. An expert group to evolve a definition of technology that is specific to industries needs to be constituted before any data on the level of technology at the firm level and in industries can be collected.

Education Policy

India is among the few countries in the world that has a rising youth population. While most countries are concerned about their ageing population profile, India continues to derive the 'demographic dividend'. India's youth population in the age-group 15 to 24 years is expected to peak only in 2024, while many Asian countries, even underdeveloped ones like Indonesia, have reached the peak (Jha 2008). While this will definitely help in continuing the remarkable growth performance as seen in the recent decade, it is also a source of worry for planners in India.

As we discussed at the beginning of this chapter, there is a debate on the kind of education that the education system in the country should provide. The 'demographic dividend' as well as increasing secondary school enrolment in India have led to a rise in demand for higher education. This, in turn, has led to a tilt in the discourse towards job-oriented education. There is an increasing demand at the policy level for 'vocationalization' of education. The debate, often led by the stalwarts of industry, places emphasis on the mismatch between skills and jobs. For example, the software industry points to the lack of appropriate lower-level skills for data entry operators, programmers and computer engineers, when the Indian educational system produces the largest number of them for the rest of the world. Similarly, the new corporate retail business ventures emphasize the lack of 'soft' skills in the retail sector. This is generally the voice of corporate industry in India, which would like to see its immediate, short-term goals fulfilled.

The ITIs have played a crucial role in providing skilled workers to the organized sector over the years. It was found that, overall, about 3–30 per cent of workers and 10–20 per cent of skilled workers trained in ITIs were in the large enterprises in the organized sector (ILO 2003). However, with the economic reforms, the public enterprises have either closed down or have stopped recruiting, and private enterprises are using other methods such as contract labour or outsourcing to conduct their business. Employment of ITI graduates has therefore come down.

In the current situation, employers want to recruit trainable workers, irrespective of whether they have vocational skills. They require workers with the basic academic skills taught in primary and secondary schools, with the ability to communicate and solve simple, day-to-day problems on the shop floor, and who have the capacity for team work. Such skills allow for cost-effective training. There is therefore an advantage in recruiting, to the extent they do, workers from the regular schooling system and training them in the necessary skills later.

If the education policy of the country succumbs to catering to the immediate demand for vocational skills and converts the higher education system into a source of supply for them, the entire higher education scenario in India will settle into a sort of low-level skills equilibrium. A broader, liberal education system that encourages curiosity, experimentation and criticism is more likely to produce skilled professionals who can take the country to the cutting edge of technology. It is this latter system of education that the advanced countries aspire for. 'Reducing the benefits of tertiary education simply to measurable economic pay-offs would appear to some as a rather impoverished vision' (Kapur and Crowley 2007).

Given the growing number of new entrants to the labour force, largely youth population, and the clearly high and growing number of educated unemployed youth, there is a reason to develop the vocational 'skills'-oriented education stream. It is the elite and economically better-off sections that can afford long years of higher education to obtain qualifications that provide them, at best, amorphous skill-sets (Kapur and Crowley 2007).

India, therefore, requires a dual education policy with a strong vocational stream as well as a liberal education stream.

Liberal education stream

There is a quiet crisis in the higher education system in India (Kapur and Crowley 2007). While there are pockets of excellence, the majority of liberal arts and science colleges do not produce employable graduates. However, this does not mean that such education is irrelevant. The Knowledge Commission has suggested rapid expansion of universities and development of at least fifty national universities. It has also made recommendations to improve the quality of education, provision of autonomy in the design of courses, better remuneration of teachers to attract committed and good faculty, etc. (GoI 2007c). A revamping of the liberal education system is definitely required before the products of this system will be able to fulfil the goals they are expected to perform.

Skill-training models

A number of countries have traditionally designed their own skill-training models. An example is the successful German system of skill-training, which adopts the famous '*dual apprenticeship system*', combining two basic models: centre-based training and enterprise-based training. The system is based on a longstanding tradition of apprenticeship that is firmly rooted in the German corporate culture. Public vocational training centres provide the theoretical training and the practical training is provided within the enterprise. Apprentices sign an employment contract with an enterprise, by which they get on average three-and-a-half years of formal training under the supervision of a certified master, and an allowance fixed by collective agreement. The graduates receive a nationally recognized diploma.

Skill-training models that take into account the needs of employers need to be designed. Two models are presented below.

Model 1: Private–Public Partnership within an On-the-Job model. As we saw in our micro study, the major form of acquiring occupational skills in small businesses and informal enterprises is through the traditional apprenticeship model or the '*ustad–shagird*' route. How best can the government and private sector cooperate to help upgrade the existing initiatives of this model? One way in which such a model can be partly formalized is for the cost borne by the worker and the enterprise to be financed by an external agency, perhaps in the form of a loan to be repaid later.

Model 2: Private–Public Partnership within 'Skill Training Centres'. The service providers charged with the responsibility of training will design curricula to suit needs that have either been established through market surveys or that can be justified based on the established skill gaps among the potential trainees. The objective of the curriculum should be to increase the employability of trainees in the local or regional context, and/or raise the ability of the trainee to absorb higher levels of skill-training available locally or at other locations. These will not be 'free' courses. A cost should be attached to each course based on overall expenditure (capital expenses amortized appropriately). Each trainee will be given a 'training loan' (without collateral) from a bank, which has to be repaid in small instalments after the trainee secures a job. The 'training loan' should include the cost of the course plus the cost of commuting to the centre if the commute is long.

Two models of skill-training are thus possible which take into account the skill-training needs of the local economy and of the trainees. Such skill-training programmes are likely to create a fast rate of absorption of trainees into the work force and growth of employment in the local economy.

Policies for Small and Unorganized Enterprises

Most studies of small and unorganized sector enterprises in India have pointed to the schism in the industrial structure (Little *et al.* 1987; Suri 1988; Morris *et al.* 2001) of the country. While the reasons for this are many, most authors consider the industrial policies of the early period of industrialization, with reservation and licensing as their main plank, to be the primary one. This schism is very much entrenched in the industrial structure today.

In the manufacturing sector in 2001, we noted that nearly half the workers were engaged in own account enterprises (Chapter Two), operated by owner–entrepreneurs either alone or with family labour. A similar situation probably existed in most of the services sector, particularly personal services. This implies that these units operate on a very small scale with low levels of technology and skills among its workers. Consequently, the productivity and earnings generated in them are likely to be very low. There also exists heterogeneity in the productivity of own account enterprises, which, to a large extent, is dependent on expanding markets for their products.

As pointed out by Morris *et al.* (2001), small firms hardly affect their environment in the way large and oligopolistic firms do. Small firms have to take their environment as a given, and respond to the threats and opportunities. The apparently 'behavioural traits' of small firms actually reflect the response of the sector to certain economic and historical contexts. We adopt a similar approach here. What we present below is not a final policy document for small and informal enterprises, but suggestions of some policy options arising from our reading of the responses of the small entrepreneurs we met and interviewed in the autocomponents sector.

Technology

Some of the macro policies introduced since the mid-1990s, like reducing import duty, have had a direct impact on the small firms as they have been able to import second-hand machines and improve their technology base in recent years. The micro study of autocomponents showed the benefits that many of the small firms gained from the policy of import liberalization of capital goods. The resulting inflow of technology helped them to improve both quality and productivity in their enterprises. Even informal enterprises, over a period of time, were able to access better technology and improve their productivity.

We made a note of two kinds of technology. One is tacit technology that is mostly transferred between and within firms, and includes brand name, goodwill and managerial practices. This kind of technology is not codified and is more compatible with the growth of skilled workers in a firm. Given the large proportion of small firms, it is necessary to devise policy that facilitates the inflow of such technology.

The second kind of technology, arms-length technology, is generally codified and standardized, and transferred through import of technology. Such technology is also very important from the point of view of keeping Indian firms on the frontiers of technological progress. It may or may not immediately benefit the workers with increased employment opportunities or upgradation of skills. However, it is essential to enable firms to remain competitive in the domestic and international markets.

Networking and the Role of Clusters

The schism in the industrial structure results in large firms producing more sophisticated and diversified products, while small firms produce cheaper and more affordable products. However, this bimodal structure has been noted to be beneficial to small enterprises. Many studies have shown that, given the labour legislations of the country, the small enterprises act as sources for the large enterprises to access cheap labour. This is done through sub-contracting linkages between large and small firms (Morris *et al.* 2001). Sub-contracting relationships also develop in the dynamic and growing industries, which help the small enterprises to gain access to new markets and technology, and increase productivity (Nagaraj 1984).

Our micro field study of the autocomponents industry revealed how clusters of small firms and informal enterprises also have the potential to become 'skill concentration networks' and allow innovations to take place. This involves horizontal sub-contracting and networking of firms. Due to the presence of a large number of specialists, there is scope for upgrading the technology in the small firms, and the large and medium enterprises surveyed by us in the regions periodically visited these small and informal units to observe the innovative ideas developed by them. There is thus a clear need to develop these clusters so that they can benefit and grow together, improving productivity for all. Networking across firms that allows for discussion of new methods, technologies and marketing strategies would help the small firms and their partners to stay ahead in the competitive environment.

We also noted the very important role played by the informal enterprises in many of these clusters in training illiterate workers and workers with low levels of education to undertake both simple and complex jobs on the shop floor. Workers in enterprises located in city centres and particularly in backward regions of the country, where there is otherwise no possibility of gaining such skills, were able to gain skills that made them upwardly mobile. There is no possibility for such workers to access the vocational education system of the country either, since it requires a minimum level of education at the entry level. These small enterprises, in that sense, do provide a very important service, and we emphasize the need for more such vocational training or providing incentives to such informal enterprises so that they can continue the training activities in their units. This is especially necessary in the dynamic context where products keep changing or are improved constantly in order for enterprises to remain in the market.

One policy option that is in vogue is the development of industrial clusters. This policy began with the development of industrial estates and District Industrial Centres in urban and rural areas. UNIDO, in collaboration with the Ministry of Small-Scale Industries, Ministry of Textiles and other ministries, has invested in and developed a number of industrial clusters in the country. More recently, the National Commission for Enterprises in the Unorganized Sector (GoI 2007a) has piloted the idea of 'Growth Poles', based on a concept of developing a cluster of clusters with private–public partnership. Such clustering of units with adequate infrastructure facilities can help to unleash the growth potential of small enterprises.

Credit

A big constraint often faced by small firms or informal enterprises is non-availability of credit in the market. A recent government report has brought out the fact that credit to small-scale industries from scheduled commercial banks as a percentage of gross bank credit has dropped from nearly 15 per cent in 1990–91 to about 6.3 per cent in 2006–07 (GoI 2007b). Micro enterprises received less than 3 per cent of the gross bank credit during 2002–05. The new policies thus have a definite bias against the flow of cheaper government and institutional funds to the small enterprises sector.

One of the reasons for this is the attack on the concept of priority sector lending. The Narasimhan Committee Report (RBI 1992) had advocated the phasing out of the 40 per cent priority sector credit. Due to political exigencies, this was not implemented. Instead, the concept of priority sector has been weakened by the inclusion of all forms of non-production loans in the category, for example, housing and education loans.

In our micro study, we found that decreased access to institutional finance did not deter the small enterprises in the autocomponents industry. For many of the owner–managers, availability of credit for expanding their business was not a constraint, as finance was easily available from various non-banking sources at lower rates of interest. The banks also provided capital subsidy up to 15–20 per cent and subsidy for quality upgradation to many of the enterprises. It needs to be pointed out, though, that easy availability of credit for the autocomponents sector could be due to the growing market for these products, and one cannot argue thereby that the problem of credit in the economy has been resolved. The growing and dynamic small industry sectors are able to manage their credit requirements through various sources, but availability of credit and concessions for improving productivity remains a problem for all sectors and different sizes of firms.

Power and Infrastructure

A major constraint faced by the informal enterprises relates to power and infrastructure. The owner–managers of the informal enterprises we surveyed reported that they were provided limited power capacity of 5 hp, which does not allow them to operate more than two or three machines, or to expand and introduce other processing machines, and that had an impact on the productivity of their enterprises forcing them to operate at lower scales. There is need at the policy level to review this issue and to allow informal enterprises to operate at higher power capacity.

Another problem faced by informal enterprises is lack of infrastructure, such as roads. Often there are no proper roads connecting clusters of these enterprises. This problem becomes very acute during the rainy season when transporting parts and components becomes difficult. Though most of these clusters have come up informally, it is essential that the industrial associations recognize their importance in the overall production process, and provide them with proper work-sheds and access to roads and other infrastructure to undertake production operations.

Pricing of Products and Raw Material

A major issue brought out by the small firms and informal enterprises we surveyed related to the pricing of the finished product. The automobile industry has not seen a revision in the prices of finished components for the last eight years, while raw material prices have shot up. In the autocomponents sector, one of the major raw materials is steel, and it was a national policy decision to increase the price of steel as China was importing large quantities from India. Power and petrol prices have also been on a steady increase over the last decade. All this has led to reduction in margins as the output prices are not being adjusted; rather, there is a downward trend in these prices due to competition.

The rising prices of raw materials and lack of upward price adjustment for finished products have actually led to a lowering of labour costs in small and informal firms. The hierarchical structure of the automobile industry allows large firms to sub-contract parts or components to smaller firms and informal enterprises, allowing them to cut costs as much as they can. We had noted that sub-contracting chains could become exploitative, and this is one instance of workers in small and informal firms bearing the brunt of downward adjustments in product prices and upward rise of input prices.

Social Security Policy

This brings us to the issue of the organization of workers in small enterprises and social security. There has been a consistent effort in small firms and informal enterprises to dissuade workers from forming unions or even attending any of the organized-sector union meetings. Firms are also making efforts to prevent workers from forming groups or undertaking any group activity. This works against the interests of the workers, as they cannot articulate and represent their concerns. The major impact is on their wage bargaining ability and on ensuring proper work contracts. In the absence of unions, there is a need for an alternative strategy that would protect the interests of the workers.

NSS data showed that in 2004–05, about 60 per cent of the work force in rural areas and 45 per cent in urban areas were self-employed (NSSO 2006). The majority of these workers were likely to be engaged in own account units. Further, nearly 33 per cent of the workers in rural areas and 15 per cent in urban areas were casual workers. Besides low wages, these workers were vulnerable to fluctuations in income. The majority of self-employed and casual workers were unlikely to receive any social security benefits.

In today's globalizing scenario that we have described, skills are at a premium and upgrading of technology is essential for workers and small enterprises to remain competitive in the market. The majority of the workers in India, since they have low levels of education or are illiterate and have little skill training, are unlikely to benefit from the process of rising skills among the work force and skill premiums as compared to the better endowed workers. This is a fact that remains and has to be faced at the policy level.

Education and skill are a route out of poverty, but if a large proportion of the working population is not equipped to take advantage of these opportunities, some form of social security has to be visualized for these workers.

Government of India has been considering a Social Security Bill for Unorganized Sector Workers. The National Commission for Enterprises in the Unorganized Sector has suggested two Bills for the conditions of work and social security, separately for workers in the agricultural and non-agricultural unorganized sectors (GoI 2007a). National Minimum Social Security for all workers, consisting of health and maternity benefits, life and disability insurance cover, and old age security in the form of either pension or provident fund, were proposed by the Commission. The National Advisory Council, Ministry of Labour and a group of non-governmental organizations also proposed a similar security cover. The government is now in the process of finalizing a proposal for social security for such workers.

To conclude, we raise a couple of larger questions that need to be addressed at the policy level, which are not directly addressed in this study. Given the growing youth labour force in the country, the 'demographic dividend', what is the absorption potential of the manufacturing sector and, particularly, of small firms? That is, to what extent can these firms remain competitive and absorb a major share of the work force in the current context? A second related question is, to what extent can these small firms and the workers absorbed by them participate in the emerging markets? Given the Eleventh Plan approach of 'inclusive growth', these questions will have to be addressed directly by the policy-makers.

QUESTIONNAIRE

Transfer of Technology and Skills

Enterprise Survey

Gujarat Institute of Development Research, Ahmedabad

A. Background Information

1. Name of the unit:

2. Respondent's name:

3. SSI/DI/DIC Registration No.:

4. Taluka: District/City: State:

5. Location: Urban   Rural
                    Semi-urban   Other

6. Address:

7. Phone/Fax/Email:

8. Year when operation began:

9. Products manufactured/activity:

10. Legal status:
    Proprietory   Partnership   Private Ltd.
    Public Ltd.   Other

11. How many factories (units) does your company have?

12. Do you have any sister concerns? Yes/No

13. How many?

14. What are their principal activities?

15. Does your factory or unit do any job work or sub-contract work?

16. Family occupational background of original entrepreneur:
    Agriculture   Manufacturing   Trade
    Services   Other

17. Educational background of principal entrepreneur

18.　Nature of activity of the enterprise:

Manufacturing product	Manufacturing parts
Assembly product	Assembly parts
Processing	Servicing
Repair	

B.　Enterprise Characteristics

1.　What is the source of your acquired technology?

Sources of Technology	Machinery & Equipment Components	Inputs, Parts & Drawing	Product Design/	Technical Assistance	Management Practices
a. No special technology required					
b. Foreign collaborator joint ventures					
c. Foreign collaborator subsidiary					
d. Licensing or local technology agreements					
e. Hired consultant or skilled employee					
f. In-house development of innovations					
g. In-house copying/ imitation					
h. Government laboratories					
i. From machinery suppliers embodied in machinery–purchased from abroad					
j. From machinery suppliers embodied in machinery–purchased within India					
k. Suppliers of inputs					
l. Vertical sub-contracting (customer order specification)					
m. Horizontal sub-contracting					

2.   What are your sales turnover export shares and capacity utilizations?

Year	Sales Turnover (in Rs.)	% Share of Exports	% Capacity Utilization
1995			
2000			
2004			

3.   What is the value of your investments in:

S. No.	Assets	Current Value (in Rs) 2004	Depreciated Stock Value	Addition in 2004	Addition since 1995	Whether Hired Yes/No
1	Land & Building					
2	Plant & Machinery					
3	Other Fixed Assets					
4	Value of all Stock (raw materials, finished goods, etc)					

4.   How much working capital do you need per month (in Rs.)?

5.   Do you take any loan for your working capital? If yes, from which source?

6.   Whether the unit has electricity? Yes/No

7.   If yes, whether the electricity supply is regular or not? Yes/No

8.   Whether the main product has changed since 1995?

9.   How many products do you manufacture? What are their shares in turnover?

S.No.	Product Name	Shares in Sales turnover		
		1995	·2000	2004

10. Have you taken any loan for the enterprise since 1995?

S.No.	Source of Loan	Year	Amount (Rs)	Interest payable
1	Central and State level term lending institutions, Government (Central, State, local bodies), banks and societies (public sector, commercial, co-operative)			
2	Other Institutional Agencies			
3	Moneylenders			
4	Business Partners			
5	Suppliers/Contractors			
6	Friends and Relatives			
7	Others			
8	Total			

11. Is it difficult to obtain finance for expansion or technological change? Explain.

C. Product Market Linkages

1. Where do you sell your products? (allow multiple answers)
    Largely locally   Statewide   Nation-wide
    Internationally

2. What is the market share of your product?
    Largely local   Statewide   Nation-wide
    International

3. Which market do you cater to? (for autocomponent parts)
    1. Replacement market
    2. Original Equipment Manufacturers

4. Do you have a brand name? Yes/ No

5. Is your product sold under any other firm's name?

6. What are the sources of competition?
    a. Small firms   b. Imports   c. Large Indian firms
    d. Multinationals   e. Both small and large firms
    f. Smuggled goods

7. Do you receive subcontract work from other firms?

8. If yes, how many firms, what is the size of the firm and where are they located?

9. What proportion of your total production do you sub-contract in?

10. Do they have a contract with any of these firms and if yes, what are the terms and conditions?

11. Do they get orders regularly from these firms?

12. Since when were they receiving orders from these firms?

13. Do you subcontract out any part of the production process?

14. Since when are you subcontracting out?

15. What percentage of your total production do you sub-contract out?

16. If yes, to whom and what stages of the production process?

17. Do you directly deal with your customers/ raw material suppliers/ sub-contractors?

18. If no, who in your unit deals with them?

19. Do you keep changing your customers/ raw material suppliers/ sub-contractors?

20. Whether this relationship with customer/ raw material suppliers/ sub-contractors has led to any change in the product or technology or management practice?

21. Do you hire consultancy services for product design/ accounts?

22. What is your perception of the business environment since 1995 (trade/industrial policy changes)?

23. What is your perception regarding prospects for this industry and the products that you manufacture since 1995?

24. How do you assess the market situation?
    a. Domestic

    | Recessionary | Growing | Stable | Volatile |

    b. Export market

    | Recessionary | Growing | Stable | Volatile |

D. Labour Market Characteristics

1. Total Number of Employees

	2003-04	2000	1995
a. Permanent Employees			
b. Contract Employees			
c. Daily Wage Employees			
Total Employees			

2. Details of the Workers (including the owner):

List of Workers	Designation of the Worker	Sex	Type of Employee (Code)	Age	Education (Code)	Wage per Month	No. of Years in Firm	No. of Years of Experience	Training at Time of Joining (Code)

Codes for Designation of the Worker (Occupation)

1 Owner- Manager
2 Professionals-Managers
3 Professionals-Engineer
4 Clerical staff
5 Supervisor
6 Accountants
7 Skilled Production Workers
8 Semi-skilled Production Workers
9 Unskilled Production Workers

Codes for Employee

1 Permanent standards
2 Contract
3 Daily Wage

Codes for Education

1-12 Schooling
13 1st year graduation
14 2nd year graduation
15 3rd year graduation
16 B.E
17 Other Tech. Degree
18 PTI/ITI/Diploma
19 Others
20 Illiterate

Codes for Training

1 Formal institutions
2 Government extension services
3 Apprenticeship in informal enterprises
4 Skill acquired from family and friends
5 On the job training
6 Others Specify

3.   When did you last recruit workers at various levels?

4.   Are your full time workers members of a union? Yes/No

5.   Do you provide any training to workers when they join? Yes/No

6.   Whether the training you provide to the workers is on the job/ from other experienced workers in the unit/ do you send them to other units/ any other method?

7.   How long is the training?

8.   How often do you provide training to your workers at different levels?

9.   Have you provided any training in the last 12 months to the workers, for all levels? (Specify at what level)

10. What is your average annual expenditure on training?

11. Are the workers rotated to other jobs, so that they can become multi-skilled?

12. How many years does it take for a new recruit to become an experienced worker?

13. Have you introduced a Voluntary Retirement Scheme? If so how many workers have utilized it?

14. What is your Wage bill?

	Total Wage Bill (in Rs.)	Wage bill of Production Workers (in Rs.)	Wage bill of Non-Production workers (in Rs.)
1995			
2000			
2004			

15. How many shifts do you operate and what is the average number of working hours of workers at different levels?

16. If new workers were hired in the last 12 months, reasons:

17. Do you find it difficult to hire workers with requisite skills?
     Unskilled workers   Yes/No
     Skilled workers   Yes/No
     Engineers   Yes/No
     Managers   Yes/No

18. How do you find workers when you need them?

19. Do you hire workers with experience or not? Why?

20. What is the mode of payment for your skilled production workers?
    1. Time rate   2. Piece rate
    3. Both time and piece rate   4. Other

21. What is the mode of payment for your unskilled production workers?
    1. Time rate   2. Piece rate
    3. Both time and piece rate   4. Other

22. Do you provide any incentives to your workers to increase productivity or innovation? (bonus, hike in wages, etc)

23. Is there any educational requirement for employees in your company?
    i. Supervisor   ii. Operator   iii. Helper
    Codes:
    0: No requirement; 1: Class 1-5; 2:Class 6-9; 3: SSC 4:HSC;
    5: Bachelors or Higher; 6: Diploma/ PTI; 7: Engineer

E.   Technology and Skill Linkages

1. Did/do you receive design/drawing or sample of the product from your customer?

2. If you receive the sample of the product, then is the drawing done in-house or do you engage outside consultants/professionals?

3. What kind of technology do you have? Simple tools and equipments, Manual, Semi-automatic or automatic? (If at different levels of the production process different technologies are used, please list them)

4. When did you last introduce:
   a. New product?
   b. New technology (machinery/ equipment)?
   c. New management practice (accounting/ movement of materials)?
   d. Expansion of existing production capacity

4. Were the same workers retained or there was retrenchment when the new product/ technology/ management practice was introduced?

5. If the workers were retrenched, why did you retrench them?

6. Did you hire any new workers when you diversified or changed? Yes/No

7. If yes, at what level did you hire these workers?

8.   If no, did you provide training to the old workers?

9.   Did the new technology lead to deskilling of workers? If so, what category of workers?

10.   If new technology has been introduced/ production capacity expanded, then what was the motivation behind it?
     a. Increasing demand for the product
     b. Increased number of suppliers
     c. Improved performance of other units in the industry
     d. Entry of powerful players like the MNCs or large firms
     e. Demanding customers
     f. Introduction of new Substitutes
     g. Easy access of second-hand imported goods
     h. Subsidies by the Government
     i. To improve the quality of the product
     j. To reduce the cost
     k. Others

11.   If the firm has not introduced any technology, then why?
     i. Lack of finance
     ii. Lack of skilled personnel
     iii. Relative factor prices
     iv. Lack of knowledge/ information
     v. Administrative hurdles to obtain import licenses
     vi. Others

12.   If no new technology was introduced, was there any in-house innovation through:
     •   Learning by doing
     •   By solving a production problem
     •   Meeting specific customer requirements
     •   Seek to improve or diversify technology by searching for it in the neighborhood areas
     •   Through new experienced workers
     •   Reverse engineering
     •   By research and development
     •   Others

13.   Do you have computers in your unit? Yes/No

14. If yes, what proportions of workers use computers on a regular basis for their work?
     a. Managers
     b. Engineers
     c. Skilled Production workers
     d. Unskilled Production workers

15. For what purpose do the workers use the computers in your unit?

16. What is your perception regarding need for technological changes in your firm to compete in the market?

17. What is your perception regarding the capability of your skilled workers to adapt to new technology?

18. How do you as an entrepreneur distinguish between skilled and unskilled worker?

F. Production Capability

1. How would you rate the quality of your product?
    Very good   Good   Average
    Poor   Very poor

2. How would you rate the average quality of your products/services in comparison to that of   your competitors (locally/nationally/ internationally)?
    Better   About the same
    A little below   Cannot be compared

3. Whether they are able to improve the quality of the product based on their customer feedback?

4. Has the cost of production changed in the recent past?
    Increased   Decreased   Remained the same

7. If increased, then under what heads have production cost increased:
    Labour   Power   Transport
    Others

8. If decreased, then under what heads have production cost decreased:
    Labour   Power   Transport
    Others

9. Do you have any certification of quality like ISO 9000, or of competence, etc.? No/Yes.

10. If, Yes Specify

11.   Have you won any awards, certificate of merit, prizes, export awards, etc.? Please list below:

G.   **Transfer of Technology, Knowledge and Skills**

1.   What was your expenditure on Research and Development in 1995, 2000 and 2004?

2.   Patent Registrations:
      Never   Rarely   Regularly

3.   Whether the production system is
      a.   Automated system (e.g. computerized interrogation for faults and repair)
      b.   Personnel based (support staff, technicians or engineers)

4.   How does the acquiring of new knowledge take place?
      a.   Documentation centre
      b.   Through exhibitions/trade fairs
      c.   Trade journals
      d.   Consultancy organisations
      e.   University/ research centers
      f.   Through Conferences/seminars
      g.   Through Internet
      h.   From other companies (knowledge transfer between business partners)

5.   Whether there has been any transfer of technology, product/ process/practice from other sub-contracted firms/large firms/small firms? Yes/No

6.   Whether the technology transferred is out-dated or new?

7.   If technology transfer took place, whether the unit got any technical help for setting it up?

8.   How is the technology transfer going to help the unit? Productivity/ quality/cost minimization/others

9.   Whether your unit has transferred any technology, product/ process/ practice to other sub-contracted firms/small firms?

10.   What is the motivation for transferring this technology?

11.   Whether the unit has received any financial support from large firms or Government organisations to upgrade their technology?

12.   If there has been any technological change, what has been the Impact of it - Quality or performance and on Workers (could compare it over two points)
a.   Output per employee
b.   Value added per employee
c.   Defect rate
d.   Environment Standards
e.   Wage/salary increases
f.   Inventory
g.   Market share
h.   R&D as percentage of sales
i.   Number of new products launched per year
j.   Number of patents granted
k.   Development of Skilled Workforce
l.   Development of Unskilled Workforce
m.   Retrenchment of Workers as a result of New technology

What is their rejection rate?

OBSERVE: Working Principles in the Company (Fives S's)
1.   Sort
2.   Systematize
3.   Sweep
4.   Sanitize
5.   Self-Discipline

Bibliography

Acemoglu, D., 2002, 'Technical Change, Inequality, and the Labor Market', *Journal of Economic Literature*, XL, March, pp. 7–72.

———, 2003, 'Patterns of Skill Premia', *Review of Economic Studies,* 70, pp. 199–230.

ADB, 2007, 'Education and Structural Change in Four Asian Countries', *Asian Development Outlook 2007* (Manila: Asian Development Bank).

Agarwal, J.P., 1976, 'Factor Proportions in Foreign and Domestic Owned Firms in Indian Manufacturing', *Economic Journal*, 86, pp. 529–95.

Ahluwalia, M.S., 2001, 'India's Economic Reforms: An Appraisal', in Jeffery Sachs, Ashutosh Varshney and Nirupam Bajpai (eds), *India in the Era of Economic Reforms* (New Delhi: Oxford University Press).

Amin, A., 1985, 'Restructuring in Fiat and the Decentralization of Production into Southern Italy', in R. Hudson and J. Lewis (eds), *Uneven Development in Southern Europe* (London: Methuen).

Amsden, A.H., 1995, 'A Strategic Policy Approach to Growth and Government Intervention in Late Industrialization', Centre for International Studies, Working Paper No. 2610, Cambridge, MA: CIS, Massachusetts Institute of Technology.

Ariga, Kenn, Giorgio Brunello and Yasushi Ohkusa, 2000, *Internal Labour Markets in Japan* (United Kingdom: Cambridge University Press).

Arrow, K., 1962, 'The Economic Implications of Learning by Doing', *Review of Economic Studies,* 29 (3), pp. 155–73.

Asai, 2002, *Competitive Power of Skill* (in Japanese) (Japan: Chuokeizaisha).

Attanasio, O., P. Goldberg and N. Pavanik, 2004, 'Trade Reforms and Wage Inequality in Colombia', *Journal of Development Economics*, 74, pp. 331–36.

Autor, David, Alan Krueger and Lawrence Katz, 1998, 'Computing Inequality: Have Computers Changed the Labor Market?', *Quarterly Journal of Economics*, 113 (4), pp. 1169–1213.

Autor, David, Frank Levy and Richard Mumane, 2001, 'The Skill Content of Recent Technological Change: An Empirical Exploration', Working Paper No. 8337, NBER Working Paper Series, Cambridge, http://www.nber.org/papers/w8337.

Banerjee, N., 1988, 'Small and Large Units: Symbiosis or Matsyanyaya?', in K.B. Suri (ed.), *Small Scale Enterprises in Industrial Development* (New Delhi: Sage Publications), pp. 184–202.

Basant, R. and P. Chandra, 2002, 'Building Technological Capabilities in a Liberalizing Developing Economy: Firm Strategies and Public Policies', *Economics of Innovation and New Technology*, 11 (4 & 5), pp. 399–421.

Beaulieu, E., M. Benarroch, J. Gasiford, 2004, 'Trade Barriers and Wage Inequality in a North–South Model with a Technology-driven Intra-industry Trade', *Journal of Development Economics*, 75, pp. 113–36.

Becker, G.S., 1964, *Human Capital* (Chicago: University of Chicago Press).

Becker, G.S. and K.M. Murphy, 1992, 'The Division of Labor, Coordination Costs and Knowledge', *The Quarterly Journal of Economics*, CVII (4), pp. 1137–60.

Berman, E., B. Johnson and S. Machin, 1998, 'Implications of Skill-Biased Technological Change: International Evidence', *Quarterly Journal of Economics*, 113 (4), pp. 1245–80.

Berman, E., J. Bound and Z. Griliches, 1994, 'Changes in the Demand for Skilled Labour within U.S. Manufacturing: Evidence from the Annual Survey of Manufactures', *Quarterly Journal of Economics*, 109 (2), pp. 367–97.

Berman, E., R. Somanathan and H.W. Tan, 2006, 'Is Skill-Biased Technological Change Here Yet? Evidence from Indian Manufacturing in the 1990s', mimeo, Delhi: Delhi School of Economics.

Berman, E. and S. Machin, 2000, 'Skill-Biased Technology Transfer around the World', *Oxford Review of Economic Policy*, 16 (3), pp. 12–22.

Bhalla, S., 2001, 'Trends in Non-Agricultural Employment', mimeo, Institute of Human Development.

Bhalla, S., 2003, *Restructuring of the Unorganized Sector in India*, Report of a project funded by the Planning Commission, mimeo, New Delhi: Institute of Human Development.

Bhavani, T.A., 2002, 'Impact of Technology on the Competitiveness of the Indian Small Manufacturing Sector: A Case study of Automotive

Component Industry', Discussion No. 2002/76, Helsinki: WIDER, UNU.

Bose, A. N., 1978, *Calcutta and Rural Bengal: Small Sector Symbiosis* (Calcutta: Minerva Associates Publication).

Bound, J. and J. George, 1992, 'Changes in the Structure of Wages in the 1980s: An Evaluation of Alternative Explanations', *American Economic Review*, 82 (3), pp. 371–92.

Braverman, Harry, 1974, *Labor and Monopoly Capital: The Degradation of Work in the Twentieth Century* (New York: Monthly Review Press).

Brown, C., James Hamilton and James Medoft, 1990, *Employers Large and Small* (Cambridge, Mass.: Harvard University Press).

Burkett, Paul and Martin Hart-Landsberg, 2000, *Development, Crisis and Class Struggle: Learning from Japan and East Asia* (London: Macmillan).

Burtless, G., 1995, 'International Trade and the Rise in Earnings Inequality', *Journal of Economic Literature*, 33, pp. 800–16.

Bustamente, J., 1983, 'Maquiladoras: A New Face of International Capitalism on Mexico's Northern Frontier', in J. Nash and M.P. Fernandez Kelly (eds), *Women, Men and the International Division of Labour*, (Albany, NY: State University of New York Press), pp. 224–56.

Cabinet Office, *Annual Report on National Accounts*, Japan.

Cappelli, P., 1993, 'Are Skill Requirements Rising? Evidence from Production and Clerical Jobs', *Industrial and Labour Relations Review*, 46, pp. 515–30.

Cappelli, P. and N. Rogovsky, 1994, 'New Work Systems and Skill Requirements', *International Labour Review*, 133, pp. 205–20.

Carre, F. and J. Herranz, 2002, 'Informal Jobs in Industrialized "North" Countries', mimeo, Boston: Radcliffe Public Policy Center, Harvard University.

Census of Manufactures, 2001, Industry, Research and Statistics Department, Economic and Industrial Policy Bureau, Ministry of Economy, Trade and Industry, Government of Japan.

Chamarbagwala, R., 2006, 'Economic Liberalization and Wage Inequality in India', *World Development*, 34 (12), pp. 1997–2015.

Chandrasekhar, C.P. and Jayati Ghosh, 2002, *The Market that Failed: A Decade of Liberal Economic Reforms in India* (New Delhi: LeftWord Books).

Charmes, J. and J. Unni, 2001, 'Employment in the Informal Sector and Informal Employment: New Insights from Recent Surveys in India, Kenya and Tunisia', paper presented at the Fifth Meeting of the

Expert Group on Informal Sector Statistics (Delhi Group), organized by the Ministry of Statistics and Programme Implementation, New Delhi, 19–21 September.

Chaudhury, D.R., 1999, 'Inter-Firm Industrial Linkages in India: Subcontracting Practices in Durgapur and Jamshedpur', in A.K. Bagchi (ed.), *Economy and Organization: Indian Institutions under the Neoliberal Regime* (New Delhi: Sage Publications), pp. 188–229.

Coase, R., 1937, 'The Nature of The Firm', *Economica*, 4 (16), pp. 386–405.

CSO, 1995a, *Annual Survey of Industries 1994–95, Summary Results for Factory Sector by State and Industry*, Department of Statistics, Ministry of Planning and Programme Implementation, Government of India.

CSO, 1995b, *Supplement to Annual Survey of Industries 1994–95, Summary Results for Factory Sector by State and Industry*, Department of Statistics, Ministry of Planning and Programme Implementation, Government of India.

CSO, 2002, *Annual Survey of Industries (Factory Sector) 1999–2000, Volume 1*, Ministry of Statistics and Programme Implementation, Government of India.

D'Costa, A.P., 1995, 'The Restructuring of Indian Automobile Industry: Indian State and Japanese Capital', *World Development*, 23 (3), pp. 485–502.

Das, D.K., 2003, 'Manufacturing Productivity under Varying Trade Regimes: India in the 1980s and 1990s', Working Paper No. 107, New Delhi: Indian Council for Research on International Economic Relations.

Das, S.P., 2002, 'Foreign Direct Investment and the Relative Wage in a Developing Economy', *Journal of Development Economics*, 67, pp. 55–77.

Economic Survey, various years, Ministry of Finance and Company Affairs, Government of India.

Employment Status Survey, Ministry of Internal Affairs and Communication, Government of Japan.

Establishment and Enterprise Census, Ministry of Internal Affairs and Communication, Government of Japan.

Feenstra, A.D. and G.H. Hanson, 1996, 'Foreign Investment, Out Sourcing and Relative Wages', in R.C. Feenstra, G.M. Grossman and D.A. Irwin (eds), *The Political Economy of Trade Policy: Essays in Honour of Jagdish Bhagwati* (Cambridge: MIT Press), pp. 89–127.

Feenstra, A.D. and G.H. Hanson, 2003, 'Global Production Sharing and

Rising Inequality: A Survey of Trade and Wages', in E. Choi and J. Harrigan (eds), *Handbook of International Trade* (Maiden, MA: Blackwell), pp. 146–85.

Fernandez-Kelly, M.P., 1983, *For We Are Sold, I and My People: Women and Industry in Mexico's Frontier* (Albany, NY: State University of New York Press).

Friedman, A.L., 1977, *Industry and Labour: Class Struggle at Work and Monopoly Capitalism* (London: Macmillan).

Ghose, Ajit K., 2000, 'Trade Liberalization and Manufacturing Employment', Employment Paper 2000/3, Geneva: International Labor Organization.

Gokarn, S. and R.R. Vaidya, 2004, 'The Automobile Components Industry', in Subir Gokarn, Anindya Sen and R.R. Vaidya (eds), *The Structure of Indian Industry* (New Delhi: Oxford University Press).

GoI, 2007a, *Report on the Condition of Work and Promotion of Livelihoods*, National Commission for Enterprises in the Unorganized Sector, Government of India, New Delhi.

GoI, 2007b, *Report on Financing of Enterprises in the Unorganized Sector and Creation of a National Fund for Unorganized sector (NAFUS)*, National Commission for Enterprises in the Unorganized Sector, Government of India, New Delhi.

GoI, 2007c, *Compilation of Recommendations on Education*, National Knowledge Commission, Government of India, New Delhi.

Gupta, D.B. and B.N. Goldar, 1995, 'Ancillarization and Subcontracting in Indian Industry', Paper No.18, Studies in Industrial Development, Ministry of Industry, Government of India, New Delhi.

Hanson, G.H. and A. Harrison, 1995, *Trade, Technology and Wage Inequality*, NBER Working Paper No. 5110.

Harrison, Rupert, 2008, 'Skill-based Technology Adoption: Firm-level Evidence from Brazil and India', IFS Working Paper W08/03, London: The Institute of Fiscal Studies.

Harris, J., 1982, 'Character of an Urban Economy: "Small Scale" Production and Labour Markets in Coimbatore', *Economic and Political Weekly*, 17 (24), pp. 993–1002.

Harrod, R.F., 1939, 'An Essay in Dynamic Theory', *Economic Journal*, 49, pp. 14–53.

Helseley, R.W. and W.C. Strange, 2002, 'Innovation and Input Sharing', *Journal of Urban Economics*, 51, pp. 25–45.

Holmes, John, 1986, 'The Organization and Locational Structure of Production Subcontracting', in Allen J. Scott and Michael Storper (eds),

Production Work Territory: The Geographical Anatomy of Industrial Capitalism (Boston: Allen & Unwin), pp. 80–106.

Holmstrom, M., 1998, 'Bangalore as an Industrial District: Flexible Specialization in a Labour Surplus Economy?', in Philippe Cadane and Mark Holmstrom (eds), *Decentralized Production in India: Industrial Districts, Flexible Specialization, and Employment* (New Delhi: Sage Publications), pp. 169–229.

ILO, 2002, *Men and Women in the Informal Economy: A Statistical Picture*, Employment Sector, Geneva: International Labor Organization.

ILO, 2003, 'Industrial Training Institutes of India: The Efficiency Study Report', Subregional Office for South Asia, International Labour Organization, New Delhi and IFP/SKILLS, International Labour Organization, Geneva.

Iyotani, Toshio, 1995. 'Japan's Policy towards Foreign Workers and the Case of Kawasaki City', *Regional Development Dialogue*, 16 (1).

Jha, Shikha, 2008, 'Young Workers in Asia', paper presented at the Asian Development Outlook Workshop, ADB, Manila, 16 January.

Jhabvala, R. and R. Kanbur, 2002, 'Globalization and Economic Reform as Seen from the Ground: SEWA's Experience in India', paper presented at the Indian Economy Conference, Cornell University, 19–20 April.

Juhn, Cinhul, K.M. Murphy and P. Brooks, 1993, 'Wage, Inequality and the Rise in Returns to Skill', *Journal of Political Economy*, 101 (3), pp. 410–42.

Kaldor, N. and J.A. Mirrlees, 1962, 'A New Model of Economic Growth, *Review of Economic Studies*, 29 (3), pp. 174–92.

Kaplinsky, R., 1995, 'Technique and System: The Spread of Japanese Management Techniques to Developing Countries', *World Development*, 23 (1), pp. 57–71.

Kapur, Devesh and Megan Crowley, 2007, 'Getting the ABCs Right: Higher Education and Developing Countries' (unpublished).

Kathuria, Sanjay, 1990, 'The Indian Automotive Industry: Recent Changes and Impact of Government Policy', mimeo, New Delhi: The World Bank.

———, 1995, 'Competitiveness of Indian Industry', in Dilip Mookherjee (ed.), *Indian Industry: Policies and Performance* (New Delhi: Oxford University Press).

Katz, L.F. and D.H. Autor, 1999, 'Changes in the Wage Structure and Earnings Inequality', in Ashenfelter and Card (eds), *Handbook of Labour Economics*, Vol. 3A (Amsterdam: Elsevier Science).

Katz, L.F. and K.M. Murphy, 1992, 'Changes in Relative Wages, 1963–1987: Supply and Demand Factors', *Quarterly Journal of Economics*, 107 (1), pp. 35–78.

Kijima, Y., 2006, 'Why did Wage Inequality Increase? Evidence from Urban India 1983-99', *Journal of Development Economics*, 81, pp. 97–117.

Kingdon, Geeta G. and Jeemol Unni, 2001, 'Education and Women's Labour Market Outcomes in India', *Education Economics*, 9 (2), pp. 173–95.

Koike, K. and T. Inoki, 1990 (eds), *Skill Formation in Japan and Southeast Asia* (Tokyo: The University of Tokyo Press).

Koshiro, Kazutoshi, 2000, *A Fifty Year History of Industry and Labour in Postwar Japan* (Tokyo: The Japan Institute of Labour).

Kucera, D. and W. Milberg, 2000, 'Gender Segregation and Gender Bias in Manufacturing Trade Expansion: Revisiting the "Wood Asymmetry"', *World Development*, 28 (7), pp. 1191–1210.

Kumar, Krishna, 2008, *A Pedagogue's Romance: Reflections on Schooling* (New Delhi: Oxford University Press).

Labour Force Survey, Ministry of Internal Affairs and Communication, Government of Japan.

Lall, Sanjay, 1980, 'Vertical Inter-Firm Linkages in LDCs: An Empirical Study', *Oxford Bulletin of Economic and Statistics*, 42 (3).

———, 1992, 'Technological Capabilities and Industrialization', *World Development*, 20 (2), pp. 165–86.

Lawrence, R.Z. and M.J. Slaughter, 1993, 'International Trade and American Wages in the 1980s: Giant Sucking Sound or Small Hiccup?', *Brookings Paper of Economic Activity*, 2, pp. 161–226.

Leamer, E.E., 1996, 'In Search of the Stopler-Samuelson Effects on US Wages', NBER Working Paper No. 5427.

Little, Ian M., D. Mazumdar and J.M. Page, 1987, *Small Manufacturing Enterprises: A Comparative Analysis of India and Other Economies* (Washington: Oxford University Press for The World Bank).

Lucas, R.E. Jr., 1988, 'On the Mechanisms of Economic Development', *Journal of Monetary Economcis*, 22 (1), pp. 3–42.

Machin, S., 1994, 'Changes in the Relative Demand for Skills in the UK Labour Market', Discussion Paper No. 952, London: Centre for Economic Policy Research.

Mathur, Ashok and Rajendra P. Mamgain, 2002, 'Technical Skills, Education and Economic Development in India', *The Indian Journal of Labour Economics*, 45 (4), pp. 1045–46.

Mazumdar, Dipak, 2000, 'Labour Markets and Employment in Economic

Growth in East and South-East Asia: Some Key Issues', *Indian Journal of Labour Economics,* 43 (3).

Moll, Peter, 1996, 'The Collapse of Primary Schooling Returns in South Africa, 1960-90', *Oxford Bulletin of Economics and Statistics,* 58 (1), pp. 185–210.

Morris, S. and R. Basant, 2004, 'Role of Small Scale Industries in the Age of Liberalisation', paper presented at the 1st Technical Workshop of the ADB Policy Networking Project, New Delhi, 25–26 October.

Morris, S., R. Basant, K. Das, K. Ramachandran and A. Koshy, 2001, *The Growth and Transformation of Small Firms in India* (New Delhi: Oxford University Press).

Murray, F., 1983, 'The Decentralization of Production: The Decline of the Mass Collective Worker', *Capital and Class,* 19, pp. 74–99.

Nagaraj, R., 1984, 'Sub-contracting in Indian Manufacturing Industries: Analysis, Evidence and Issues', *Economic and Political Weekly,* 19 (30, 31 and 32), pp. 1435–56.

Nagaraj, R., 1989, *Sub-contracting in Indian Manufacturing Industries: The Bangalore Experience* (unpublished thesis), Trivandrum: Centre for Development Studies.

Najmabadi, F. and S. Lall, 1995, *Developing Industrial Technology: Lessons for Policy and Practice* (Washington DC: The World Bank).

Nakamura, Tadashi, 1992, 'Labour Market and Manpower Policy 1945–1985', in Kazutoshi Koshiro(ed.), *Employment Security and Labour Market Flexibility: An International Perspective* (Detroit: Wayne State University Press).

Nakamura, Takafusa, 1995, *The Postwar Japanese Economy: In Development and Structure, 1937–1994* (Tokyo: University of Tokyo Press).

Nelson, R. and S.G. Winter, 1982, *An Evolutionary Theory of Economic Growth* (Cambridge, MA: Harvard University Press).

Nouroz, H., 2001, *Protection in Indian Manufacturing: An Empirical Study* (New Delhi: Macmillan India).

NSSO, 1989, *Tables with Notes on Survey of Unorganized Manufacture: Non-Directory Establishments and Own Account Enterprises, Part I, Part II (Volume 1 and 2),* NSS 40th Round, July 1984–June 1985, No. 363/1, Department of Statistics, Government of India, New Delhi.

NSSO, 1994a, *Tables with Notes on Survey of Unorganized Manufacture: Non-Directory Establishments and Own Account Enterprises, Part I (All India),* NSS 45th Round, July 1989–June 1990, No. 396/2, Department of Statistics, Government of India, New Delhi.

NSSO, 1994b *Tables with Notes on Survey of Unorganized Manufacture:*

Non-Directory Establishments and Own Account Enterprises, Part II (States), Volume 1 and 2, NSS 45th Round, July 1989–June 1990, No. 396/2, Department of Statistics, Government of India, New Delhi.

NSSO, 1998a, *Unorganized Manufacturing Sector in India: Its Size, Employment and Some Key Estimates, Directory Establishments and Own Account Enterprises*, NSS 51st Round, July 1994–June 1995, No. 433 (51/2.2/1), Department of Statistics, Government of India, New Delhi.

NSSO, 1998b, *Unorganized Manufacturing Sector in India: Salient Features*, NSS 51st Round, July 1994–June 1995, No. 434 (51/2.2/2), Department of Statistics, Government of India, New Delhi.

NSSO, 1998c, *Assets and Borrowings of the Unorganized Manufacturing Sector in India*, NSS 51st Round, July 1994–June 1995, No. 435 (51/2.2/3), Department of Statistics, Government of India, New Delhi.

NSSO, 2002a, *Unorganized Manufacturing Sector in India: Characteristics of Enterprises*, NSS 56th Round, July 2000–June 2001, No. 478 (56/2.2/2), Ministry of Statistics and Programme Implementation, Government of India, New Delhi.

NSSO, 2002b, *Unorganized Manufacturing Sector in India: Employment, Assets and Borrowings*, NSS 56th Round, July 2000–June 2001, No. 479 (56/2.2/3), Ministry of Statistics and Programme Implementation, Government of India, New Delhi.

NSSO, 2002c, *Unorganized Manufacturing Sector in India: Input, Output and Value Added*, NSS 56th Round, July 2000–June 2001, No. 480 (56/2.2/4), Ministry of Statistics and Programme Implementation, Government of India, New Delhi.

NSSO, 2006, *Employment and Unemployment Situation in India: 2004–05, Part I*, NSS 61st Round, July 2004–June 2005, No. 515 (61/10/1), Ministry of Statistics and Programme Implementation, Government of India, New Delhi.

OECD, 1997, *Industrial Competitiveness in the Knowledge-based Economy: The New Role of Governments* (Paris: OECD).

Ogawa, 1996, *New Management of Opening Business* (Japan: Chuokei-zaisha).

Okada, A., 2004, 'Skills Development and Interfirm Learning Linkages under Globalization: Lessons from the Indian Automobile Industry', *World Development*, 32 (7), pp. 1265–88.

Pandit, B.L. and N.S. Siddharthan, 2008, 'MNEs, Product Differentiation, Skills and Employment: Lessons from the Indian Experience', in

S.R. Hashim and N.S. Siddharthan, *High-tech Industries, Employment and Global Competitiveness* (New Delhi: Routledge).

Papola, T.S., 2005, 'Emerging Structure of Indian Economy: Implications of Growing Inter-sectoral Imbalances', Presidential Address of 88th Annual Conference of Indian Economic Association, Visakhapatnam, 27–29 December.

Papola, T.S and R.S. Mathur, 1979, *Inter-Sectoral Linkages in Manufacturing: A Study of Metal Engineering Industry in Kanpur*, mimeo, Lucknow: Giri Institute of Development Studies.

Pingle, V., 2000, *Rethinking the Developmental State: India's Industry in Comparative Perspective* (New Delhi: Oxford University Press).

Planning Commission, 2001, *Report of the Task Force on Employment Opportunities*, New Delhi: Government of India, July.

Planning Commission, 2001a, *Special Group on Targeting Ten Million Employment Opportunities per Year: Employment Generating Growth*, New Delhi: Government of India, May.

Planning Commission, 2002, *Employment Generating Growth: Special Group in Targeting Ten Million Employment Opportunities per Year.* New Delhi: Government of India.

Psacharopoulos, G., 1994, 'Returns to Investment in Education: A Global Update', *World Development*, Vol. 22, No. 9, pp. 1325–44.

Ramachandran, H., 2002, 'Education, Skill Development and Changing Labour Market", *The Indian Journal of Labour Economics*, Vol. 45, No. 4, pp. 999–1014.

Ramaswamy, K.V., 1999, 'The Search for Flexibility in Indian Manufacturing: New Evidence on Outsourcing Activities', *Economic and Political Weekly*, 34 (6), pp. 363–68.

Ramsey, F.P., 1928, 'A Mathematical Theory of Savings', *Economic Journal*, 38, pp. 543–59.

Rani, U., 2006, 'Economic Growth, Labour Markets and Gender in Japan', *Economic and Political Weekly*, 41 (41), pp. 4369–77.

Rani, Uma and Jeemol Unni, 2004a, 'Unorganized and Organized Manufacturing in India: Potential for Employment Generating Growth', *Economic and Political Weekly*, 39 (41), pp. 4568–80.

——, 2004b, 'Impact of Inflow of Goods from China on Small-scale Manufacturing and Labour in Ahmedabad', in Shuji Uchikawa (ed.), *Trade, Investment and Economic Cooperation between China and South Asia,* Joint Research Program Series No. 131, Chiba, Japan: Institute of Developing Economies, IDE-JETRO.

RBI, 1992, 'Report on the Committee on Financial Systems (Narasimhan Committee)', *Reserve Bank of India Bulletin,* No. 371, February.

Reve, T., 1990, 'The Firm as a Nexus of Internal and External Contracts', in Aoki, M., B. Gustafsson and O.E. Williamson (eds), *The Firm as a Nexus of Treaties* (London: Sage Publications), pp. 133–61.

Rigolini, J., 2004, 'Education Technologies, Wages and Technological Progress', *Journal of Development Economics*, 75, pp. 55–77.

Robbins, D., 1996, 'Evidence on Trade and Wages in the Developing World', OECD Development Centre Technical Paper No. 119.

Rodrik, Dani, 1997, *Has Globalization Gone Too Far?*, mimeo, Washington DC: Institute of International Economics.

Romer, P.M., 1986, 'Increasing Returns and Long-run Growth', *Journal of Political Economy*, 94 (5), pp. 1002–37.

Rubery, J. and F. Wilkinson, 1981, 'Outwork and Segmented labour Markets', in F. Wilkinson (ed.), *The Dynamics of Labour Market Segmentation* (London: Academic Press), pp. 115–32.

Rush, H. and J.C. Ferraz, 1993, 'Employment and Skills in Brazil: The Implications of New Technologies and Organizational Techniques', *International Labour Review*, 132 (1), pp. 75–93.

Sabel, C.F., 1982, *Work and Politics: The Division of Labour in Industry* (Cambridge: Cambridge University Press).

——, 1986, 'Changing Models of Economic Efficiency and their Implications for Industrialization in the Third World', in A. Foxley, M. Mesherson and G.O. Donel (eds), *Development, Democracy and Art of Trespassing: Essays in Honour of Albert O'Hirschman* (University of Notre Dame), pp. 27–55.

Sahay, B.S., K.B.C. Saxena and A. Kumar, 2004, 'Cyber-age Manufacturing', *Industry 2.0*, 18–26 March.

Sargeant, J. and L. Mathews, 1997, 'Skill Development and Integrated Manufacturing in Mexico', *World Development*, 25 (10), pp. 1669–81.

Schultz, Theodore, 1975, 'The Value of the Ability to Deal with Disequilibria', *Journal of Economic Literature*, 13, pp. 827–46.

Schultz, T.P., 1988, 'Education Investments and Returns', in H. Chenery and T.N. Srinivasan (eds), *Handbook of Development Economics*, Vol. 1 (Amsterdam: North-Holland).

Scott, A.J., 1983, 'Industrial Organization and the Logic of Intra-metropolitan Location. I: Theoretical Considerations', *Economic Geography*, 59 (3).

Scott, M.F.G., 1989, *A New View of Economic Growth* (Oxford: Clarendon Press).

Sen, A.K., 1979, *Growth Economics*, Penguin Modern Economic Readings (London: Penguin).

Seth, Vijay K. and Suresh C. Aggarwal, 2004, *The Economics of Labour Markets: Policy Regime Changes and the Process of Labour Adjustment in the Organized Industry in India* (New Delhi: Ane Books).

Sheard, P., 1983, 'Auto-Production Systems in Japan: Organizational and Locational Features', *Australian Geographic Studies*, 21 (1), pp. 49–68.

Siddharthan, N.S. and K. Lal, 2003, 'Liberalization and Growth of Firms in India', *Economic and Political Weekly*, 38 (20), p. 1983.

Slaughter, M.J., 1998, 'What are the Results of the Product Price Studies and What can We Learn from their Differences', NBER Working Paper No. 6591.

Solow, R., 1957, 'Technical Change and the Aggregate Production Function', *Review of Economics and Statistics*, 39 (3), pp. 312–20.

Standing, G., 1999, 'Global Feminization through Flexible Labour: A Theme Revisited', *World Development*, 27 (3), pp. 583–602.

Stopler, W.F. and P.A. Samuelson, 'Protection and Real Wages', The *Review of Economic Studies*, 9 (1), pp. 58–73.

Suri, K.B. (ed.), 1988, *Small Scale Enterprises in Industrial Development: The Indian Experience* (New Delhi: Sage Publications).

Survey on Overseas Business Activities, Ministry of Economy, Trade and Industry, Government of Japan.

Tinbergen, Jan, 1975, *Income Difference: Recent Research* (Amsterdam: North-Holland).

The Small and Medium Enterprise Agency, 2000, *New Manufacturing of Small and Medium Enterprises*, Japan.

Thurow, L., 1992, *Head to Head: The Coming Economic Battle among Japan, Europe and America* (New York: William Morrow).

Topel, R.H., 1997, 'Factor Proportions and Relative Wages: The Supply-Side Determinants of Wage Inequality', *The Journal of Economic Perspectives*, 11 (2), pp. 55–74.

Uchikawa, S., 2003, 'Employment in the Manufacturing Organized Sector in India: The Rise of Medium Scale Units', in Shuji Uchikawa (ed.), *Labour Market and Institutions in India: 1990s and Beyond* (New Delhi: Manohar).

UNCTAD, 1994, *World Development Report 1994: Transnational Corporations, Employment and the Workplace* (New York: United Nations Publication).

United Nations, 1999, *World Survey on the Role of Women in Development: Globalization, Gender and Work*, Report of the Secretary-General, General Assembly, United Nations.

Unni, Jeemol, 2003, 'Economic Reforms and Labour Markets in India: Organized and Unorganized Sectors', in Shuji Uchikawa (ed.), *Labour Market and Institutions in India: 1990s and Beyond*.

———, 2004, 'Globalization and Securing Rights for Women Informal Workers in Asia", *Journal of Human Development*, 5 (3), pp. 335–54.

Unni, J and U. Rani, 2003, 'Changing Structure of Workforce in Unorganized Manufacturing', *Indian Journal of Labour Economics*, 46 (4).

Unni, J. and U. Rani, 2004, 'Technical Change and Workforce in India: Skill-biased Growth?', *Indian Journal of Labour Economics*, 47 (4), pp. 683–92.

Unni, J. and U. Rani, 2005, 'Impact of Recent Policies on Home-Based Work in India', Discussion Paper Series No. 10, New Delhi: Human Development Resource Centre, UNDP.

Unni, Jeemol, N. Lalitha and Uma Rani, 2001, 'Economic Reforms and Productivity Trends in Indian Manufacturing', *Economic and Political Weekly*, 36 (41), pp. 3915–22.

van der Hoeven, R., 2001. 'Labour Markets and Economic Reforms under the Washington Consensus: What Happened to Income Inequality?', *The Indian Journal of Labour Economics*, 44 (3).

Watanabe, S. (ed.), 1983, *Technology, Marketing and Industrialization: Linkages between and Small Enterprises* (Delhi: Macmillan).

White Paper on Small and Medium Enterprises, 2003, Government of Japan.

White Paper on Manufacturing Base, 2004, Ministry of Education, Culture, Sports, Science and Technology, Government of Japan.

Whittaker, D.H., 1997, *Small Firms in the Japanese Economy* (Cambridge: Cambridge University Press).

Wilkinson, B., 1983, *The Shopfloor Politics of New Technology* (London: Heinemann Educational Books).

Williamson, O. E., 1975, *Markets and Hierarchies: Analysis and Antitrust Implications* (New York: Free Press).

———, 1979, 'Transaction-cost Economics: The Governance of Contractual Relations', *Journal of Law and Economics*, 22, pp. 233–62.

Wilson, P., 1992, *Foreign Trade and Local Development: Mexico's New Maquiladoras* (Austin, Texas: University of Texas Press).

Wood, A., 1994, *North–South Trade, Employment and Inequality: Changing Fortunes in a Skill-driven World* (Oxford: Clarendon Press).

———, 1997, 'Openness and Wage Inequality in Developing Countries: The Latin American Challenge to the East Asian Conventional Wisdom', *World Bank Economic Review*, 11, pp. 33–57.

World Bank, 1998, *World Development Report 1998–99: Knowledge for Development* (New York: Oxford University Press).

———, 2005, 'The Vocational Education and Training System in India', draft paper, Delhi, September.

Zeira, Joseph, 2006, 'Wage Inequality, Technology and Trade', *Journal of Economic Theory,*

Index